IMAGES
of America

GREENVILLE AND BOND COUNTY

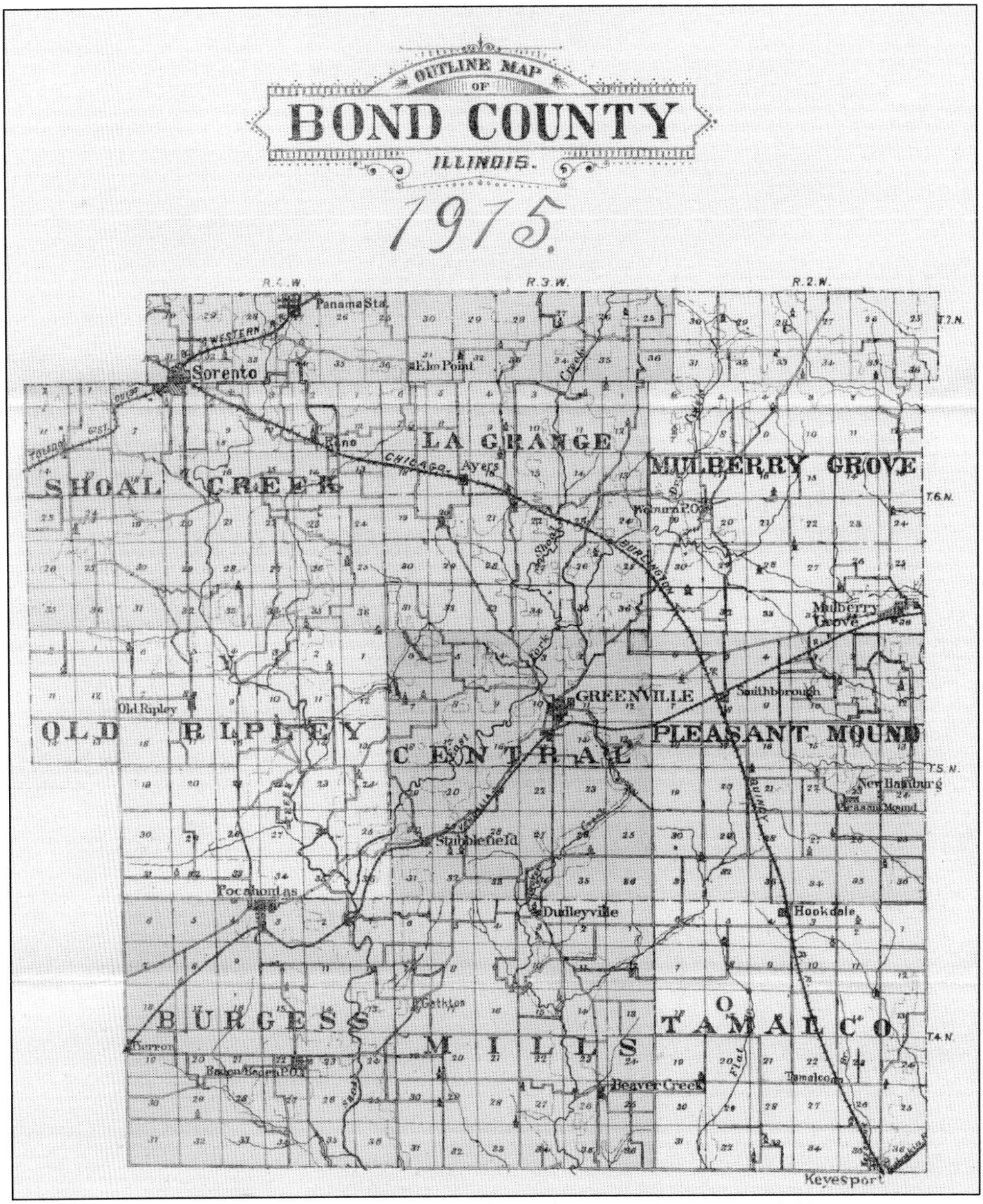

Bond County was established by the Territorial Legislature on January 4, 1817—one year prior to statehood. It was 24 miles wide and ran north to the Wisconsin Territory Line. By 1821, it was reduced to its present size. In 1889, the county adopted a township form of government with boundaries as shown above on this 1915 map. The chapters of this book are arranged by township and run clockwise from Shoal Creek at the upper left, to Greenville in the center. (Map courtesy Bond County Historical Society.)

IMAGES
of America

GREENVILLE AND BOND COUNTY

Kevin John Kaegy
and the
Bond County Historical Society

ARCADIA
PUBLISHING

ISBN 978-0-7385-2316-3

Published by Arcadia Publishing
Charleston, South Carolina

Printed in the United States of America

Library of Congress Catalog Card Number: 2002116909

For all general information contact Arcadia Publishing at:
Telephone 843-853-2070
Fax 843-853-0044
E-mail sales@arcadiapublishing.com
For customer service and orders:
Toll-Free 1-888-313-2665

Visit us on the Internet at www.arcadiapublishing.com

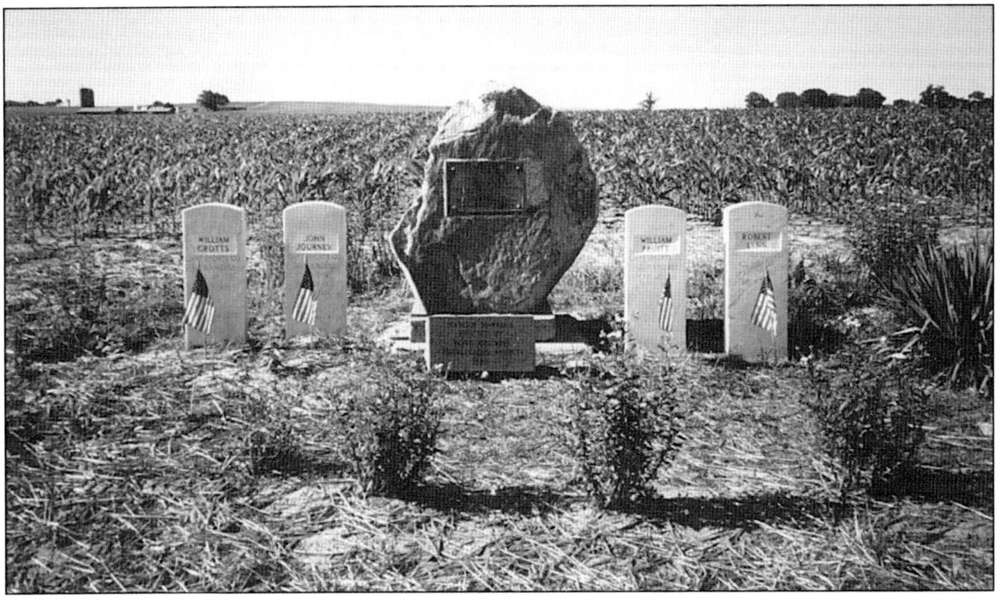

Located west of Millersburg Road on what is now Hill's Fort Avenue, this stone marker was erected in 1918 by the Daughters of the American Revolution in memory of the four Illinois rangers who were ambushed by a native tribe outside of Hill's Fort on September 9, 1814. Killed were William Grotts, John Journey, William Pruitt, and Robert Lynn. Their tombstones were added in recent years by the Bond County Genealogical Society. Hill's Fort was Bond County's first seat of government. In 1817, the county seat was relocated from Hills Fort to the newly formed city of Perryville, farther east. When Bond County was reduced in size in 1820, the county seat of Perryville ended up in Fayette County. (Courtesy Kevin Kaegy.)

Contents

ACKNOWLEDGMENTS

This book has been the result of many hours donated by a dedicated group of volunteers. From April through December 2002, the following members worked together to find, sort, and identify all of the photos used in this book:

Kevin Kaegy, Chairman/Editor: Kevin is the sixth generation of his family to live in Bond County. He has collected photos for 26 years, and served as president of the Bond County Historical Society for 8 years. He is a kitchen designer and has two children.
Kathy Brewer, Assistant Editor: Kathy is a member of the Historical Society's Board of Directors. She and her husband, Bill, run Indian Images, a home-based business. They recreate authentic Native American costumes for collectors and the movie industry, and made principal props and set decorations for the film "Dances with Wolves."
Dr. Everett Sanders: Everett is a retired professor of music at Greenville College. He used his considerable talent with the computer to scan all of the photos used in this book. He was able to restore some of the worn images, making them look like new again.
John Goldsmith: John is program director and assistant manager at WGEL radio in Greenville. He collects local memorabilia with a special interest in DeMoulin Bros. artifacts. He is the current president of the Bond County Historical Society.
Jeff Leidel: Jeff is the editor of the *Greenville Advocate*, the only newspaper of record in Greenville. He has accumulated one of the largest collections of local post cards known to exist—and he gladly shared them! He is currently secretary of the Bond County Historical Society.
Bill Johnson: Bill has served as Bond County Treasurer for 32 years. He collects courthouse photos and has been very active with the Boy Scouts. Bill has also served as vice pres of the Bond County Historical Society.
Martha Radcliff: Martha is president/event coordinator for the non-profit group Our Common Ground, which promotes the humanities within the region. She is editor of ourcommongroundmag.com. Martha works at WGEL radio in Greenville. It was her job to edit and retype the text within this book.
Dr. James Wilson: Jim wrote the captions for the college shots. He is a retired professor of music at Greenville College. In the fall of 2001, he published a history of the college choir, which he directed for 36 years.

Other significant contributors include Dean and Nelda Anthony, Bill Donnell, for Greenville; Janice Baldwin for Pleasant Mound; Norman Compton for Panama; Leah Hans for Mulberry Grove; David Meyers for Keyesport; Jerry Nance for Pocahontas; and John and Jeanette Coleman for Smithboro. Thanks to Bob Wilson, Kathie Wiedenhoeft, and Susan Hulvey for the copy work.

On behalf of the Bond County Historical Society, we would like to express our great appreciation to those who shared their photographs, for without their trust and assistance, this publication would not have been possible.

INTRODUCTION

In 1809, Captain Issac Hill came to what is now Bond County, Illinois, with a group of 11 rangers. They surveyed the region for President Thomas Jefferson, built Hills Fort, and staked claims throughout the area, making Bond County one of the earliest settled counties within the state of Illinois.

During the War of 1812, most of the early settlers moved back to the Mississippi River, joining most of the state's population. When Indian hostilities ceased and the war ended, the settlers returned.

They came up the Mississippi in flatboats; later, they came from the west on horseback. In the 1830s the National Road brought them by stage from the east. In 1868, the St. Louis Vandalia and Terre Haute (Pennsylvania) Railroad came through Bond County, planting towns like Johnny Appleseed planted trees—towns with names like Pierron, Stubblefield, and Smithboro. Established towns like Greenville, Mulberry Grove, and Pocahontas flourished. The Jacksonville Southeastern Railroad (CB&Q) was built in 1882, and Sorento, Reno, Ayers, Durley, Hookdale, Tamalco, and Keyesport sprouted as it went. When the St. Louis Toledo & Western crossed the northwest corner of the county in 1882, Panama and Donnellson took root.

The Pennsylvania Railroad hooked Bond County to the rest of the nation. It brought folks like William Jennings Bryan and Theodore Roosevelt through Greenville. It brought the Liberty Bell on an open car so school children could see it. The railroads brought businessmen from St. Louis and Chicago, making Greenville's hotels and restaurants bustle.

Greenville grew until it became the largest town in Bond County. In 1821, it was designated the county seat. Its square became the center of the county's historical and cultural identity: Civil War soldiers camped and drilled around it. Indians passed by it on their way to trade before disappearing from the area around 1820. Preachers like Reverend Hynes, and presidential candidates like Abraham Lincoln and Stephen A. Douglas, expounded for those who gathered to hear. "White Mule" whiskey was poured into its gutters during Prohibition, and unemployed protesters carried their placards around it during the Great Depression.

Today, you'll find the 21st century alive and well in Greenville—it exists side-by-side with the past: new homes neighbor historic homes, computers and state-of-the-art school buildings sit just down the road from the One Room Schoolhouse Museum. Discount store and fast-food chains prosper on its outer edges, while the historic square remains lined with family-owned businesses. These days, visitors enter Bond County from I-70, Eisenhower's concrete river of commerce. They land in our airport and they tour our streets by bus.

Over 17,000 people live in Bond County. Many descendants of the families that once came to town on Saturday nights still live within the county. Several of the earlier businesses have stood the test of time as well: the *Greenville Advocate*, founded in 1858 to support Abraham Lincoln, is still a privately owned newspaper. The Bradford National Bank dates back to 1867, and Watson's Drug Store has anchored their corner of the square since 1881. Greenville College and the DeMoulin Bros. Factory were founded in 1892. Today, each remains an integral part of Greenville, bigger and better than ever. Each learned to adjust to the demands progress makes in order to maintain their own vitality.

The area's rich history is gathered and recorded by the Bond County Historical Society, founded in 1955. A committee of eight selected the photos used in this book, with the desire to fairly and equally represent all of the townships within the county. It is their wish that as you peruse its pages you'll gain an appreciation for those who settled Bond County—those earliest settlers who came here before us, broke the first soil on the prairie, made sacrifices, took risks, endured hardships, and kept the faith. I am grateful to the historians that keep before us those reminders that will strengthen and wisen us for our journey into the future.

Martha Radcliff

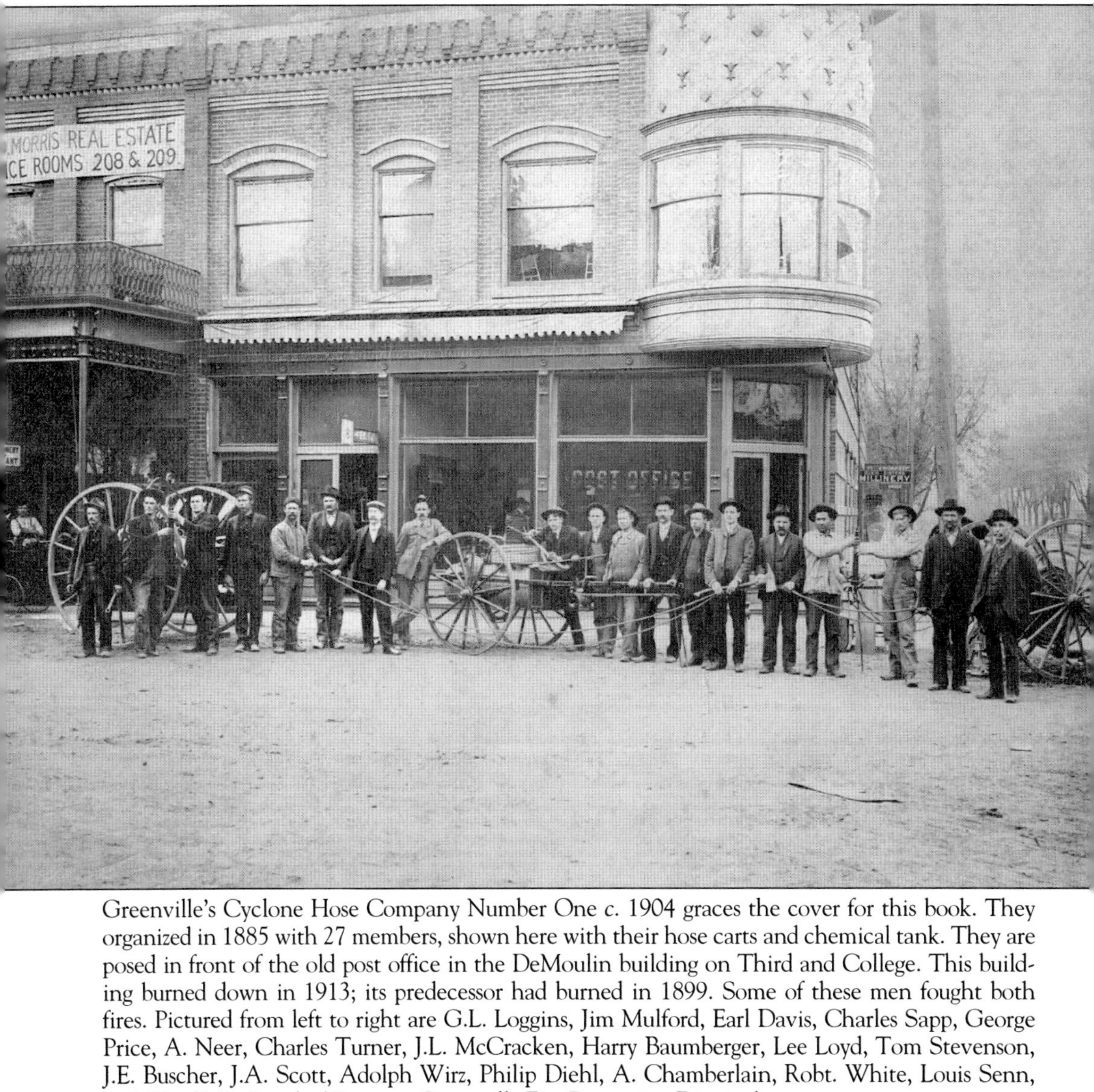

Greenville's Cyclone Hose Company Number One *c.* 1904 graces the cover for this book. They organized in 1885 with 27 members, shown here with their hose carts and chemical tank. They are posed in front of the old post office in the DeMoulin building on Third and College. This building burned down in 1913; its predecessor had burned in 1899. Some of these men fought both fires. Pictured from left to right are G.L. Loggins, Jim Mulford, Earl Davis, Charles Sapp, George Price, A. Neer, Charles Turner, J.L. McCracken, Harry Baumberger, Lee Loyd, Tom Stevenson, J.E. Buscher, J.A. Scott, Adolph Wirz, Philip Diehl, A. Chamberlain, Robt. White, Louis Senn, and Chief L.E. Derith. (Courtesy Greenville Fire Protection District.)

One

Shoal Creek Township

Shoal Creek Township, named for the county's main watercourse, is located in the northwest corner of the county. Before townships were established in the county in 1889, most of the area was known as Cottonwood Grove Precinct. The first settlers came to the area in 1816 or 1817, drawn to the saltworks along Shoal Creek, which had first been used by Native Americans. The communities of Shoal Creek Township include Sorento, founded in 1885. Reno replaced a smaller town known at various times as Bethel, Augusta, and Cottonwood Grove. Panama straddles the Bond/Montgomery County line. A community called Harrisonville, surveyed and platted in 1838, was never populated. Pleasant Prairie, which in 1861 had a church, a school, a store, and a post office, ceased to exist after the railroad established a station a mile west, in what later became Sorento. A few localities that were more neighborhoods than towns were Stringtown, southeast of Panama and Roubideux (also spelled Ruby-Do), west of the Ripson Bridge.

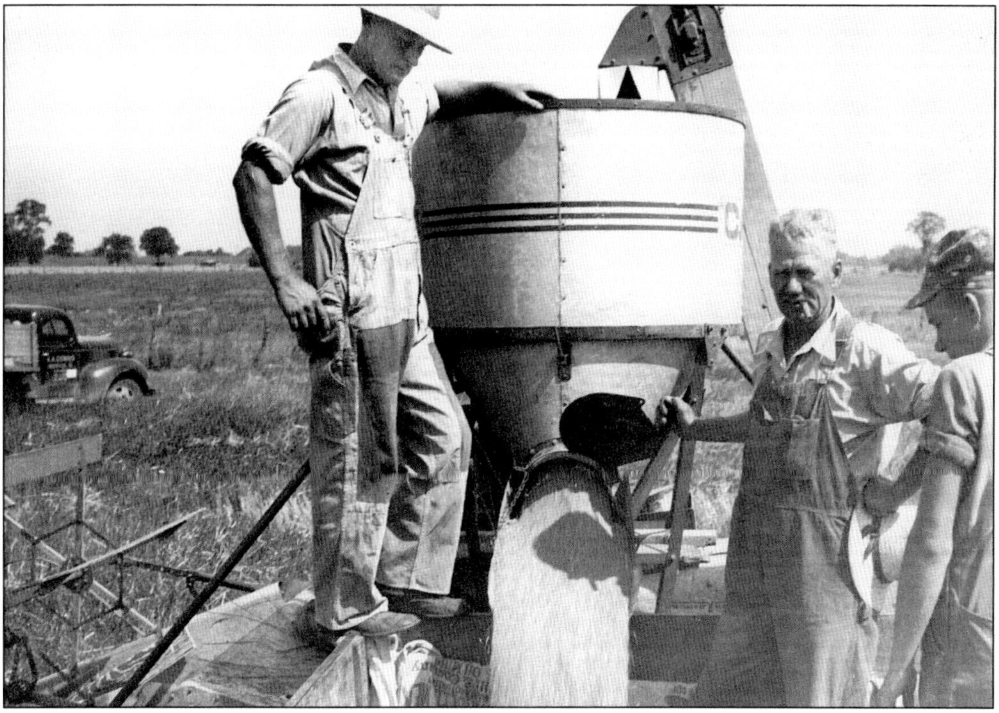

Farming was and continues to be the main business of Bond County. The Baumberger farm is located a couple of miles south of Reno, in south central Shoal Creek Township. Pictured here dumping wheat from the combine to the grain truck in the 1940s are Hubert Gruner, Nathaniel "Than" Baumberger, and Stanley Allen. (Courtesy Fred Baumberger.)

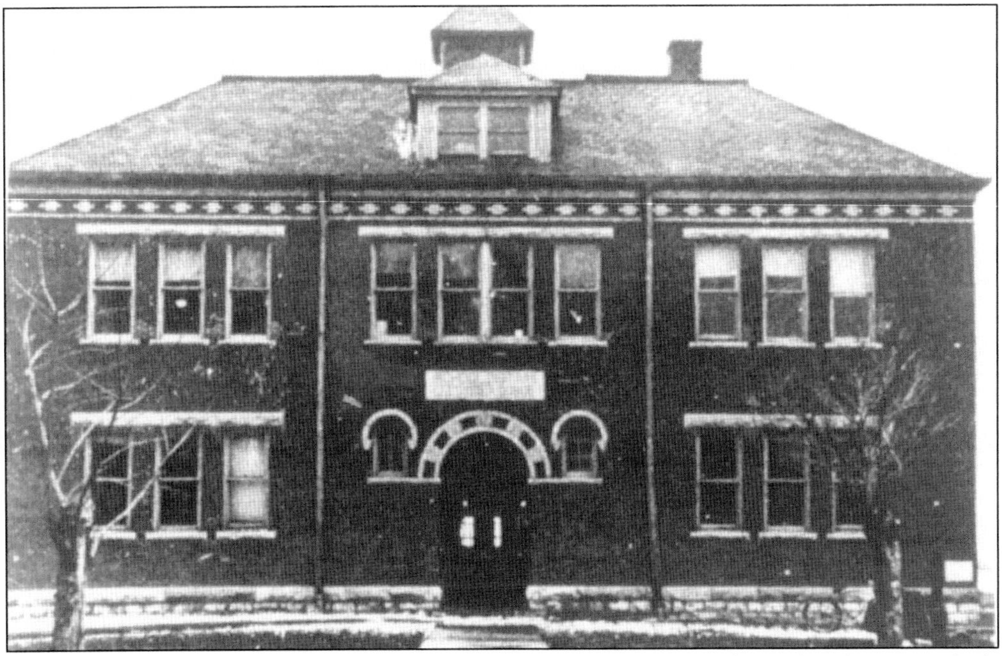

The Sorento school was built in 1905. It housed eight primary grades and a three-year high school. Seniors had to board in Greenville for their senior year. Several additions were made through the years. All high school students have been bussed to Greenville since the early 1950s. The original portion of this building was taken down in 1968. (Courtesy Lillian Dauderman.)

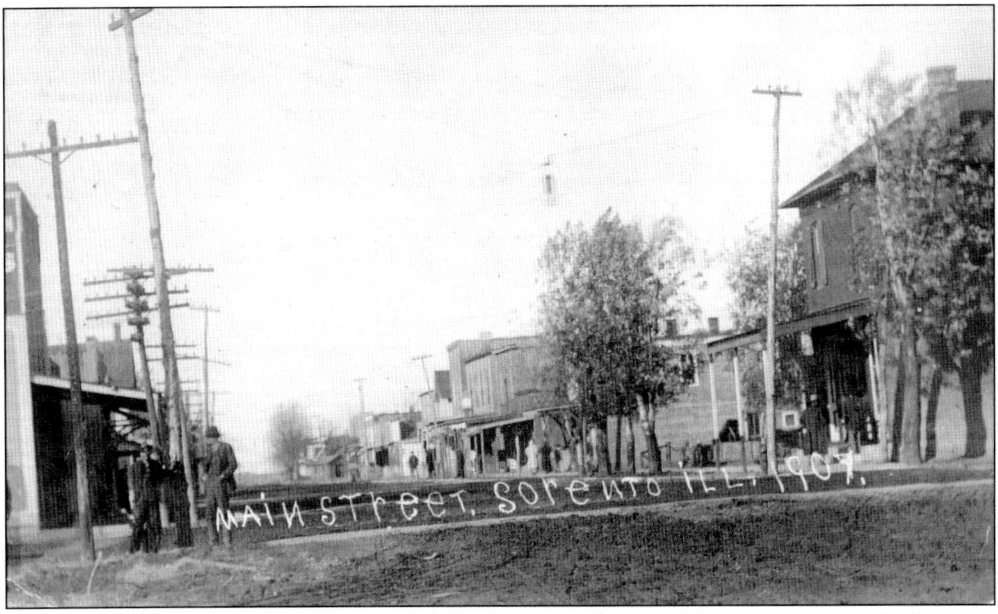

Mr. Scharf's 12-acre wheat field provided the first town lots, and by 1884, Sorento had grown to over 60 acres. With two railroads and a coal mine, the village grew rapidly. By 1909, thriving businesses lined both sides of Main Street. The town was named for Sorento, Florida, after Mr. Scharf's son returned from the area and suggested the name. (Courtesy Ron Mrischen.)

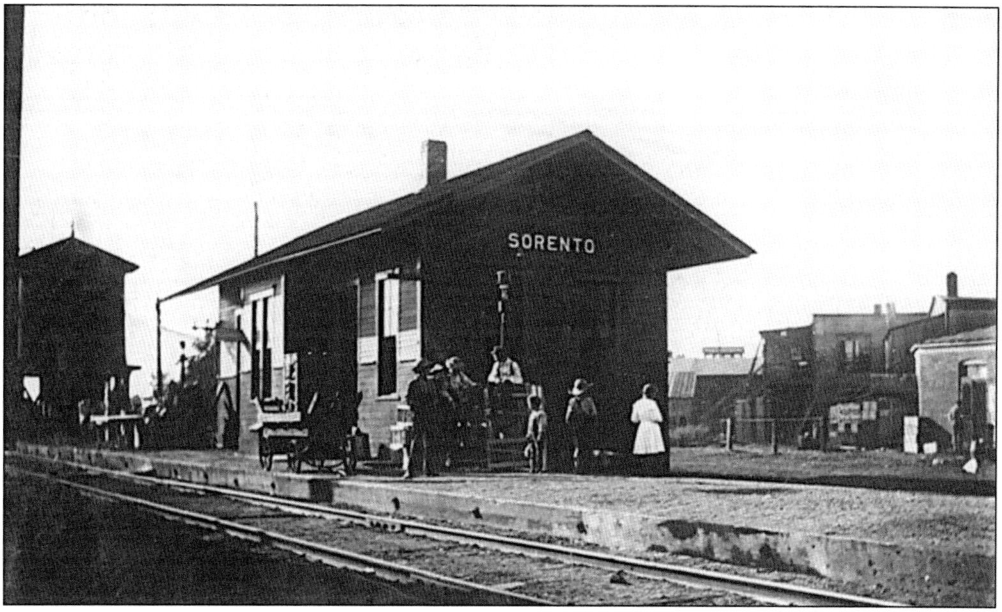

The Sorento C.B.& Q. Depot was the hub of activity for passengers boarding and getting off trains in the village. Sorento was built at the crossing of the Jacksonville Southeastern Railroad and St. Louis Western Railroad. The Jacksonville Southeastern became a part of the Chicago Burlington and Quincy (C.B.& Q.) in 1900. The depot was south of the crossing on Main Street. The railroad was also important as a means to haul coal from the Sorento Coal Company. The mine closed in 1914. (Courtesy Jeff Leidel.)

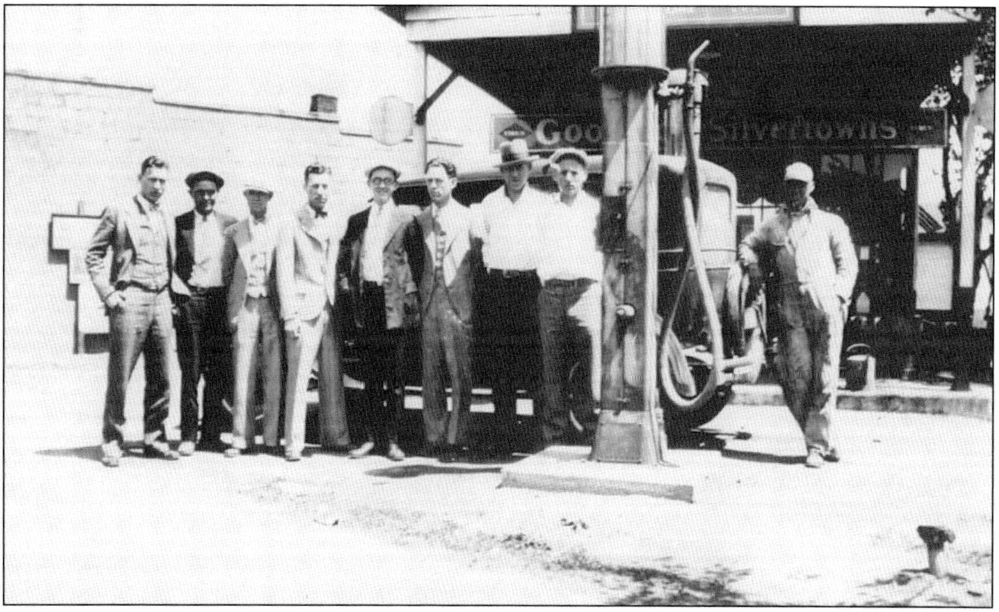

A group of Sorento residents pose around the gas pump at a village filling station in the late 1920s. Pictured from left to right are Dan Tyler, Rufus Saathoff, Tod Johnson, J.W. Boleria, Red Cowen, Dove McCreaken, Harry Moss, Sherm Tipsword, and Seth Young. (Courtesy Sorento Homecoming Association.)

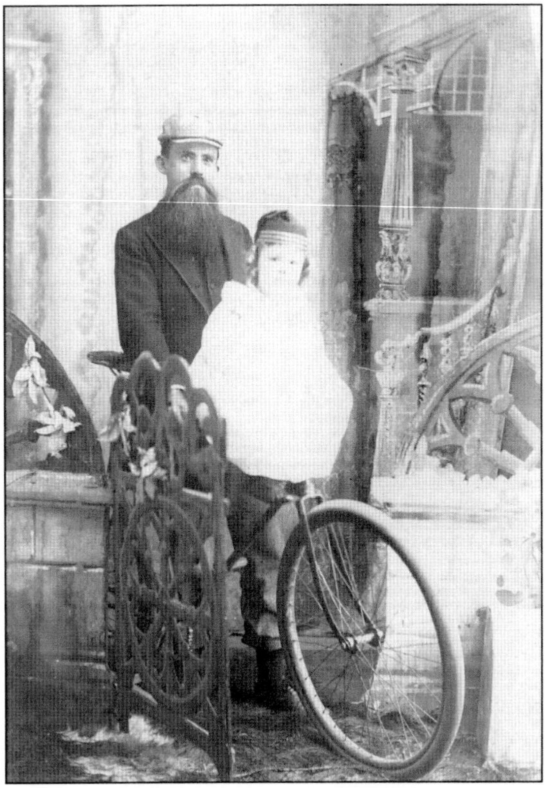

The year is 1898 and Dr. Jason (J.D.) Chittum is shown above with his 2-year-old daughter, Mae. He started practicing medicine in Sorento in 1895, in a small two room office on the corner of State and Taylor Streets. He made house calls, first on his horse, Daisy, and later, in his Plymouth. He died in 1955 after 60 years of practice. During his career, Dr. Chittum delivered 1,360 babies. (Courtesy Sorento Homecoming Association.)

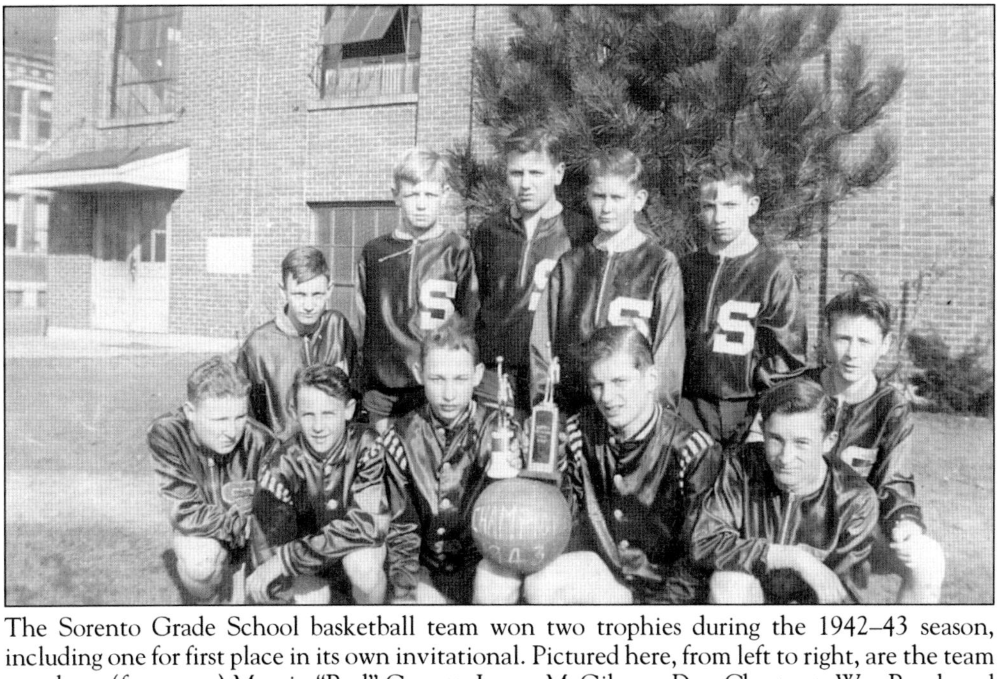

The Sorento Grade School basketball team won two trophies during the 1942–43 season, including one for first place in its own invitational. Pictured here, from left to right, are the team members: (front row) Marvin "Red" Garrett, Loren McGibany, Don Chestnut, Wes Reed, and Herschel Reed; (back row) Francis Ingles, Owen McCracken, Robert Collman, Leon Linnin, Harvey Cruthis, and George Redfern. (Courtesy Sorento Homecoming Association.)

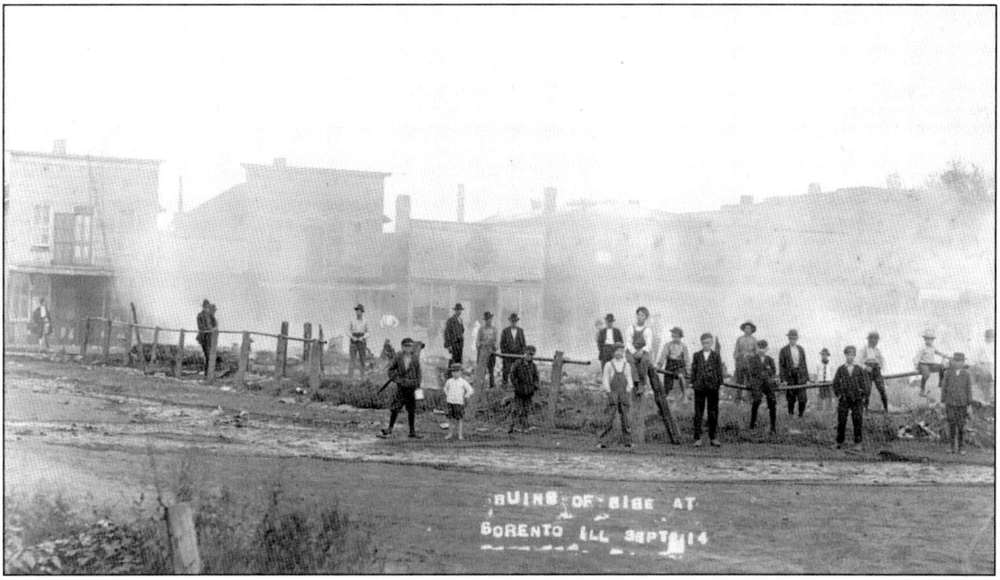

The Nickel Plate and Jacksonville Southeastern Railroads crossed each other on William Scharf's farm. He laid out the village of Sorento in 1882 and within one year, over 200 people lived in the "boom town." Hastily constructed frame buildings were always at risk of fire. In this c. 1914 postcard, residents look over the remains after several buildings burned down in the business district. (Courtesy Ron Mrischen.)

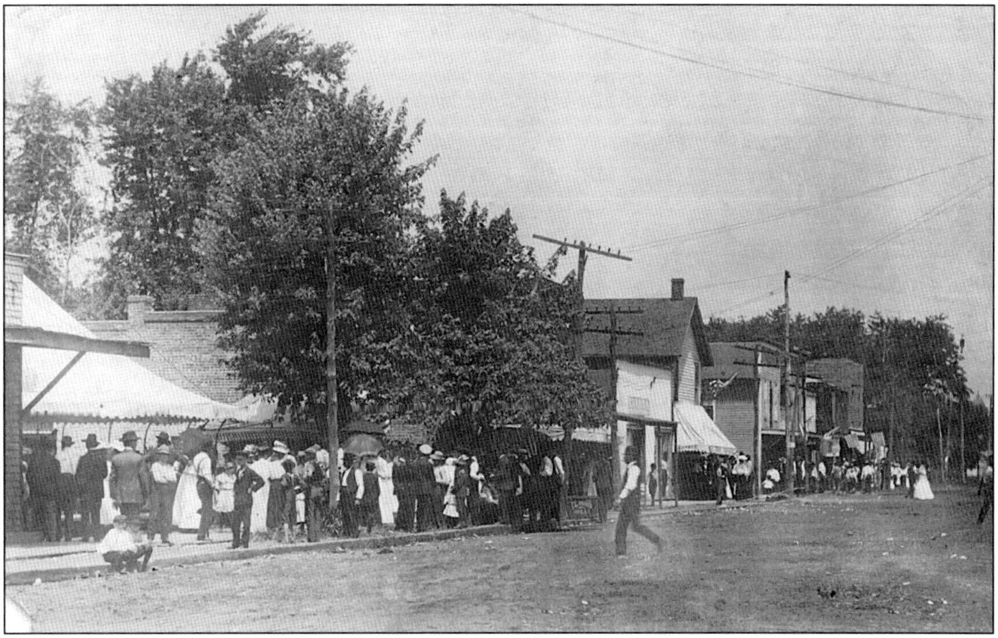

The Fourth of July was an important day for all rural communities in the 19th and early 20th centuries and every community had its own celebration. Residents of Sorento celebrated Independence Day here in 1908, with the annual Old Settlers Day in downtown, honoring those who first came to the region, many of whom were still alive at the time. (Courtesy Jeff Leidel.)

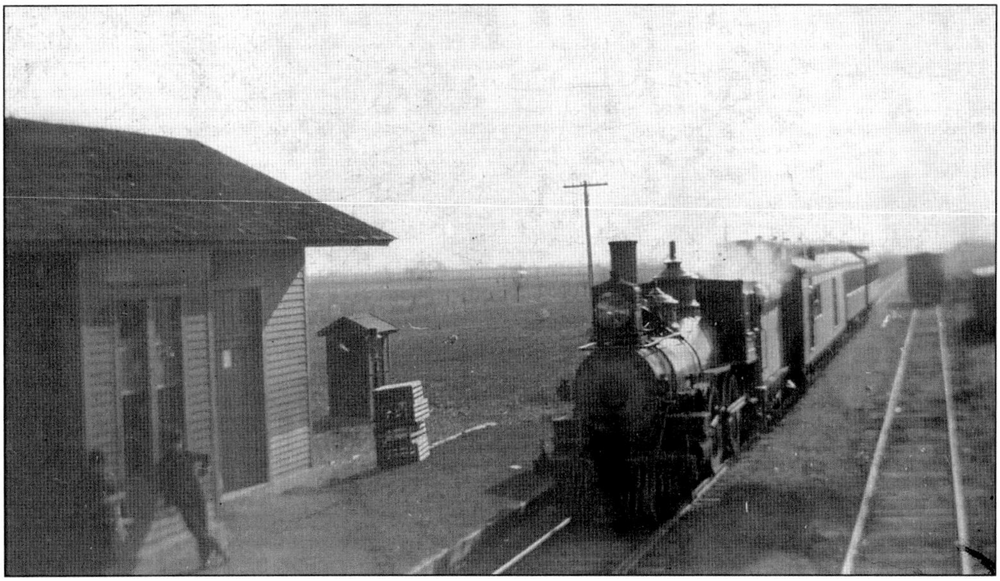

A train pulls into the Reno Depot from the east as two men look on, *c.* 1910. Settlers were in the area in the 1820s and the community was first known as Bethel, after the church. The village was called Augusta in the 1830s and became Cottonwood Grove Post Office in 1851. The C.B.& Q. Railroad passed a half mile south of the village and Reno was laid out in 1883. The post office then changed its name from Cottonwood Grove to Reno. (Courtesy Jeff Leidel.)

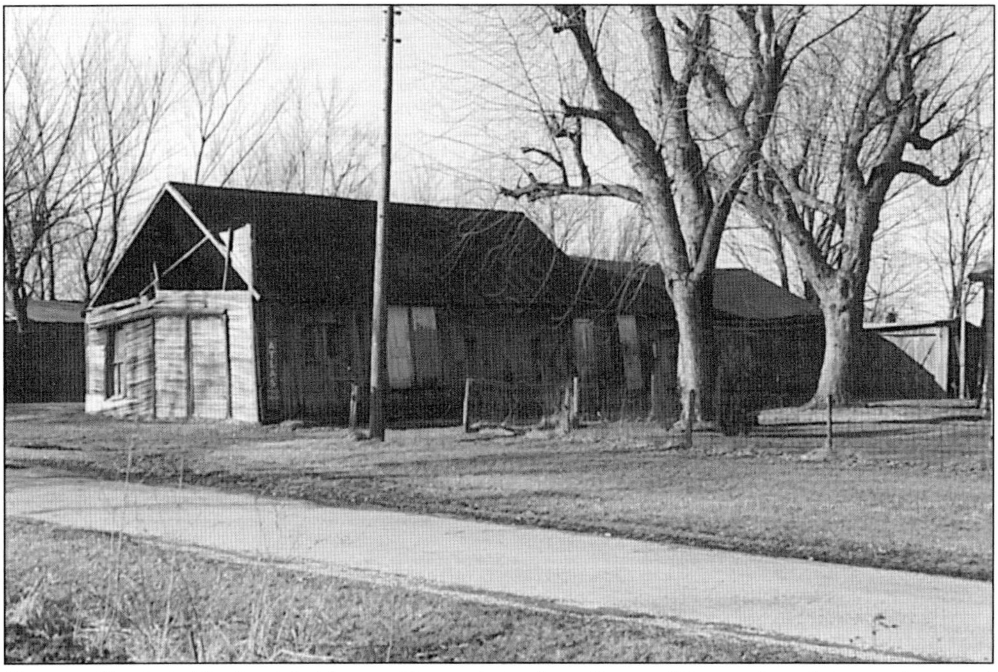

Herman Henke's Blacksmith Shop still stands in the village of Reno, though it was last used in the 1940s. His son Adolf sold McCormick Deering implements there. Other blacksmiths in this village were Henry Weber, John Duffy, George Schwenderman, and Mr. Coleman. (Courtesy Kevin Kaegy.)

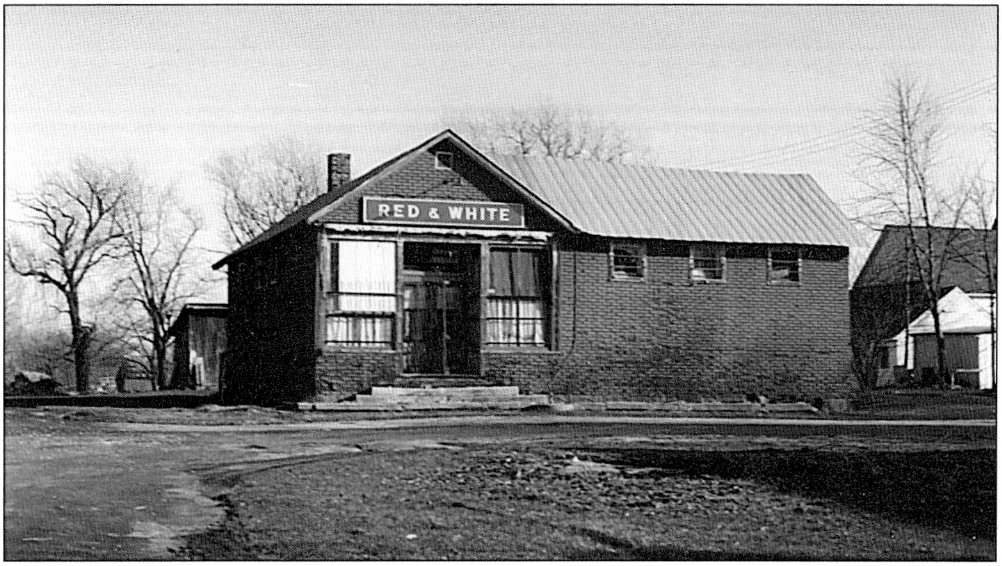

Blackburn's Red and White Grocery Store, originally built as a blacksmith shop by Henry Weber, still stands in Reno today. It was located in Cottonwood Grove. Weber converted it into a store, and after the railroad was built in 1883, moved it to its present location. George Weber ran it for many years and was the last postmaster. The Blackburns ran it from 1961 to 1964. (Courtesy Kevin Kaegy.)

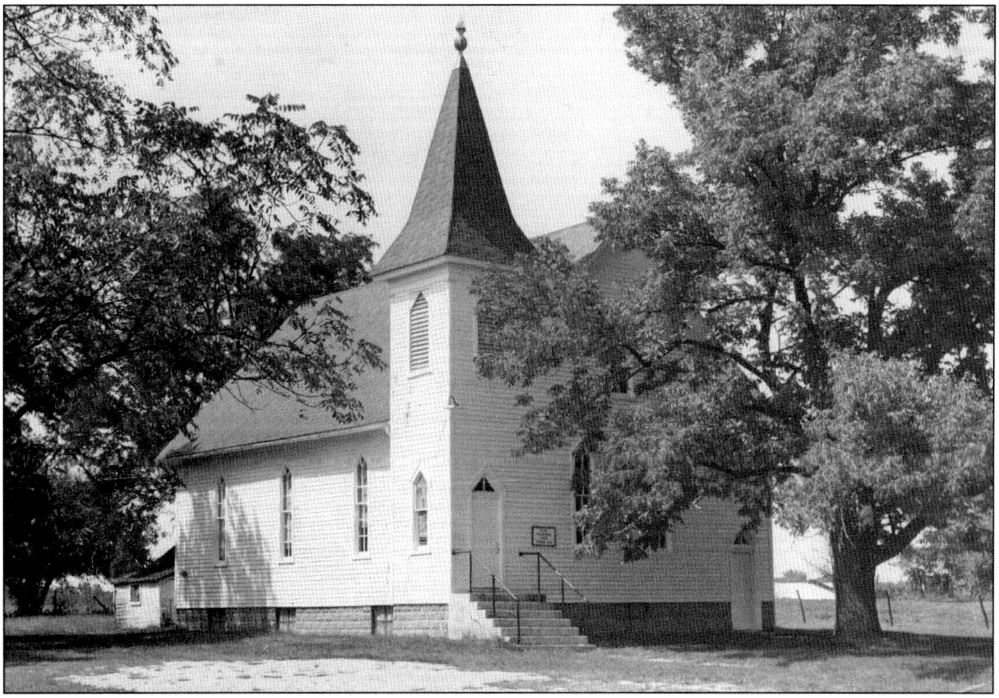

The Reno/Bethel Presbyterian Church was established in 1825. The original log church stood within the site of the Bethel Cemetery. Several operators of the Underground Railway were among its early members. In 1837, Elijah P. Lovejoy, the abolitionist, spoke there. Built in 1899, the structure is the third building to serve this congregation. (Courtesy Fred Baumberger.)

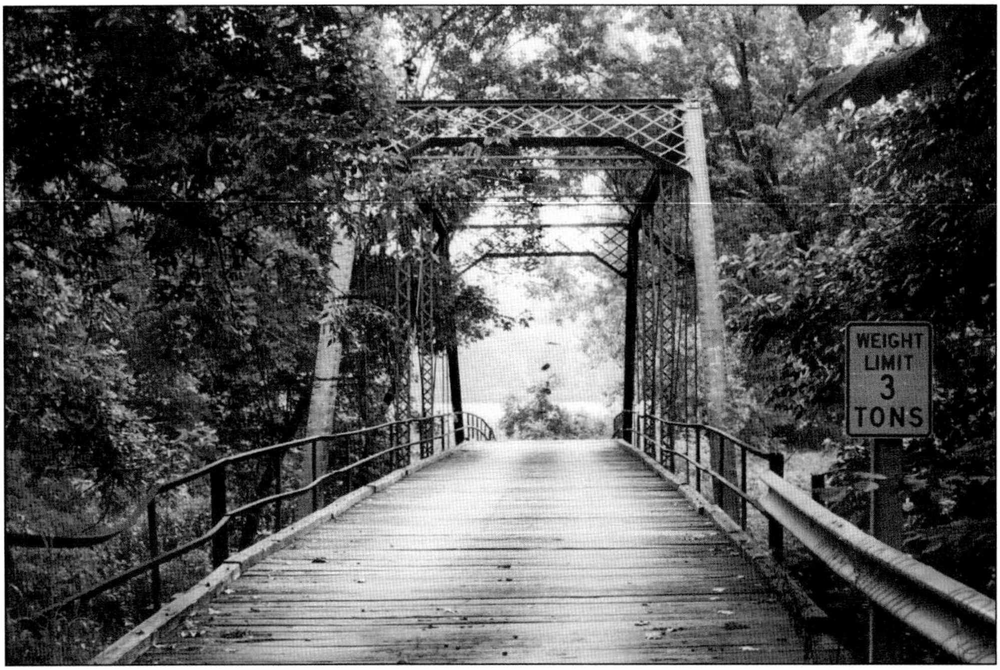

Ripson Bridge was built in 1895, replacing the original all-wood bridge that crossed Shoal Creek on Cyrus Ripson's property. It is the last pony truss iron bridge left in Bond County. Each October, residents from Bond County and the surrounding area flock to Ripson Bridge for the fall festival. (Courtesy Jeff Leidel.)

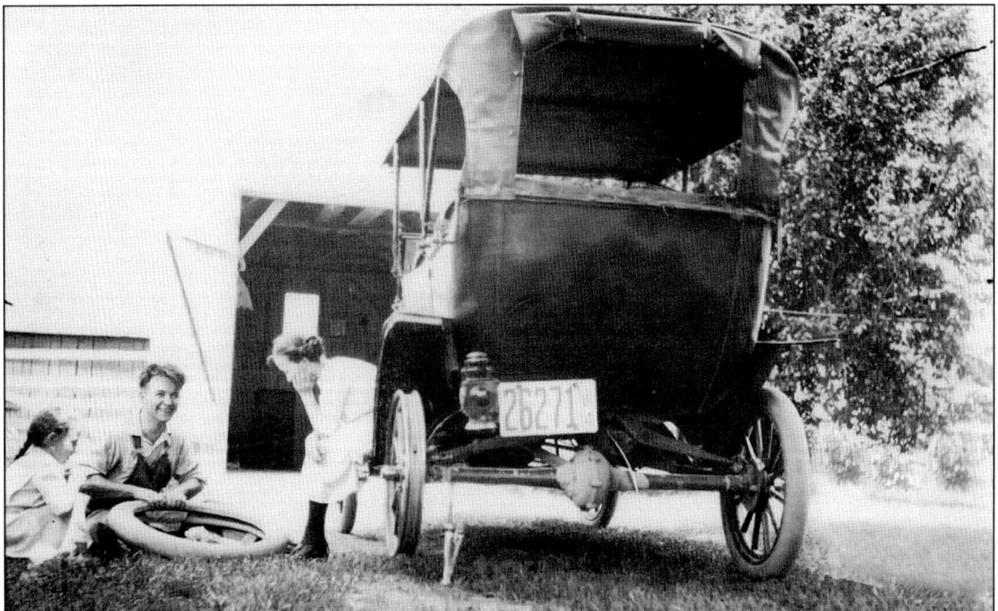

George Weber repairs a tire on his first car, a Model T Ford. This photo was taken prior to 1920 at his home in Reno. Two of his sisters watch and provide encouragement. Several generations of the Weber family lived in Reno and operated the general store there. (Courtesy Fred Baumberger.)

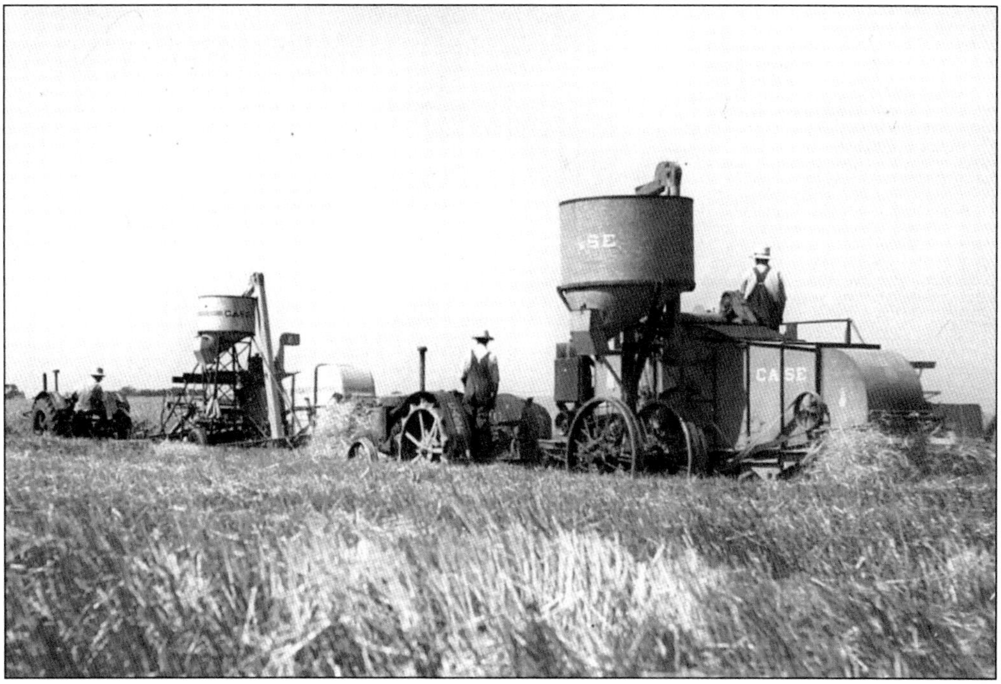

Neighbors helping neighbors during the harvest was common throughout the 19th and most of the 20th centuries, as this scene during World War II shows. Pictured here, from left to right, are Hubert Gruner with his 6-foot Case combine, Lee Nash driving the tractor pulling the second combine, and "Than" Baumberger at the controls of the Case 12-foot combine. (Courtesy Fred Baumberger.)

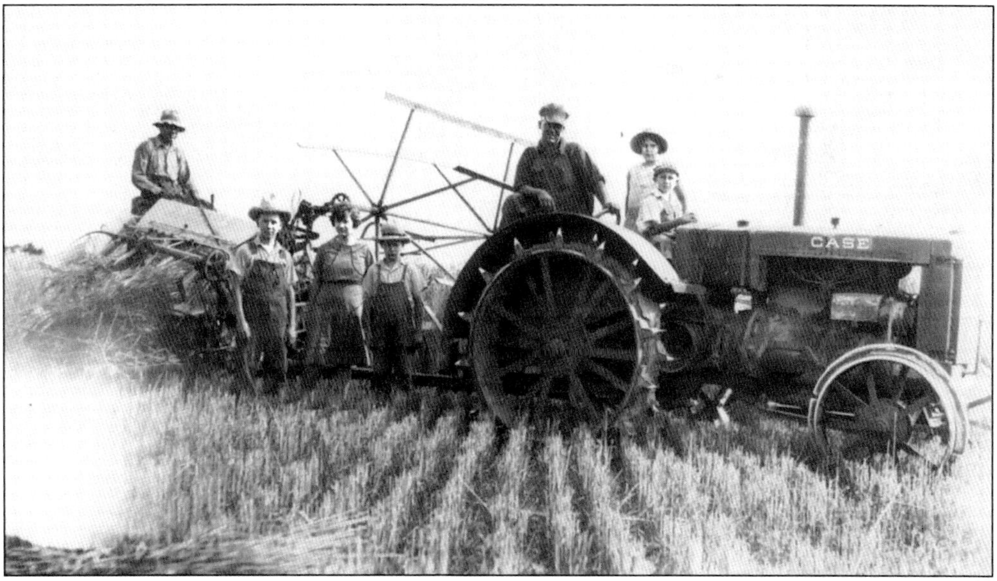

The Baumberger family takes a break from cutting wheat with an old fashioned reaper in the early 1930s. Fred Baumberger Sr. is on the grain binder. On the ground from left to right are Fred, Jean, and Ed Baumberger. On the Model L Case tractor are Nathaniel "Than" (at the wheel), Helen, and Keith Baumberger. (Courtesy Fred Baumberger.)

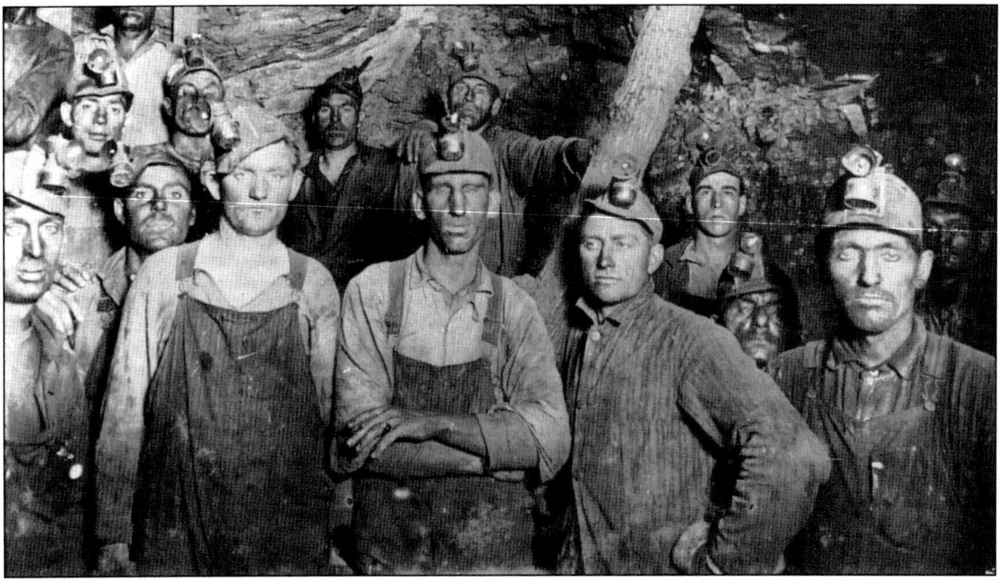

These miners were photographed in the Panama Mine around 1910. Most are unidentified except for the following: Clyde McReaken, front row, far left; "Dutch" Cunningham, pictured next to McReaken; and second from right, Ivor Williams. The most famous Panama miner of all is also present—the man in the rear wearing a dark shirt, second left from the post—John L. Lewis, founder of the United Mine Workers and head of the AFL-CIO. (Courtesy Norman Compton.)

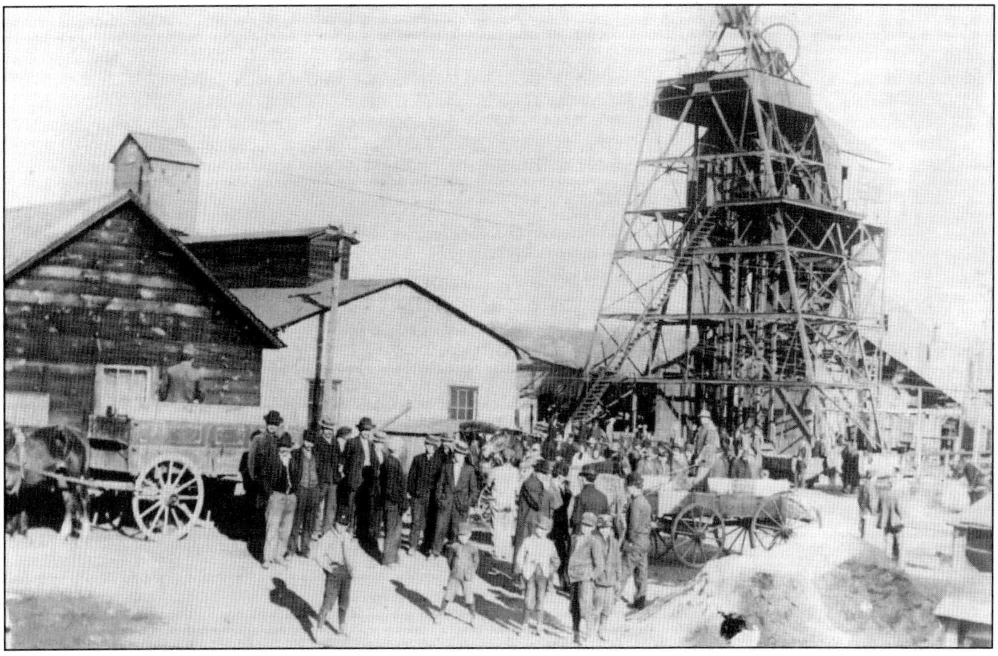

On November 11, 1910, a gas explosion at the Panama mine killed five miners. The sixth man to die, a resident of Sorento, perished as a result of trying to help recover bodies. He succumbed to "blackdamp," a low-lying cloud devoid of oxygen. Twenty-three miners were badly injured in the explosion, but all recovered. This photo depicts men and boys gathered at the mine, awaiting news of the injured and dead. (Courtesy Norman Compton.)

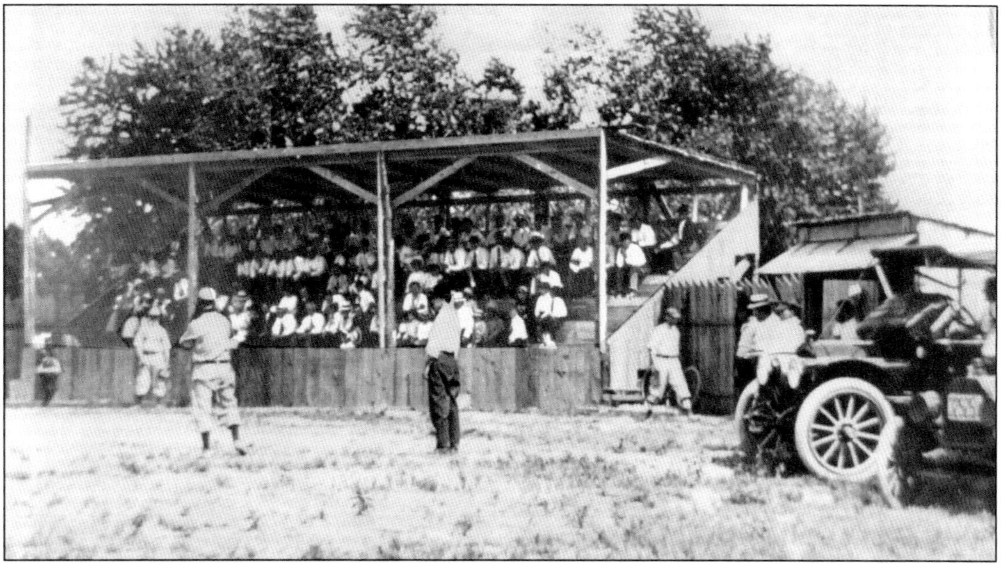

The Panama Ball Park was located several hundred yards west of where the present schoolhouse now stands. This game, *c.* 1915, involves a team sponsored by the American Brewing Company. Note the white shirts and dark ties on almost all of the spectators in the grandstand! (Courtesy Norman Compton.)

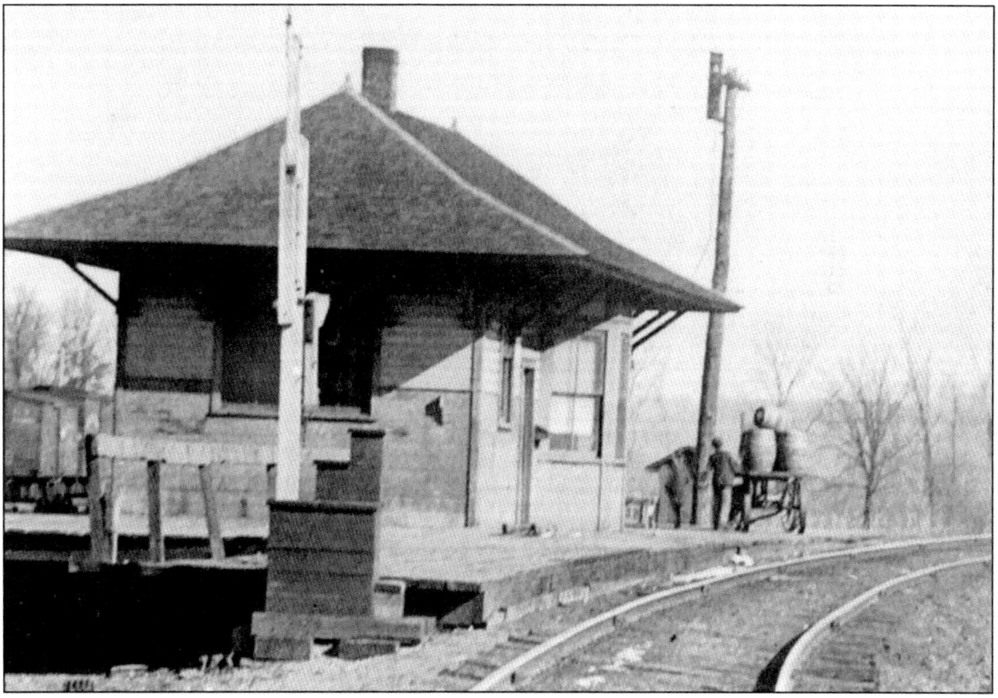

This shows the second Panama train depot *c.* 1910. The first, a larger building, was destroyed by fire. The tracks behind the building (with the box car visible) were one of two spurs leading to the coal mine. The mine brought the railroad to the area; as a result, Panama was established in 1904. The depot was located south of town at the foot of Depot Street. (Courtesy Norman Compton.)

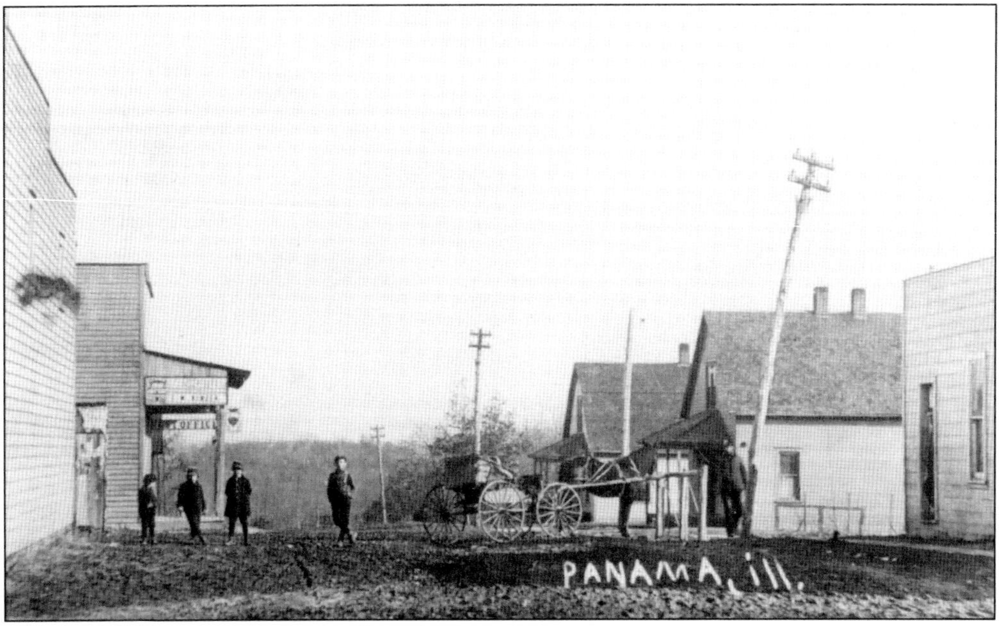

Here is a view east in Panama on Plum Street, around the turn of the century. The side of the building visible at far left was the restaurant/pool hall that belonged to J.D. Williams before he built an impressive opera house on North Avenue. The second building at left was the Kinzer Hardware Store, which also served as the post office. (Courtesy Norman Compton.)

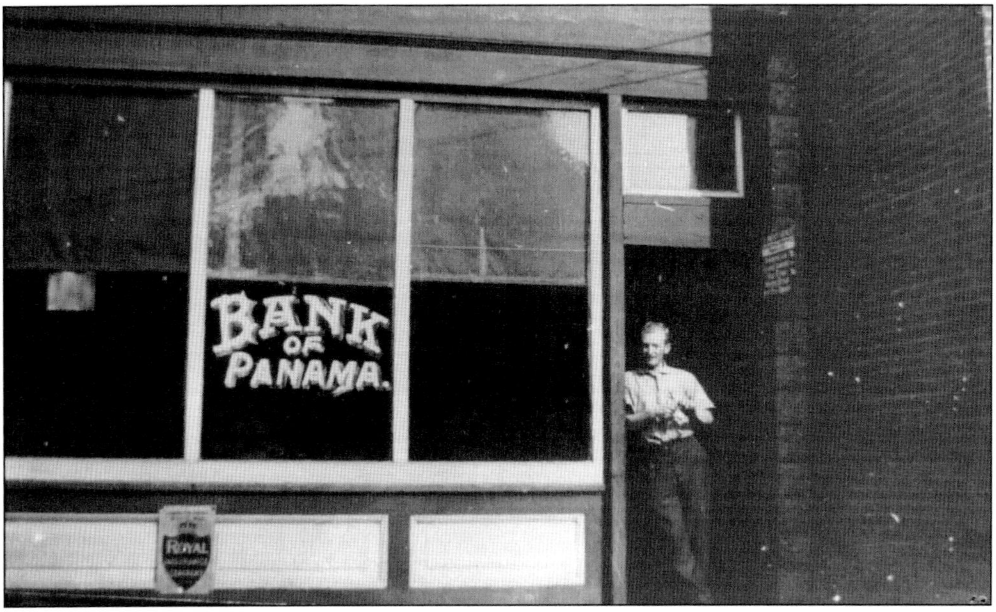

An unidentified man stands in front of the Panama Bank on Main Street. On December 12, 1921, bank robbers stole the mine payroll. Implicated in the crime was Bond County's own sheriff, John W. Wilson. Not all of the robbers were caught nor was the money recovered. In 1923, after a particularly heavy spring downpour, $10 bills, later identified as part of the loot, were discovered washing down Mill Hill in Greenville—ironically, right across from the county jail! (Courtesy Norman Compton.)

Two

LaGrange Township

LaGrange Township's name refers to "the grange" or farmland, and to this day, has remained a rural area with no major villages. It is located in the north central part of Bond County and was previously called LaGrange Precinct. The first neighborhood established in the area was the Ohio Settlement about 1820, so-called for the several families who came from that state. The Ohio Settlement became the Union Grove community. Elm Point, established in 1837, had a large mill, a church, school, and post office, but it died out when the railroad bypassed it, and nothing remains where it once stood.

Donnellson, established in 1850 as Bear Creek, straddles the Montgomery County line. Ayers, founded in 1895, along the Jacksonville-Southeastern Railroad had a post office, store, and coaling station for the railroad. Betterton, though never platted, had a school, store, and post office from 1883 to 1891. This neighborhood was on the Red Ball Trail, three miles north of Greenville. Farther north along the Red Ball Trail, a neighborhood known as Jett's Prairie had a post office around 1893.

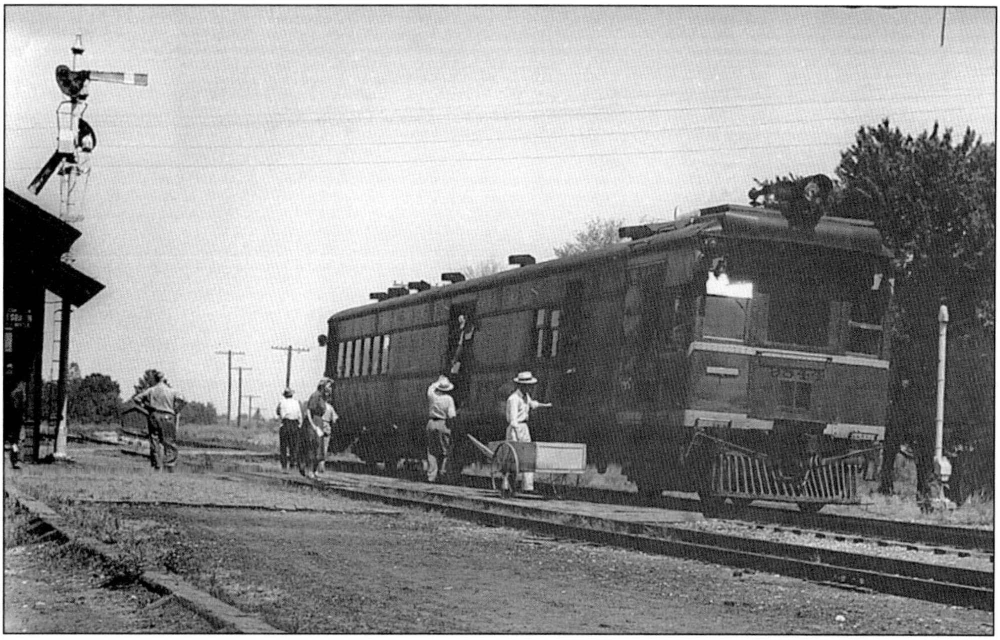

In the late 1920s, the Burlington Northern Railroad ran a daily passenger and mail car between Beardstown and Herrin. It made nine stops throughout Bond County. Each neighborhood had a different nickname for it, including the Dinkey, Puddle Jumper, and the Toonerville Trolley. In Ayers, they called it the Doodlebug. For only 25¢ you could ride to Centralia's Woolworth's Store for Christmas shopping and be back home by 6 p.m. Its last run was April 27, 1957. (Courtesy Marvin Knight.)

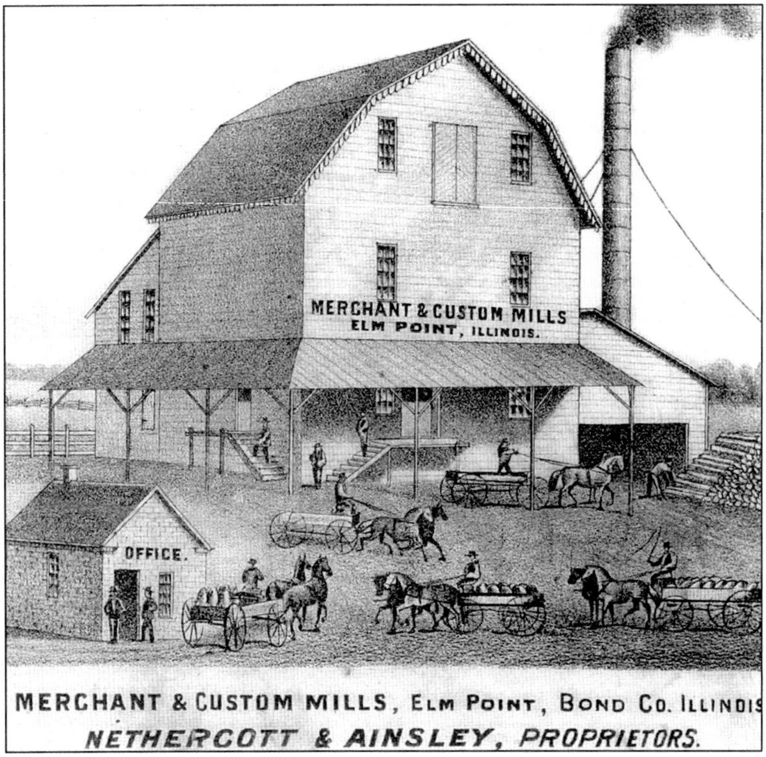

This lithograph of the Elm Point Mill is from the 1875 Bond County Plat Book. The business was at its high point then, as was the village. Laid out in 1856, Elm Point had a school, church, store and post office. When local farmers refused to sell right-of-way near Elm Point, the Nickel Plate Railroad went to Donnellson instead. (Courtesy the Bond County Historical Society.)

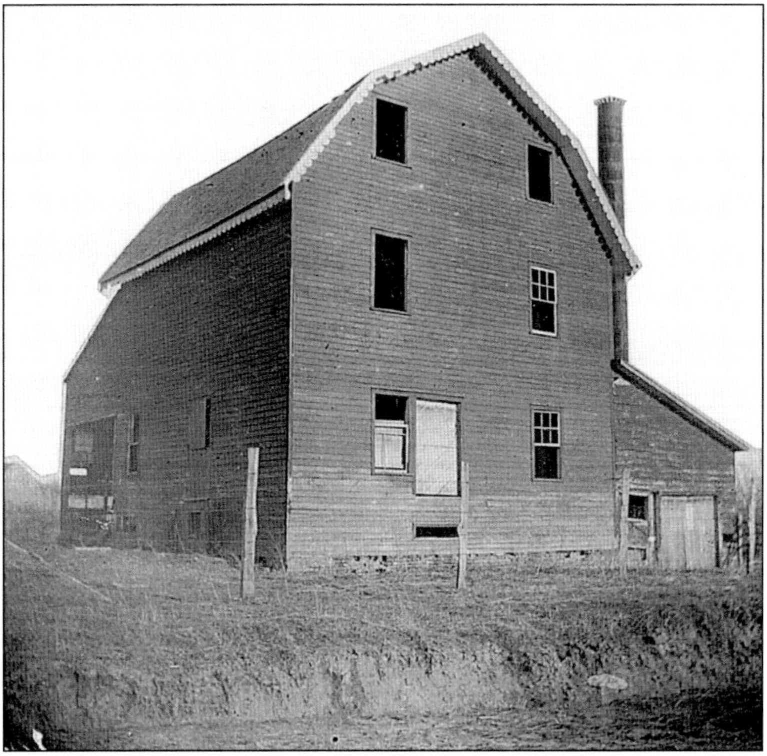

The steam powered flour mill at Elm Point was built by N.W. McClain and operated by Nethercott and Ainsley. It is shown here before being dismantled. The railroad passed the town in 1881. Within one year, the post office, store, blacksmith, and most of the residents had left. Pownell's home and the old school house are all that remain of the once thriving town. (Courtesy Bill Donnell.)

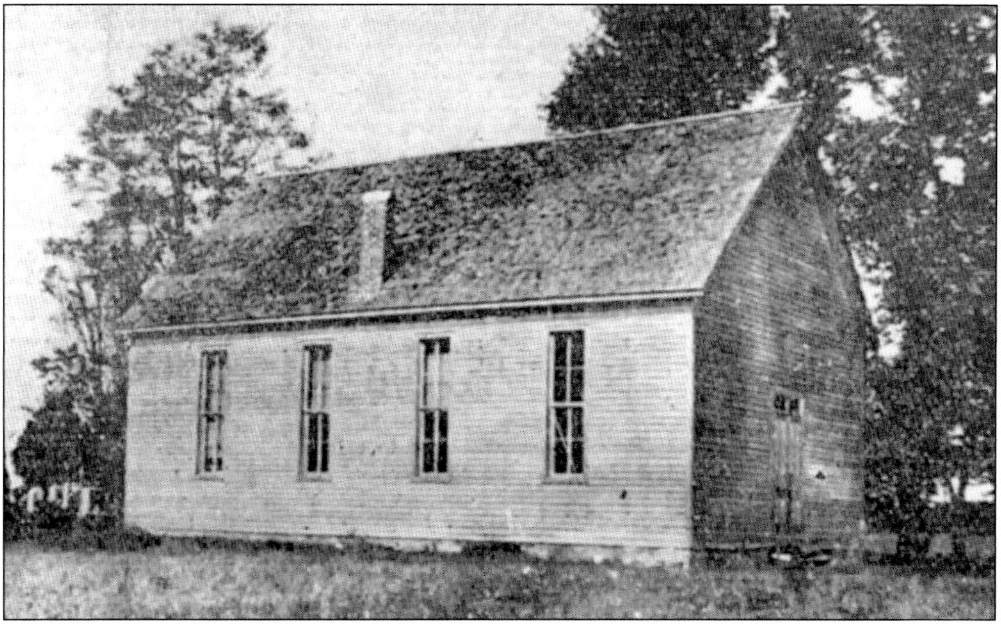

The Elm Point Presbyterian Church was organized c. 1854, one mile south of the site where the village was laid out. Pictured here is their second church, which was dedicated in 1884. The old church continued to serve the neighborhood after the town had vanished. It closed in the 1920s and was taken down in 1938. (Courtesy the *Montgomery County News*.)

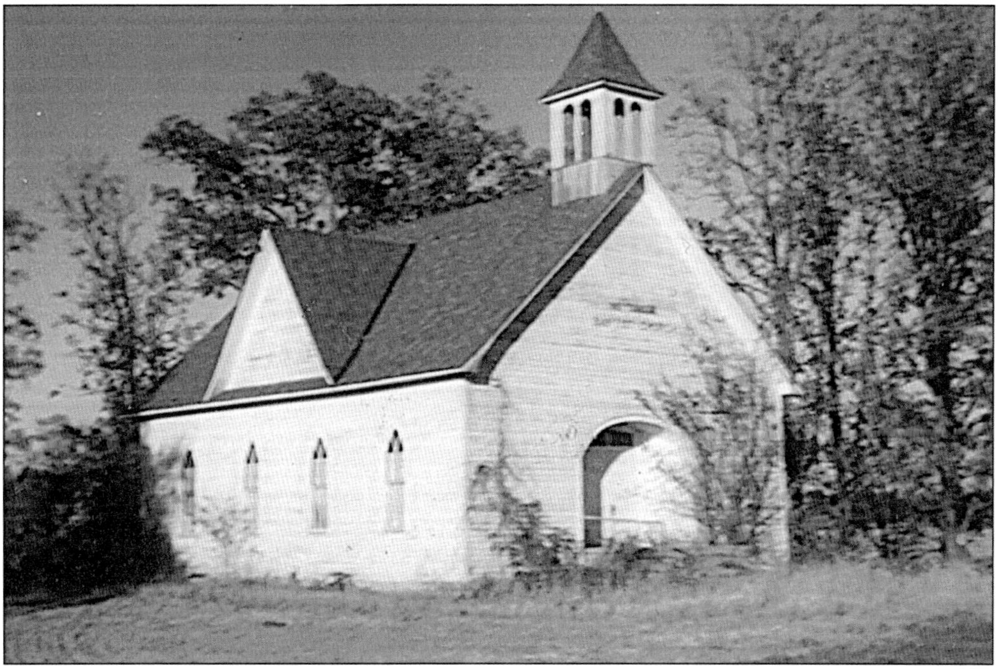

The Mount Tabor Baptist Church was organized in 1857 by Richardson Grigg. Originally built as a Union church, the Methodists, Baptists, and the Presbyterians of Jett Prairie worked together to get it established. The Baptist congregation prospered and built this structure in 1909. It closed in 1969 and has since been razed. (Courtesy Kevin Kaegy.)

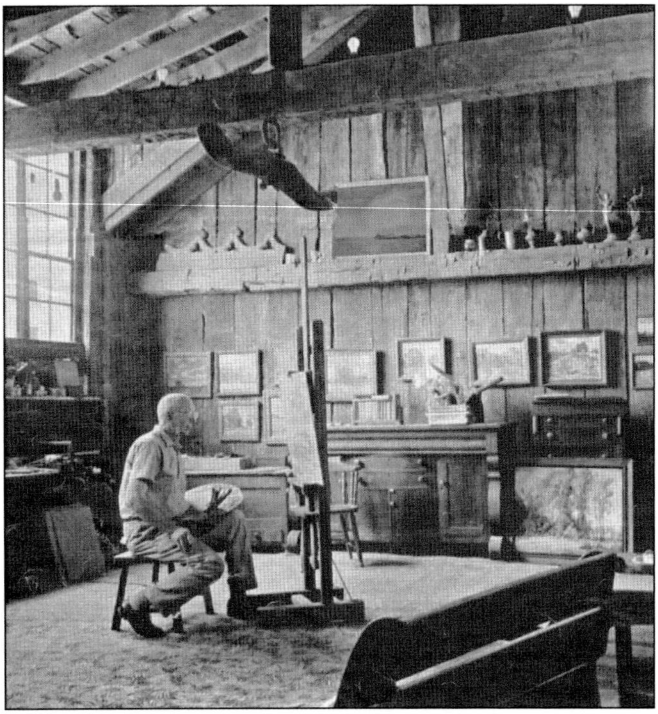

Local artist Carson Donnell worked at his easel located in the center of his barn studio. This photo was taken in 1961.The far wall is lined with his paintings. The barn was built in the 1840s by his grandfather, who also founded the town of Donnellson. Donnell's sought-after wood block prints and impressionistic oil paintings often depicted Bond County scenes and landmarks, and are the cherished possessions of Donnell art collectors. (Courtesy Wilma Baumberger.)

The village of Donnellson was laid out in 1854 by James Hutchinson on Thomas Donnell's land and named for both of them. Located just north of the county line on Route 127, it prospered after the railroad came through town in 1881. The Cloverleaf Railroad later became the Toledo, St. Louis & Western, then the Nickel Plate Road, and finally, the Norfolk & Western. The depot was razed a few years ago. (Courtesy Kevin Kaegy.)

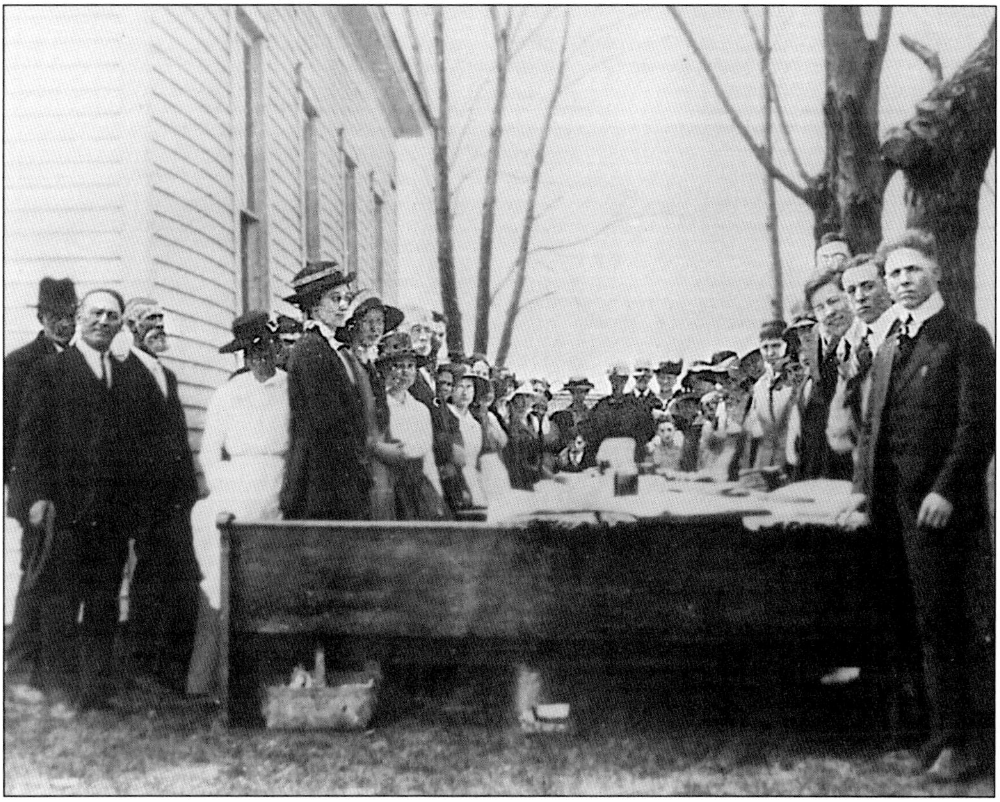

About 50 Cumberland Presbyterians are gathered together on the north side of the old Maple Grove Church for a potluck dinner in this *c.* 1920 photo. Members of the Mt. Gilead Church were also present. As the rural population moved to larger towns throughout the 1940s and 50s, many of Bond County's rural churches like Maple Grove closed. Mt. Gilead still serves its congregation. (Courtesy Lavinia McFarland.)

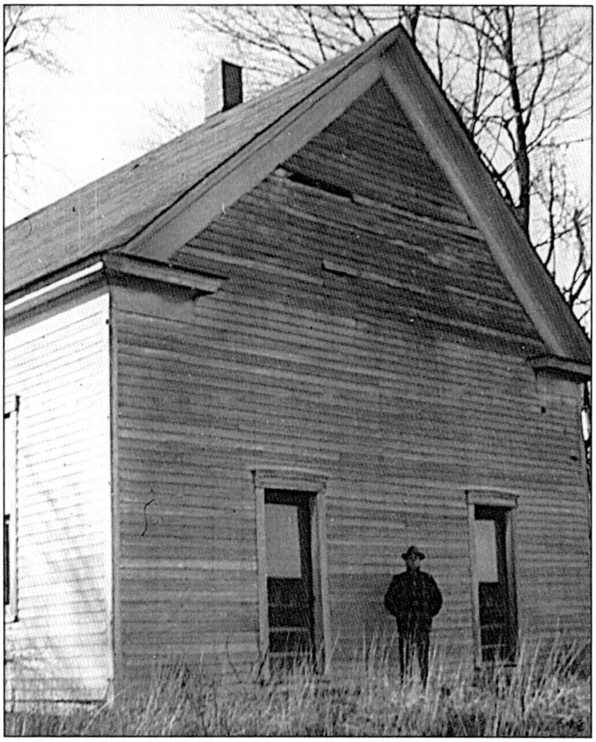

The Maple Grove Cumberland Presbyterian Church was organized in 1855 at the Union Grove Church site, where they had shared the single church with Baptist and Methodist congregations. They built their own building in 1868, over a mile north of Union Grove and changed their name to Maple Grove. (Courtesy Gib Clementz.)

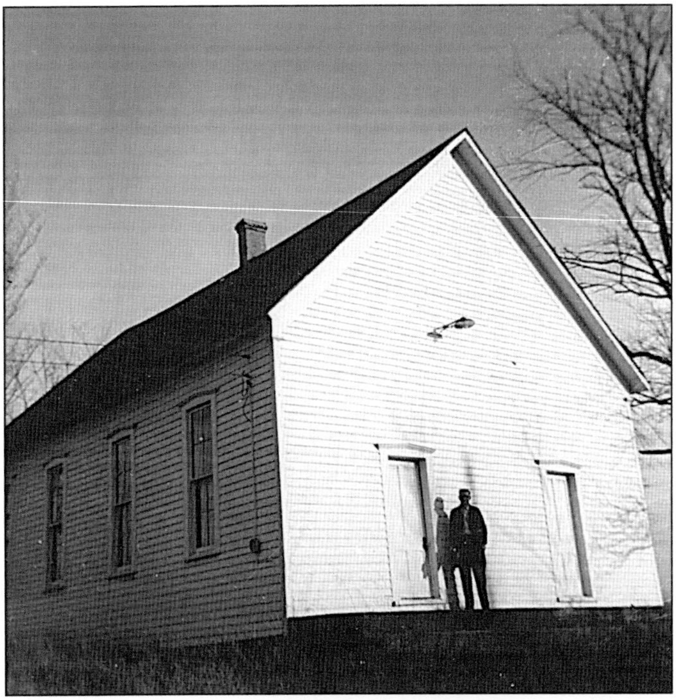

The Union Grove Free Methodist Church was the fifth and last congregation to worship at this location. They attended here from around 1880 to 1958. The old Shoal Creek Presbyterian Church was organized in 1819 on this site when the area was known as the Ohio Settlement. They split in 1825 to form the Greenville, Bethel, and Union Grove churches. A Union church was built that was shared among the Baptists, Methodists, and Cumberland Presbyterians. (Courtesy Gib Clementz.)

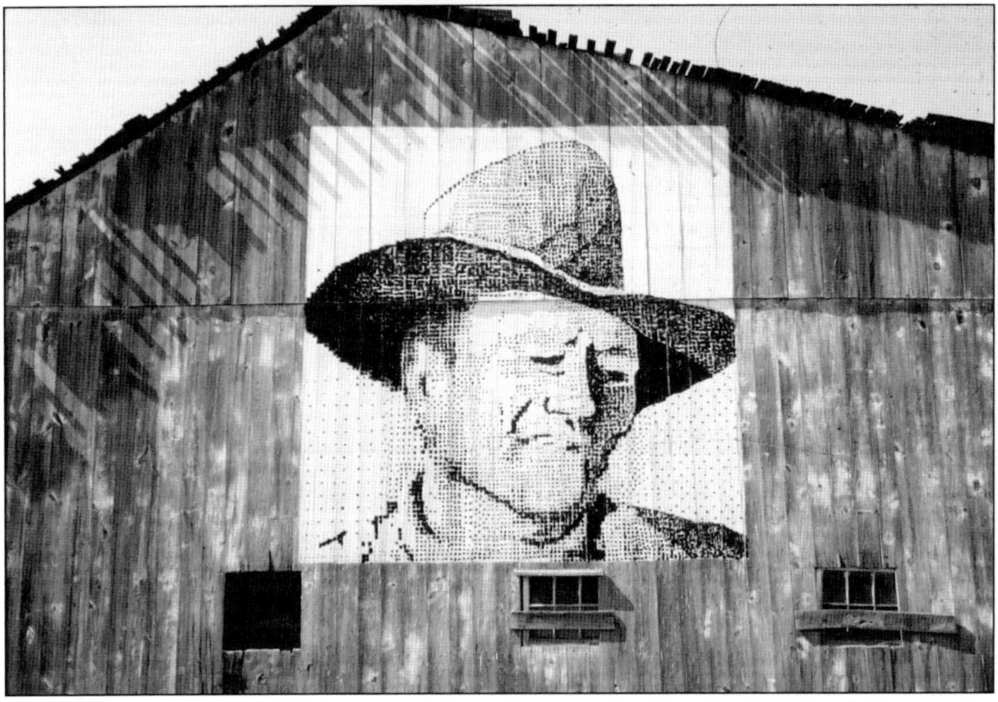

The Hubbell farm near the community of Ayers became a local landmark in Bond County after artist John Hubbell painted a large mural of John Wayne on his father's barn in 1970. The 12-by-12-foot mural could be seen for quite a distance. John Hubbell continued his mural painting in other towns, including Bloomington, Illinois, and most recently Greenville, where examples of his work can be seen on the walls of several businesses around the square. (Courtesy John Hubbell.)

Three

Mulberry Grove Township

Mulberry Grove Township is located in the far northeast section of the county. The post office of Mulberry Grove was established in 1834 and the village lots were laid out in 1841. Early names for the community were Houston, Bucktown, and Shake Rag. The latter was a nickname that came from the habit of the hotel keeper flagging down the stagecoach with a rag when they wanted it to stop for passengers. Being on the Old National Trail and the St. Louis, Vandalia & Terre Haute Railroad, Mulberry Grove was a hub of freight shipping. Along Zion Creek, which later became Kingsbury Creek, was the Zion Springs Church and campground, which was first settled around 1818. Woburn was laid out as Newport in 1856, and had the nickname of Cross Roads. Durley was established as a stop and post office along the railroad in 1884. A newer community of Royal Lakes was laid out in the 1950s southwest of Mulberry Grove.

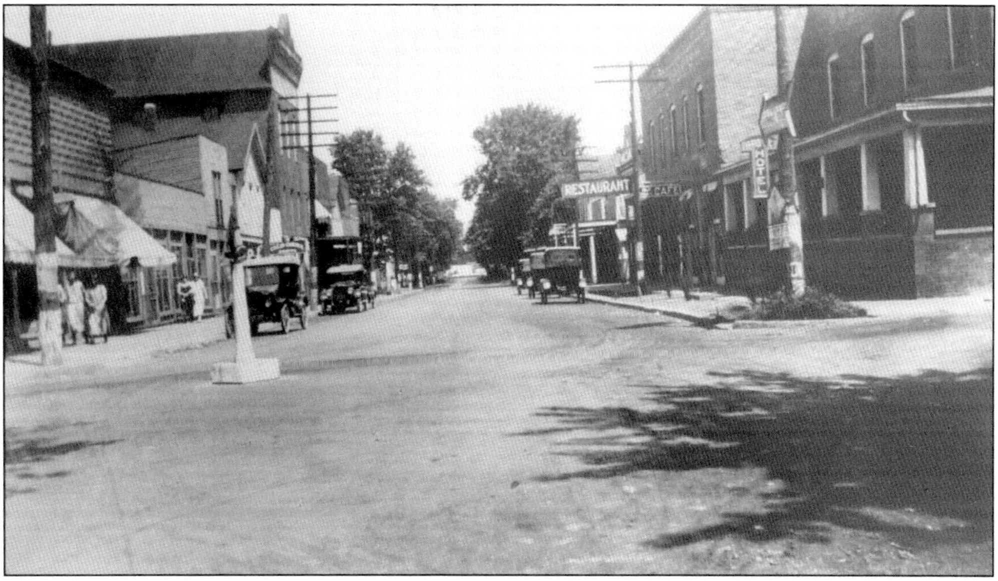

This photo of downtown Mulberry Grove was taken in 1926, looking north from the intersection of Maple and Wall Streets. At the far right (east side of the street) is the Grove Hotel, formerly the Davis House, situated where the present bank is now located. The Old Trail Cafe can be seen farther up the street on the right. (Courtesy Leah Hans.)

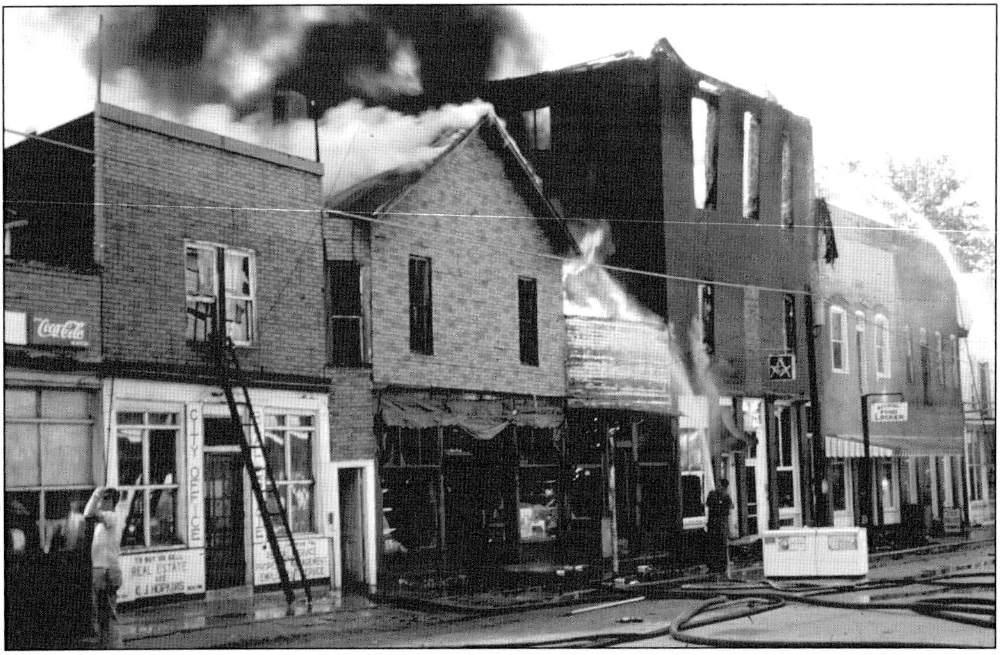

Three businesses were destroyed and others damaged when fire broke out the afternoon of June 13, 1959, in downtown Mulberry Grove. The fire started in the Mulberry Grove Locker Plant, which was on the first floor of the three-story Masonic building. Locker plant workers reported hearing a muffled explosion. At one time, the fire threatened the entire business district. Fire departments from throughout the area raced to the scene to battle the blaze. (Courtesy Bond County Historical Society.)

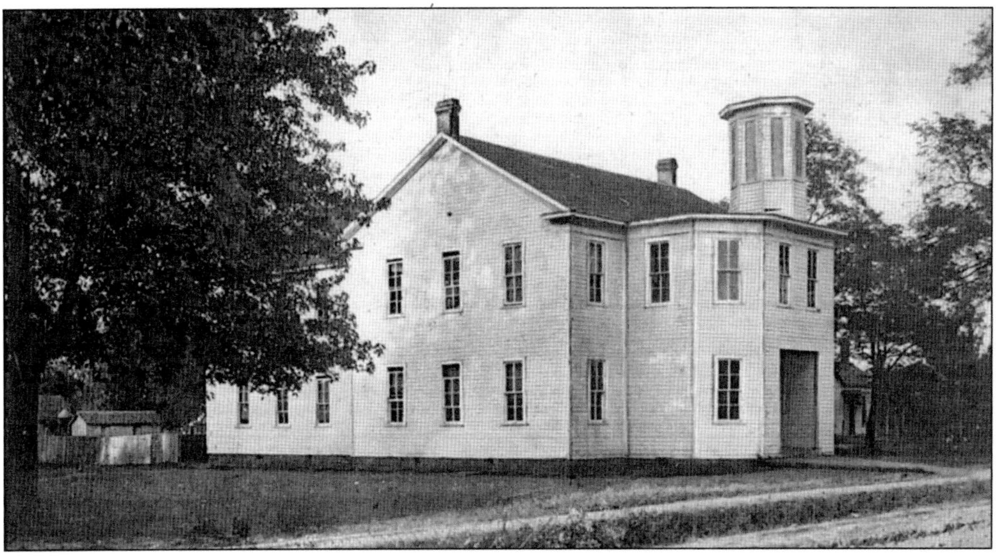

The first large public school building in Mulberry Grove was a white frame structure on School Street, between Church and Wood Streets. It served the community until 1917, when it was replaced with a brick school house, which still exists in private hands. Starting in 1917, four years of high school were offered in Mulberry Grove. In 1953 the consolidated Unit 1 high School was built west of town. (Courtesy of Jeff Leidel.)

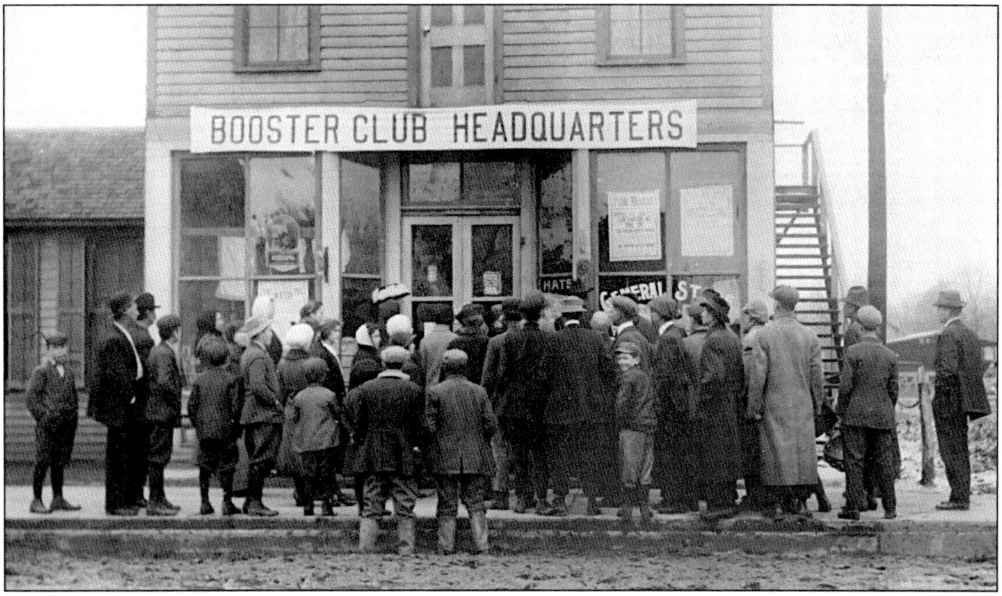

The General Store, owned by "Teen" Sellers, was located at the corner of Maple and School Streets. It later became Eckard Durr's grocery store, and later a feed store operated by Hayden Olive. This *c.* 1910 photo shows a crowd gathering in the muddy street for a contest in which a gold watch was to be given away. The Sellers once owned much of the business district on Maple Street. (Courtesy Leah Hans.)

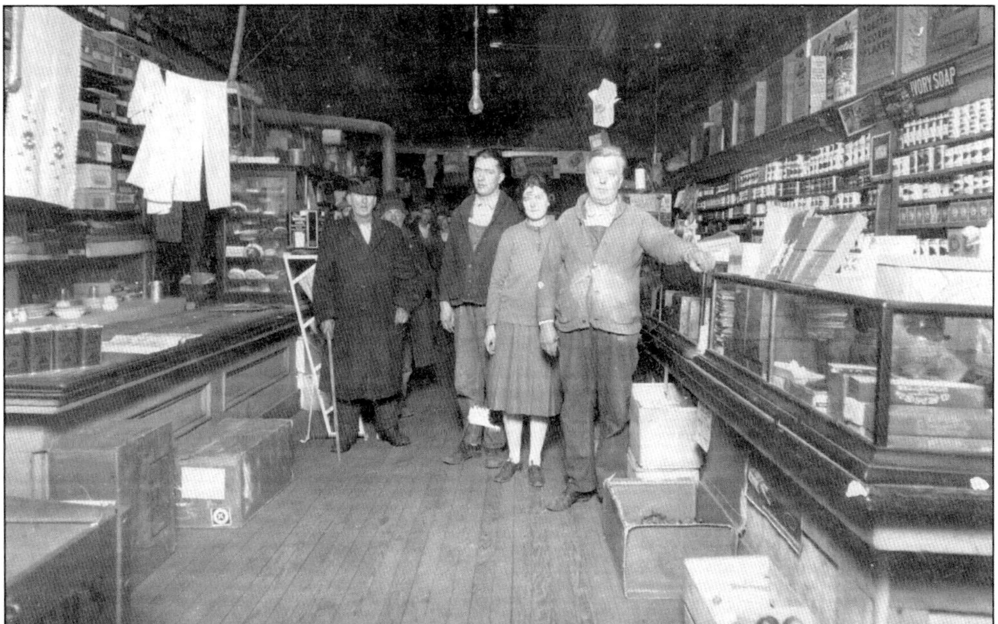

Eckard Durr moved to Mulberry Grove from VanBurensburg around 1917 and operated a general store with his son Walter. His daughter Faye also helped out at the Durr and Son store, which was a favorite haunt of school children. This photo was taken *c.* 1930. From left to right are Ben Elam, Walter Durr, Faye Durr McFarland, and Eckard Durr. (Courtesy Leah Hans.)

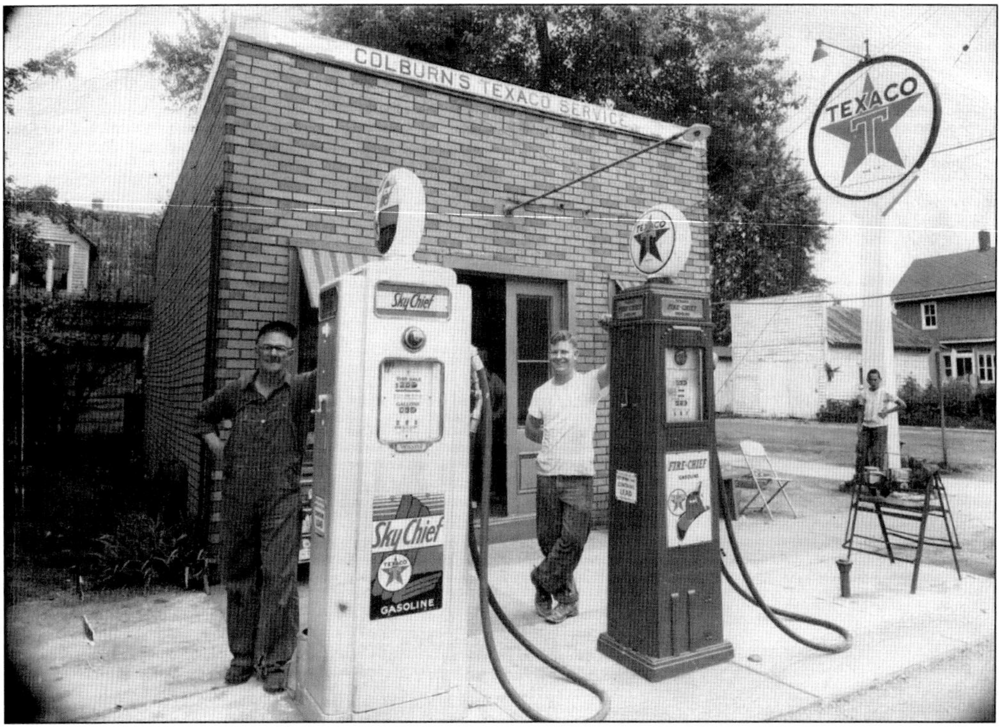

John "Jolly" Colburn opened his Texaco Station in November 1950 at the corner of School and Maple Streets in Mulberry Grove. Colburn later served as Town Clerk and water plant operator. He is pictured with his son Danny. (Courtesy Leah Hans.)

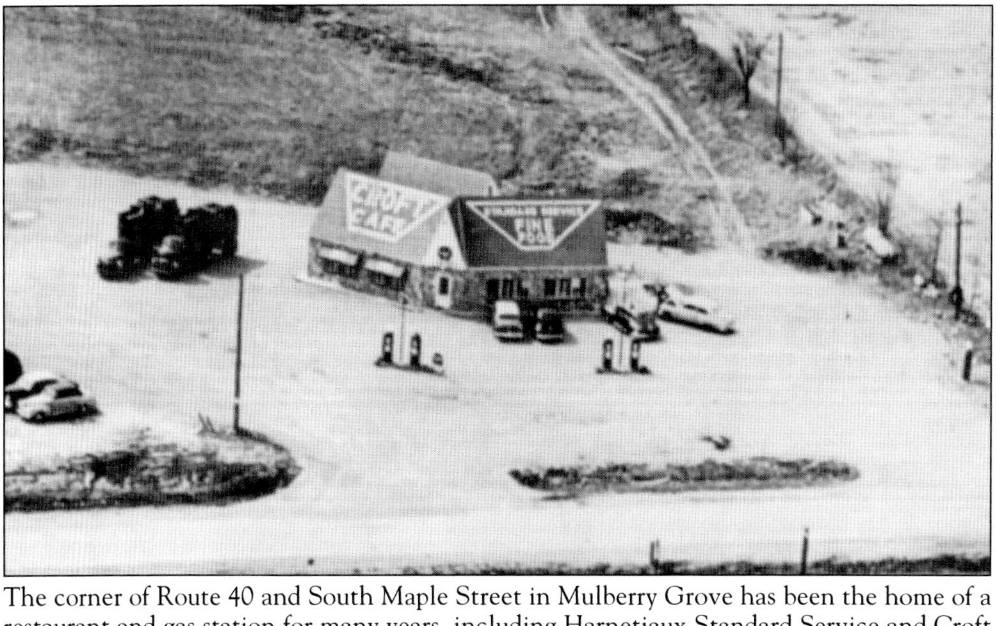

The corner of Route 40 and South Maple Street in Mulberry Grove has been the home of a restaurant and gas station for many years, including Harnetiaux Standard Service and Croft Cafe in the 1950s. (Courtesy Leah Hans.)

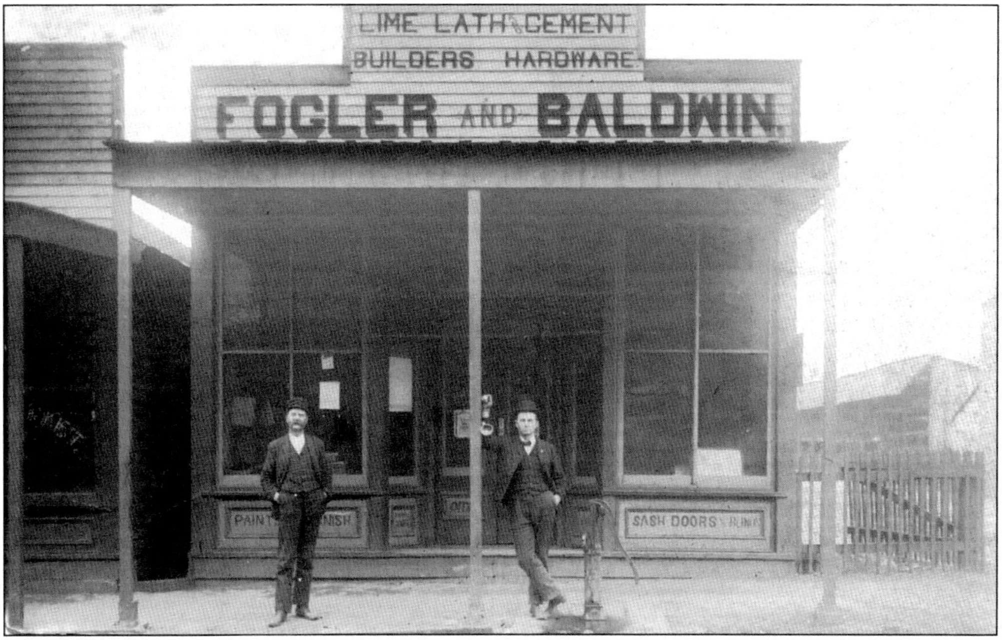

This lumber yard was operated in Mulberry Grove by William Henry Baldwin and Mr. Fogler. This photo, *c.* 1900, shows the proud owners in front of their store. It stood north of the hotel that was on the east side of Maple Street. (Courtesy Vera Furry.)

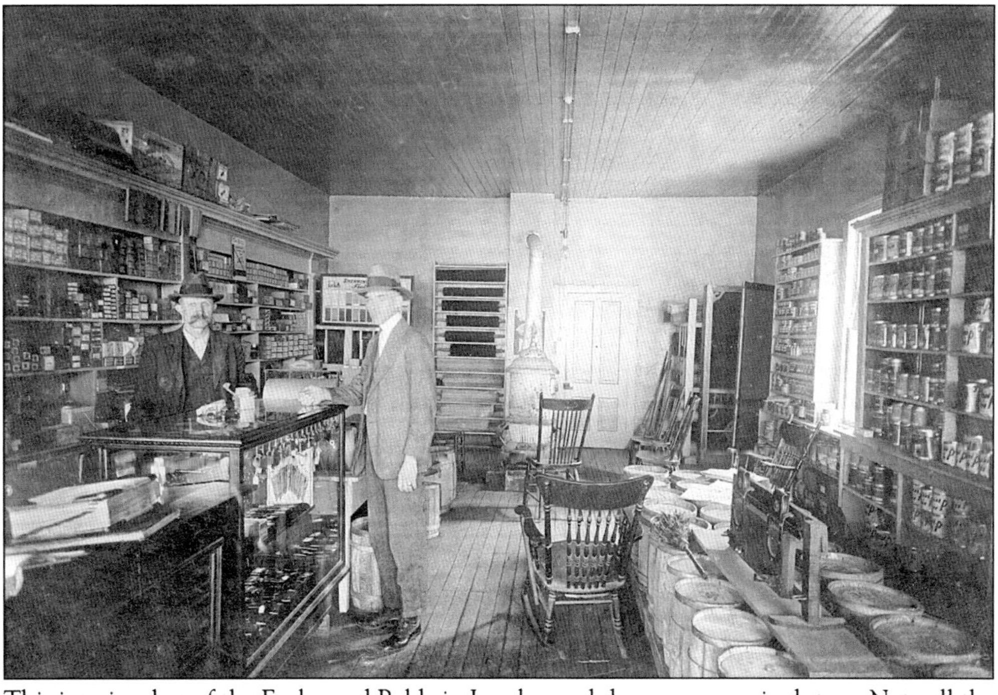

This interior shot of the Fogler and Baldwin Lumberyard shows an organized store. Note all the small barrels around the room, which are nail kegs. Once a common sight, they are seldom seen today. Notice, too, the chairs in the aisle, ready for patrons to pull up around the pot-bellied stove. This is where they whittled, loafed, and caught up on local gossip. (Courtesy Vera Furry.)

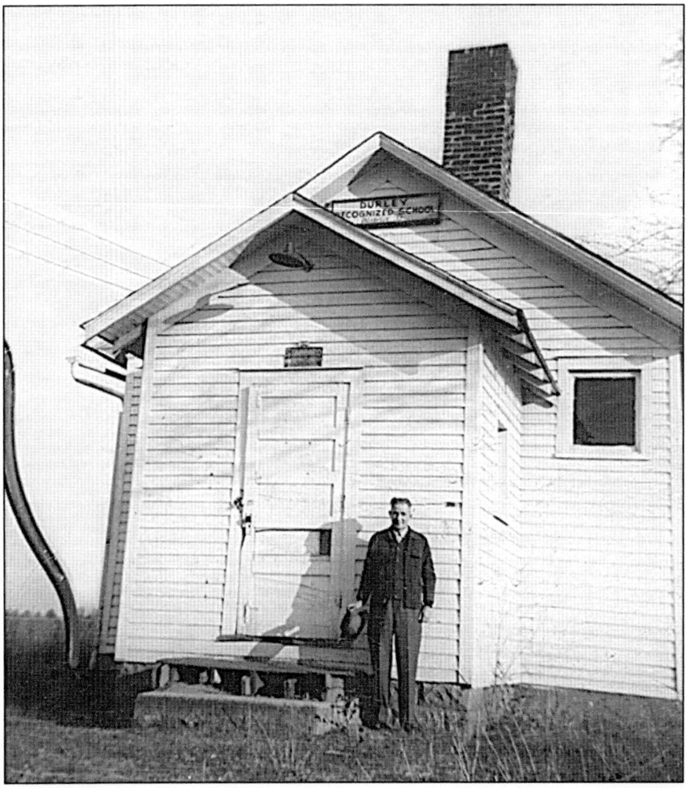

The Durley Schoolhouse along Woburn Road was the only remainder of a community that once existed on the C.B.&Q. Railroad. A store with post office was here from 1880 to 1903. A spur railroad track was built from Durley four miles southwest to Greenville. The Chicago, Greenville & Southern Railroad was supposed to go farther, but ended in Greenville, prompting wags to call it the "Chicago, Greenville and Stop." The old school was moved and is now a home. (Courtesy Gib Clementz.)

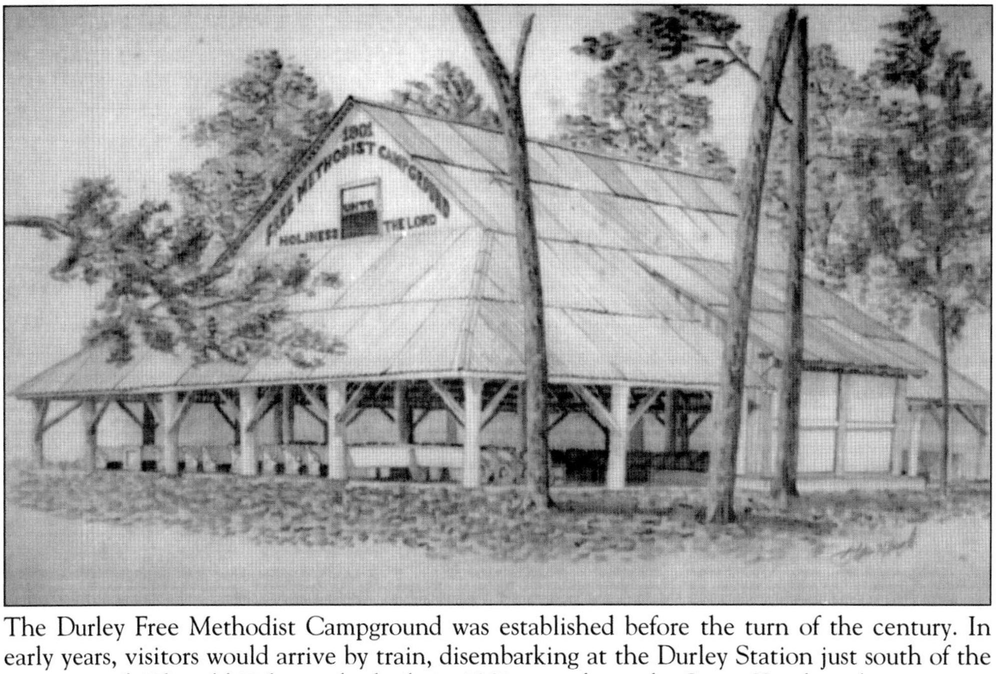

The Durley Free Methodist Campground was established before the turn of the century. In early years, visitors would arrive by train, disembarking at the Durley Station just south of the campground. The old Tabernacle, built in 1901, was drawn by Steve Knight, whose parents were the resident caretakers for many years. Retreats, youth camp, and family camp events still take place every summer. (Courtesy Marvin Knight.)

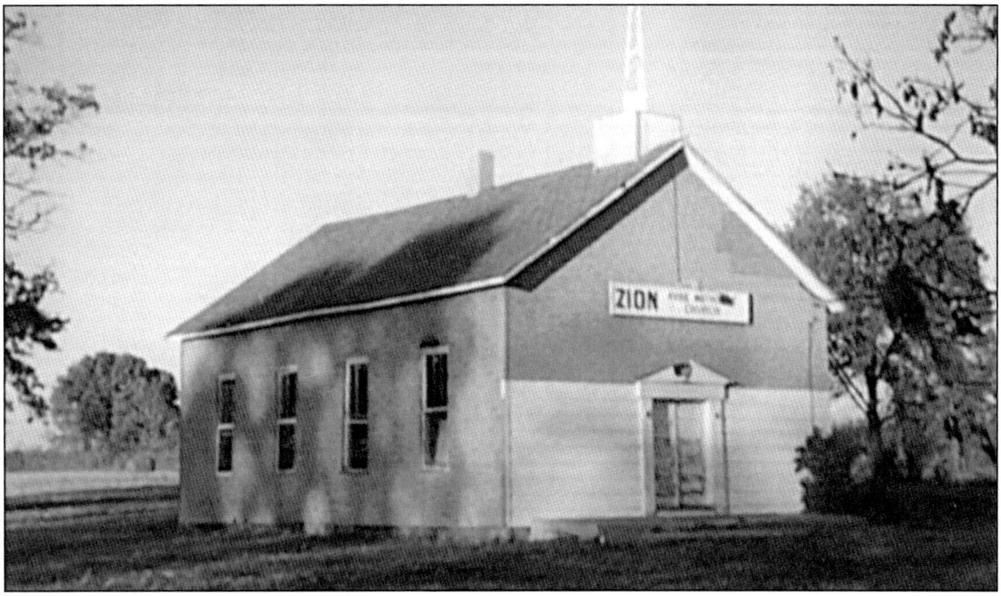

The Mt. Zion Free Methodist Church was built in 1881. It originally had two doors, one for men and the other for women. It served the Woburn neighborhood for over 80 years, closing around 1960. It has since been taken down, but the adjacent Zion Cemetery continues to be well maintained. The site was first known as Zion Springs Campground, and a Methodist Church stood there from 1828 to 1861. (Courtesy Kevin Kaegy.)

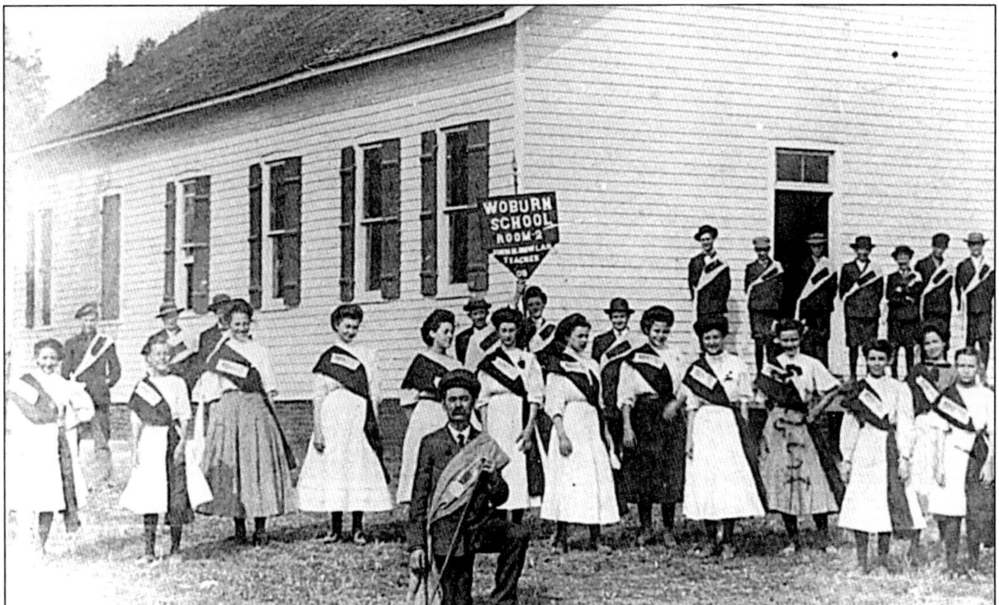

The older students at Woburn School are dressed for a school parade during the 1908 Greenville Farmer's Institute. Their teacher, John Nowlan, was also a Bond County surveyor. Nowlan wrote a history column called "Bond County Records and Traditions" for the local papers from 1927 to 1961, which was based on information he found in the early survey reports. He was the founder of the Bond County Historical Society. (Courtesy Glen Diamond.)

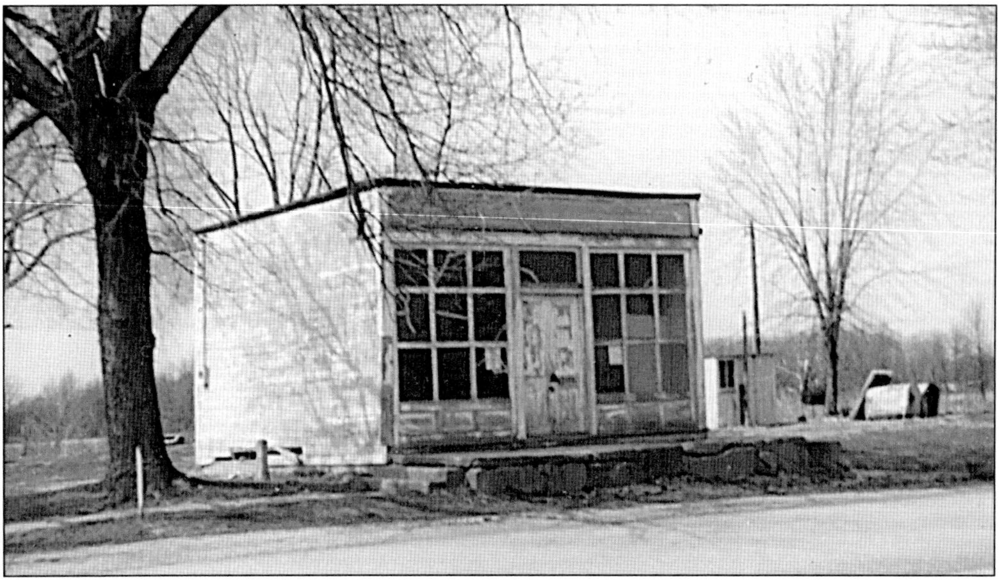

The village of Newport was laid out by John Hughes in 1856. The post office was established in 1860, but since there was already a Newport post office in the state, the town changed its name. An early resident, John B. Reid, suggested naming it for his hometown of Woburn, Massachusetts, and the name stuck. The town hall, pictured here, served as a polling place for the township until about 1980. (Courtesy Kevin Kaegy.)

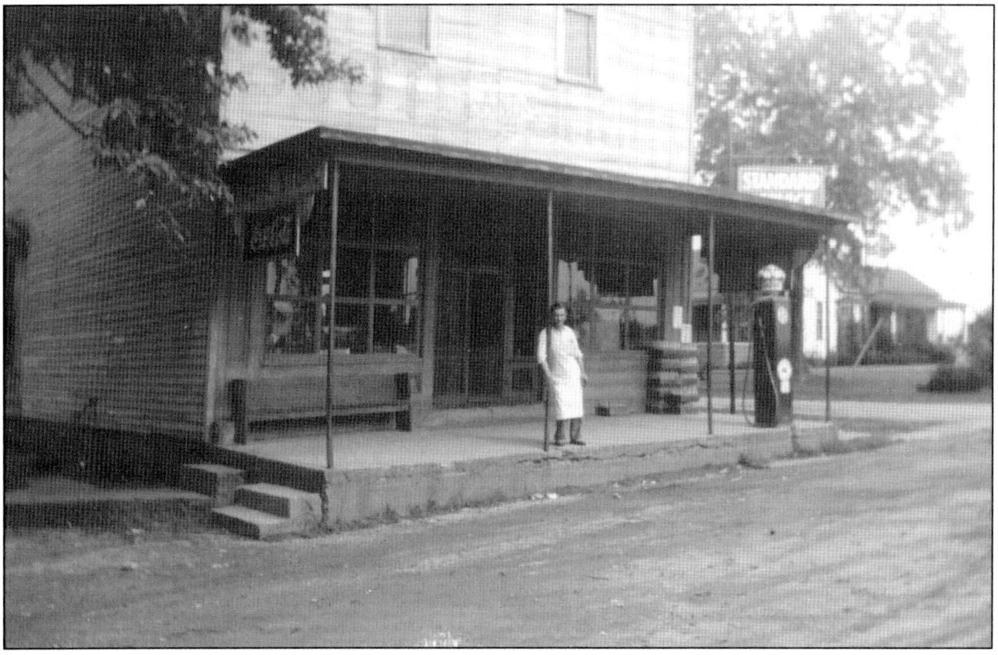

The Woburn General Store once had a second floor for holding public meetings and showing silent films in the 1920s. This photo, taken by Marvin Knight in the early 1940s, shows the owner, Charles Johnson, under the original front porch. The Rust brothers owned and remodeled the store in the fifties. Pete and Charlene Harnetiaux were the last owners, operating it from 1960 to 1976. (Courtesy Marvin Knight.)

In the fall of 1859, Brother John Williams held a revival in the old Woburn Schoolhouse. Many souls were saved, and the Woburn Church of Christ was organized. There was a strong anti-instrument element in this congregation, so no organ or piano was used until the 1890s. The present church was built in 1903, and with many modern additions, continues to serve the community. (Courtesy Glen Diamond.)

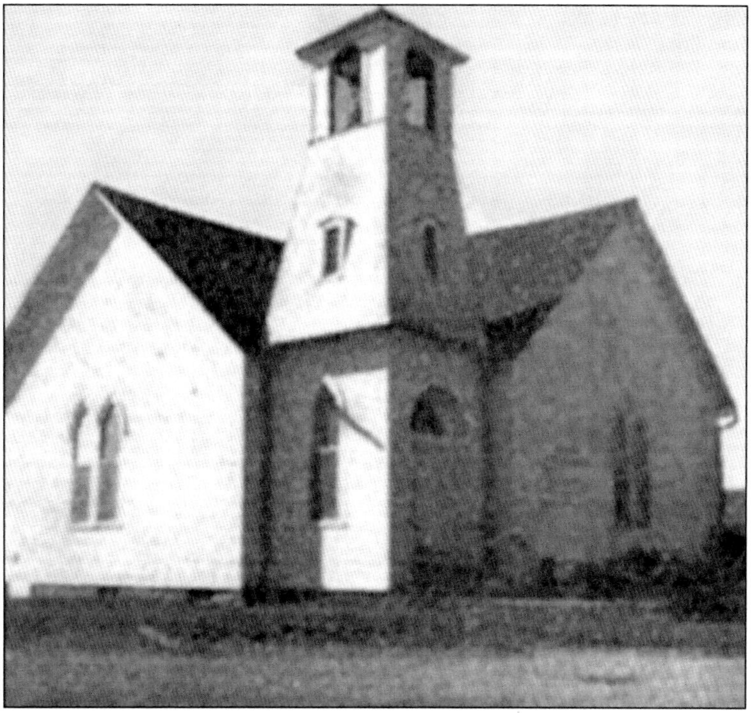

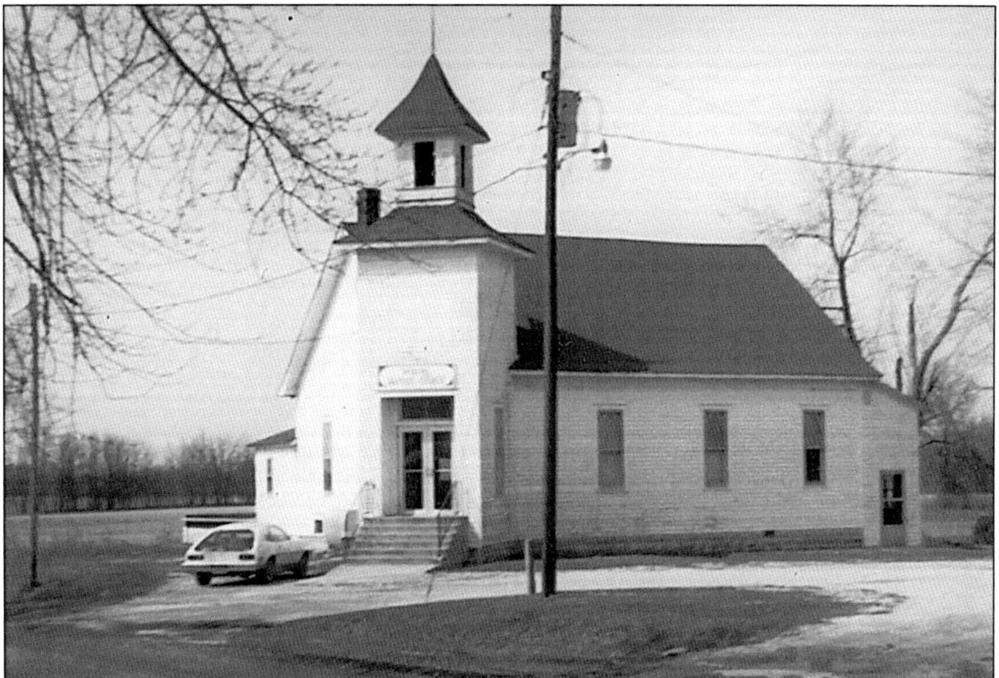

The Woburn Baptist Church was organized in 1896 by the Rehoboth Association of Baptist Churches, and the building was constructed in 1920. In early years, services were only held once a month with a minister traveling to town by horseback or buggy. Today, a full-time minister serves the congregation and lives in the adjacent parsonage. (Courtesy Wayne Snow.)

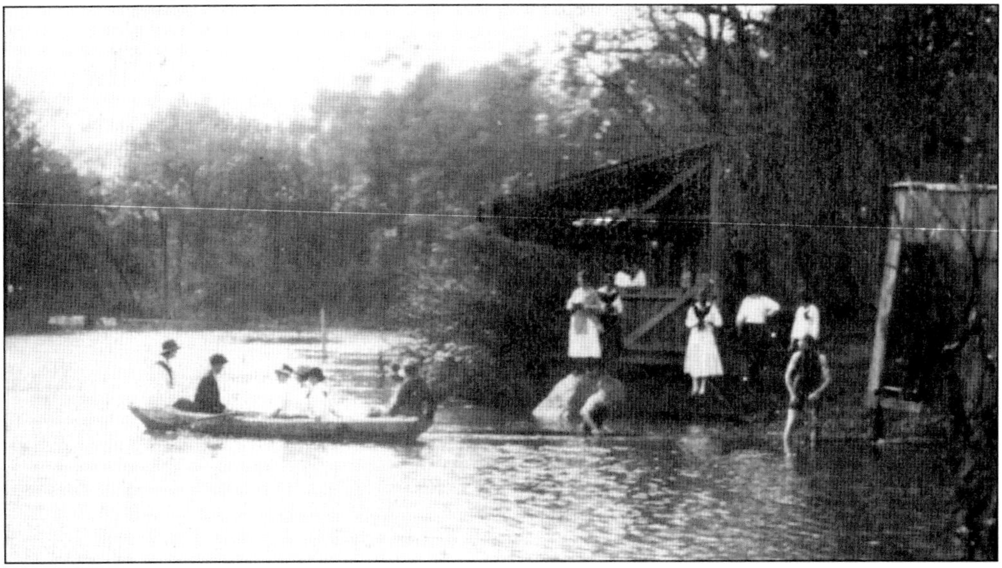

Hudson Park, a half-mile north of Mulberry Grove, was a popular recreational spot from the late 1800s through the 1930s. Activities included swimming, roller skating, canoeing, and picnicking. Charles Watson took this photo of his Greenville High School class of 1919 trip to Hudson Park. Watson wrote that the "boat leaked and the water was ice cold." (Courtesy Frank Watson.)

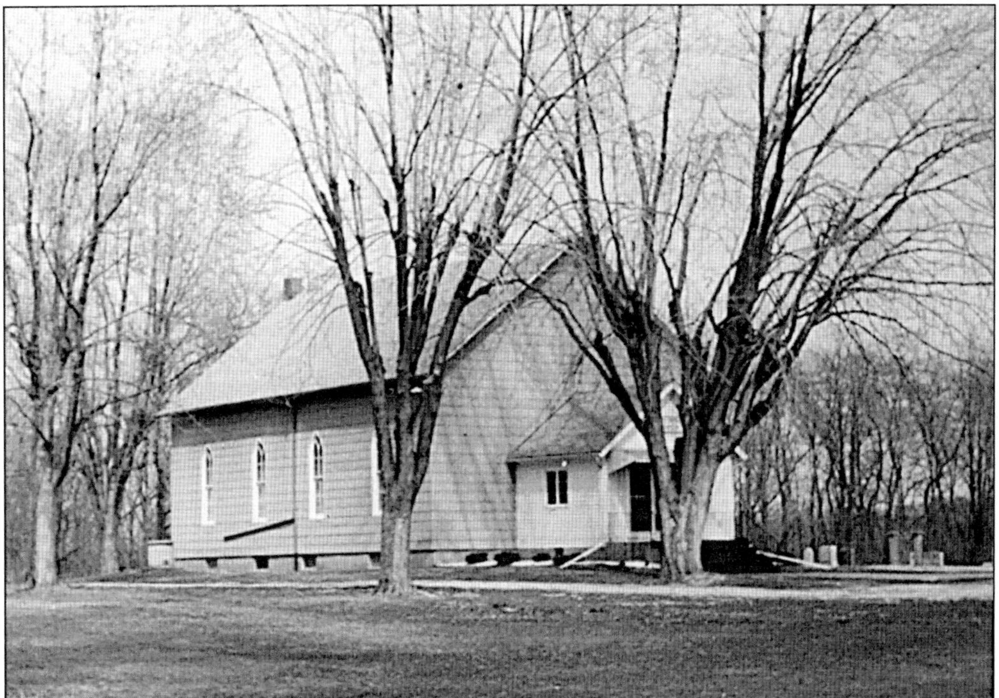

The Liberty Baptist Church was organized in 1853 after a five-day revival. They met at various locations and homes until building their first church in 1858. The present church was built in 1894 and is part of the Rehoboth Association of Baptist Churches. (Courtesy Kevin Kaegy.)

Four

Pleasant Mound Township

Pleasant Mound Township is in the east central portion of Bond County. It was previously the Fairview Precinct. It consists of three main communities: Fairview, New Hamburg, and Smithborough. Fairview, now more commonly known as Pleasant Mound, was established in 1857. New Hamburg was nicknamed Sorghumtown for its four sorghum mills. Smithborough was founded in 1870 by Henry L. Smith, a wealthy entrepreneur, whose influence and efforts got the Jacksonville-Southeastern Railroad, later the CB&Q, to come through in 1882. The railroad dubbed the village Henderson Station, and the spelling of the town was shortened to Smithboro in 1893. Brookside was platted just north of Smithboro around the turn of the century, but now consists of only a few houses. The area in the south part of the township just northwest of Hookdale was known as Dutch Flats, for all the German farmers that settled there.

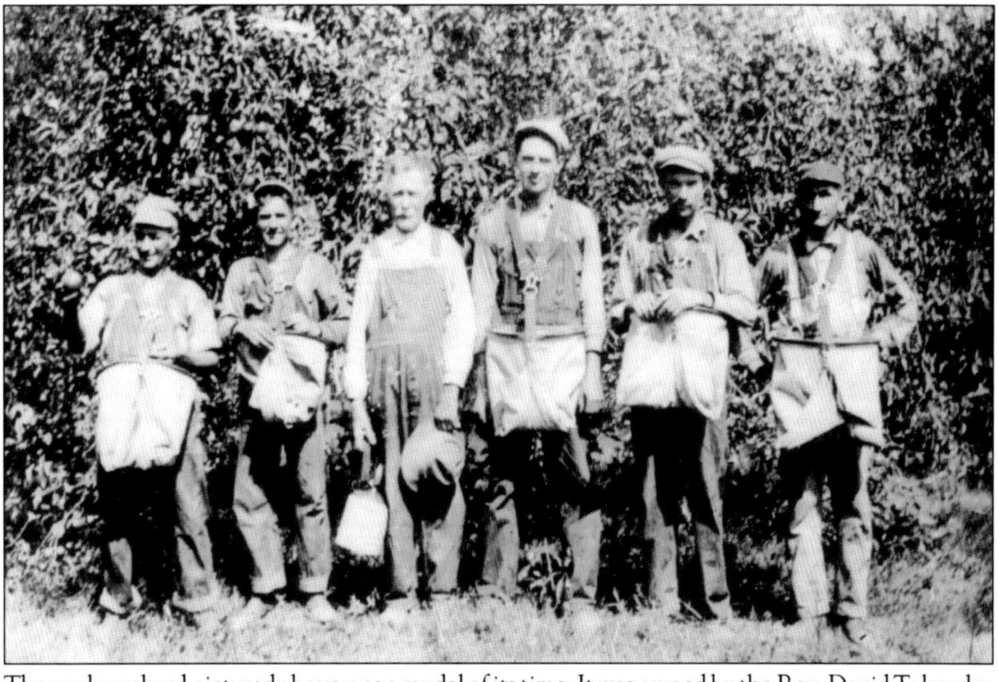

The apple orchard pictured above was a model of its time. It was owned by the Rev. David Talmadge "Tally" Defrees, who also served as an officer in various agricultural associations. The orchard was located two miles east of Smithboro and local men were hired to harvest the crop. Apple pickers shown in this c. 1930 photo are, from left to right, Gilbert Kious, Douglas Wheatley, unidentified, Luther Moore, Albert Steiner, and Bill Stark. (Courtesy Janice Baldwin.)

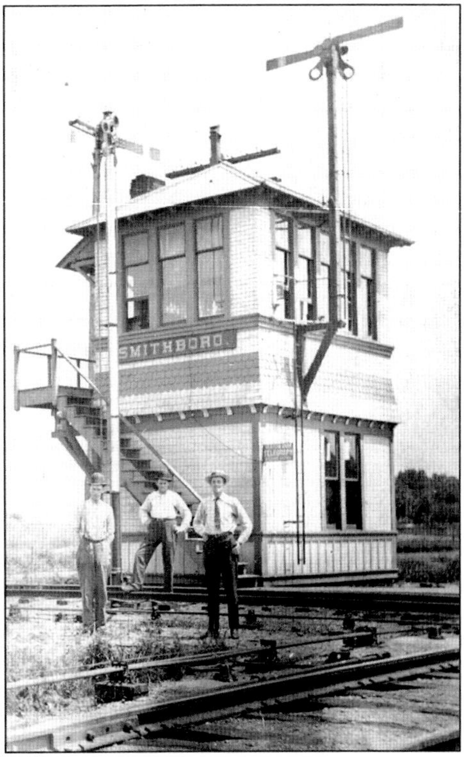

Smithboro's switch tower watched over the busy intersection of the C.B.& Q. railroad interchange with the Pennsylvania Railroad. Note the detail on this structure: bracketed eaves, fishscale shingles, and wainscot siding. It was replaced by a rather plain brick building around 1940. The men in this 1910 photo are unidentified. (Courtesy Janice Baldwin.)

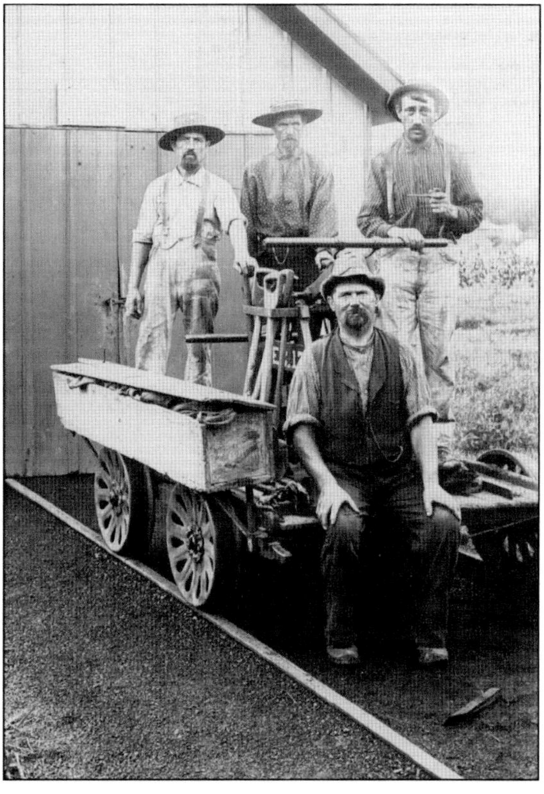

This handcar shed stood along the C.B.& Q. tracks in Smithboro. This c. 1890 work crew is ready to go out for maintenance duty. Tools and the handcar were stored in the shed when they were not in use. (Courtesy Paulette Bandelow Kelly.)

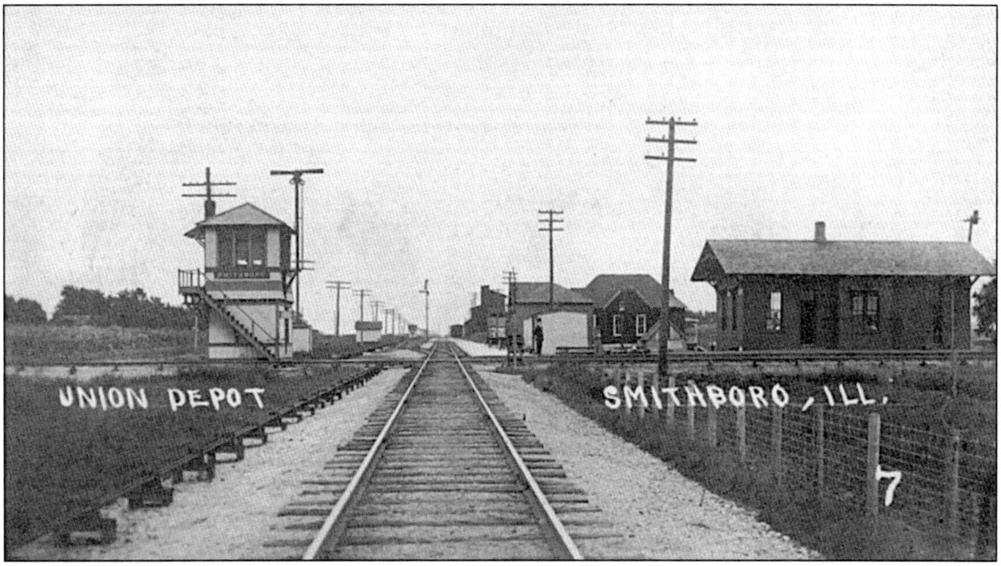

Smithboro Union Station c. 1910, was one of two separate stations when rail was America's main form of transportation. The Pennsylvania and the C.B.& Q. (Jacksonville) Railroads provided North-South and East-West transport for mail, people, and Smithboro area rural and industrial products. Along the tracks were the railroad control tower and telegraph office, Pennsylvania Station, the waterworks, creamery, livestock holding facilities, grain elevator, and coal mine. (Courtesy John Coleman.)

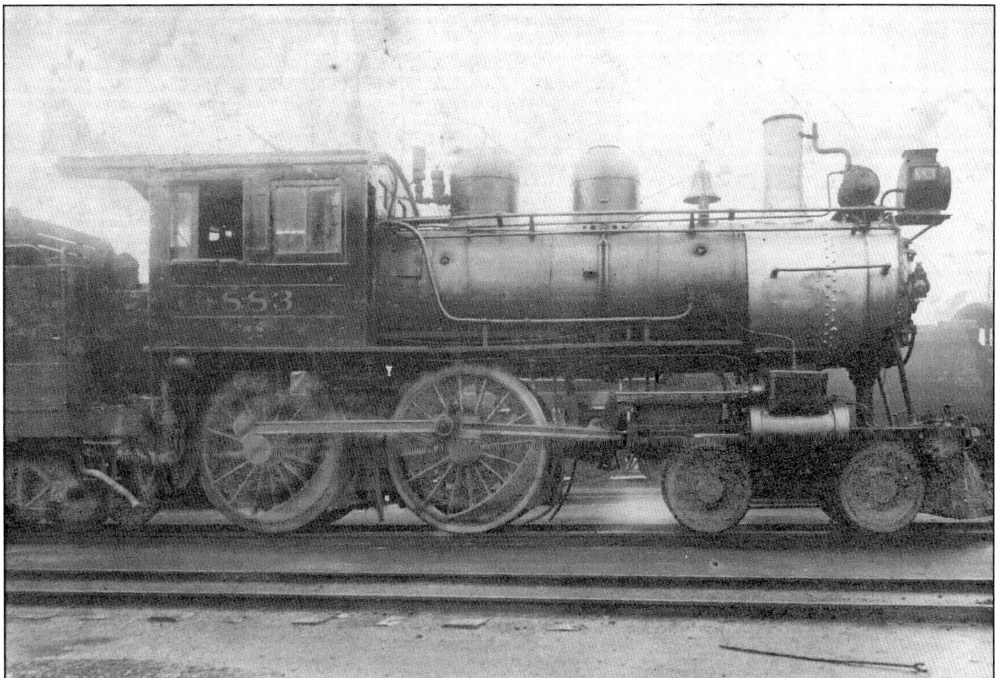
This small steam engine, #883, remained in service on the C.B.& Q. Railroad until 1955. It was used on a daily passenger run from Centralia to Beardstown. In later years, a diesel rail coach replaced the steam engine. (Courtesy Paulette Bandelow Kelly.)

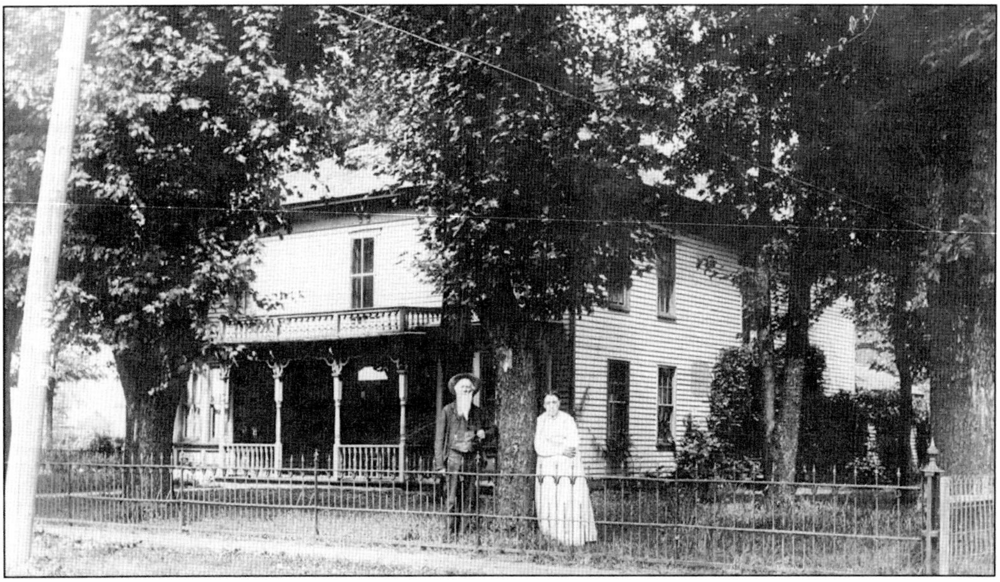

Henry and Eleanor Smith, in front of their home on Main Street before 1908, were wealthy and well-educated Easterners. Smith, the founder and promoter of Smithboro, almost succeeded in having the county seat moved to Smithboro after winning the C.B.& Q. line away from Greenville. After this home was destroyed by fire, a second home was built, which later served as the Smithboro Library and the Eleanor Home. The Smiths are buried below concrete in the back yard. (Courtesy John Coleman.)

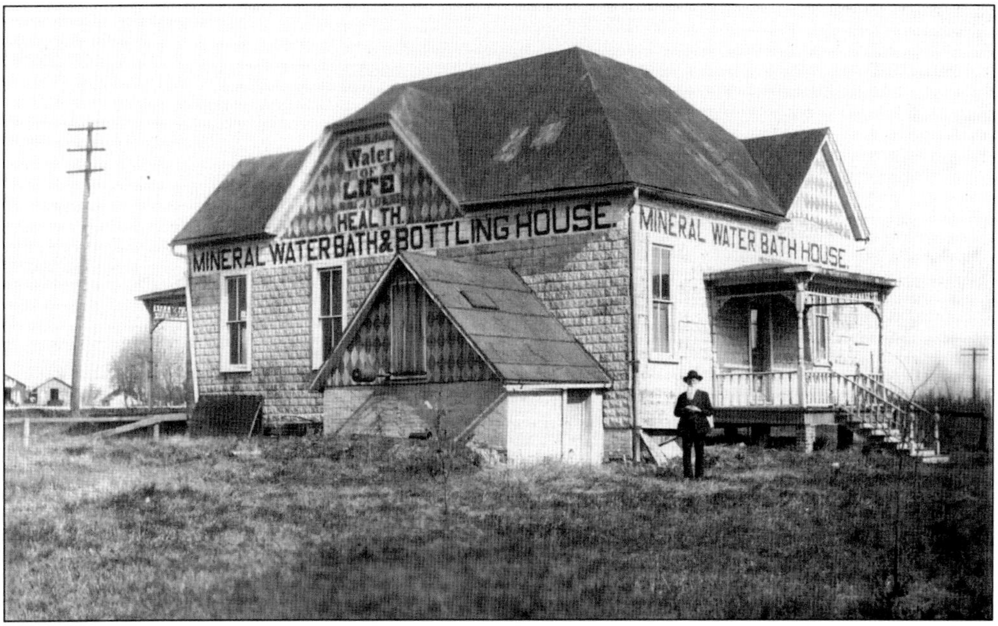

Smithboro Waterworks and Bath House was located along the rail line and the much touted mineral water was bottled and served in the Pennsylvania Railroad dining cars. A buggy transported patrons between the hotel and bath house, where they received the healthful benefits of the mineral water spa. The structure was torn down in 1940 when the Route 40 bridge was built through Smithboro. (Courtesy John Coleman.)

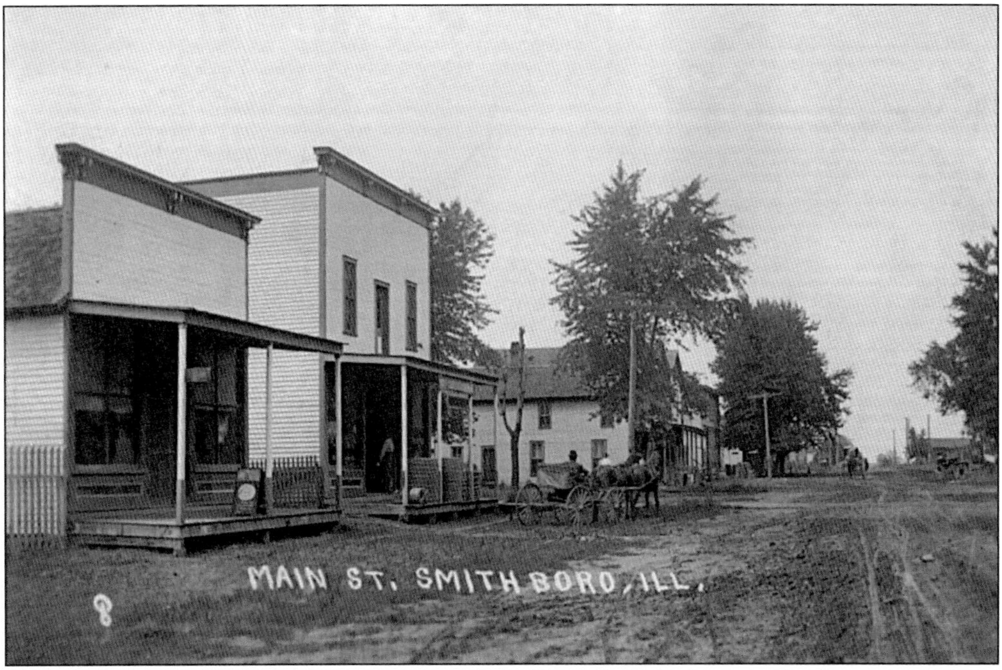

The west side of Main Street, *c.* 1910, included the Elam buildings, which comprised the following: an undertaker's parlor (later the Smithboro Post Office), a hardware store with a lumber yard in the rear, the mine door factory, another hardware store, a grocery store, and a restaurant. (Courtesy John Coleman.)

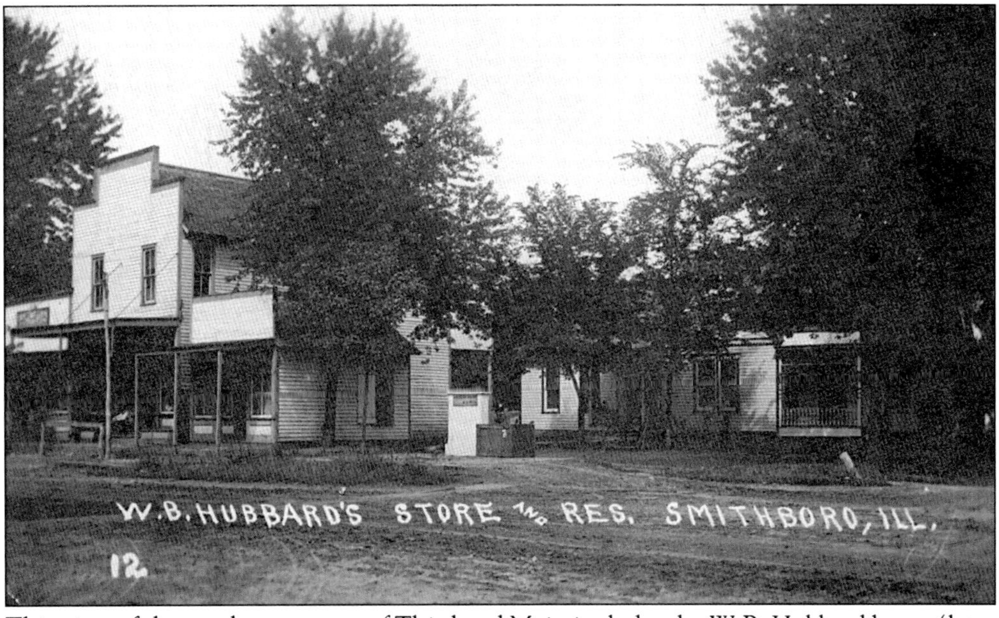

This view of the northeast corner of Third and Main includes the W.B. Hubbard home (later a doctor's office and residence) a weight station (later a barber shop) and W.B. Hubbard's grocery store. At the far left is the Smithboro Bank, now the Smithboro Village Hall. (Courtesy John Coleman.)

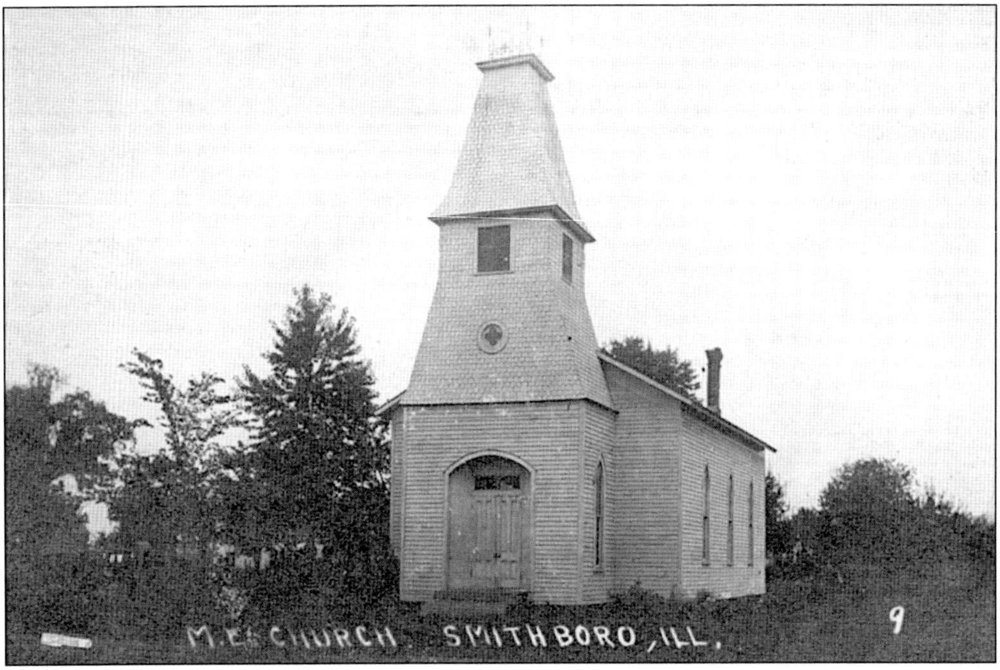

The Methodist Episcopal Church was one of three churches in Smithboro. The others were a Brethren Church and a Christian Church. The Methodist Church was built by Henry Smith and was part of his estate at death. The Smiths, staunch Methodists, bequeathed their large home to the denomination as the Eleanor Home for elderly Methodist women. (Courtesy John Coleman.)

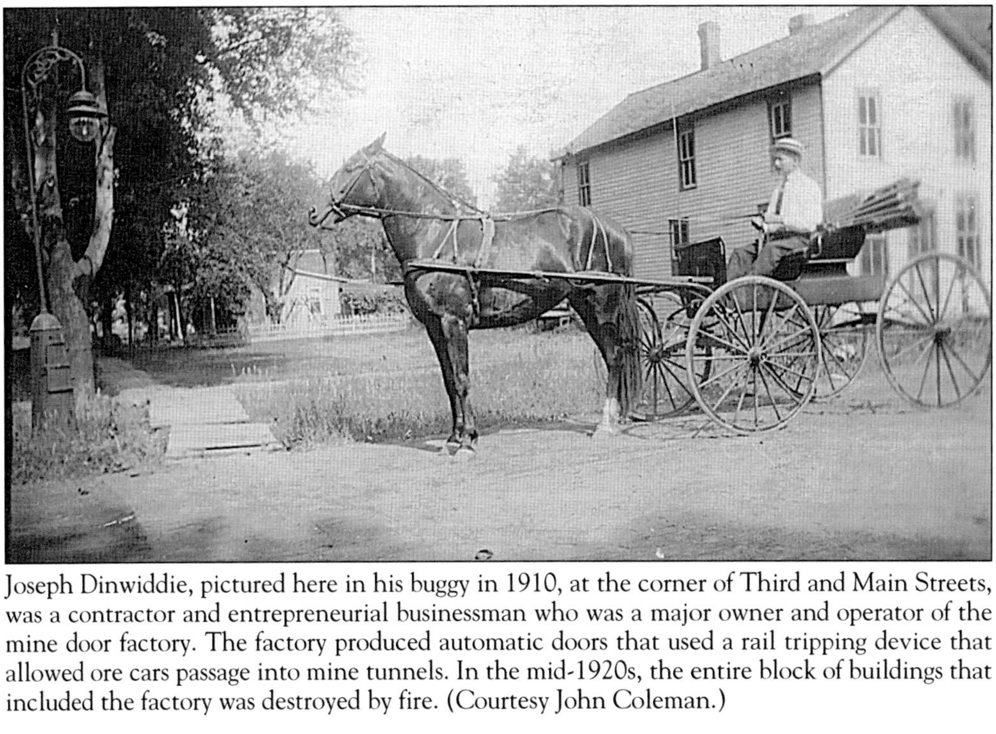

Joseph Dinwiddie, pictured here in his buggy in 1910, at the corner of Third and Main Streets, was a contractor and entrepreneurial businessman who was a major owner and operator of the mine door factory. The factory produced automatic doors that used a rail tripping device that allowed ore cars passage into mine tunnels. In the mid-1920s, the entire block of buildings that included the factory was destroyed by fire. (Courtesy John Coleman.)

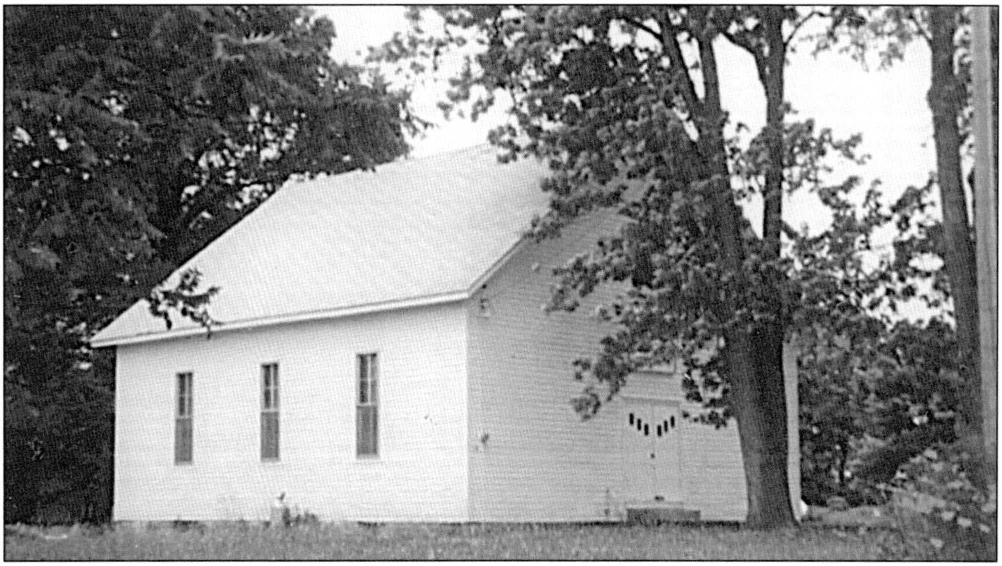

The Hurricane Creek Church of the Brethren was built in 1874, then moved a mile northward into town in 1908. The basement was completed in 1942. With additional improvements as needed through the years, it still serves the community of Pleasant Mound as the Church of the Brethren. It is often referred to by outsiders as the "Dunkard" Church. (Courtesy Kevin Kaegy.)

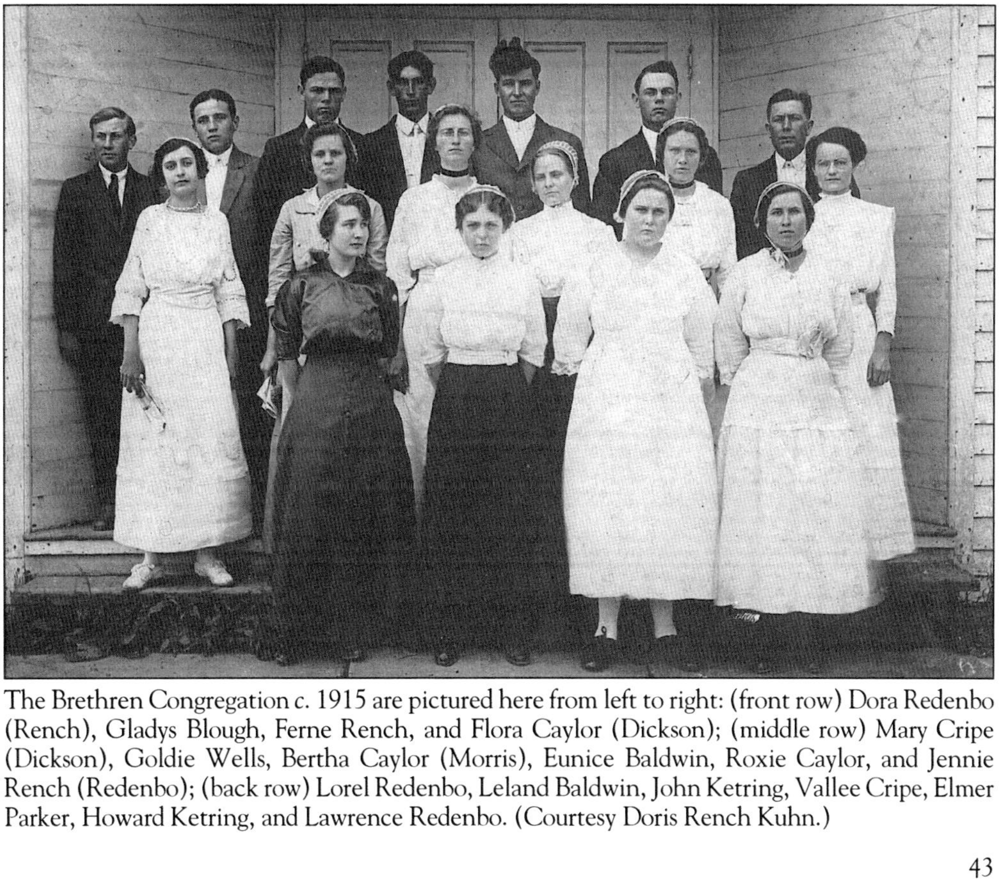

The Brethren Congregation c. 1915 are pictured here from left to right: (front row) Dora Redenbo (Rench), Gladys Blough, Ferne Rench, and Flora Caylor (Dickson); (middle row) Mary Cripe (Dickson), Goldie Wells, Bertha Caylor (Morris), Eunice Baldwin, Roxie Caylor, and Jennie Rench (Redenbo); (back row) Lorel Redenbo, Leland Baldwin, John Ketring, Vallee Cripe, Elmer Parker, Howard Ketring, and Lawrence Redenbo. (Courtesy Doris Rench Kuhn.)

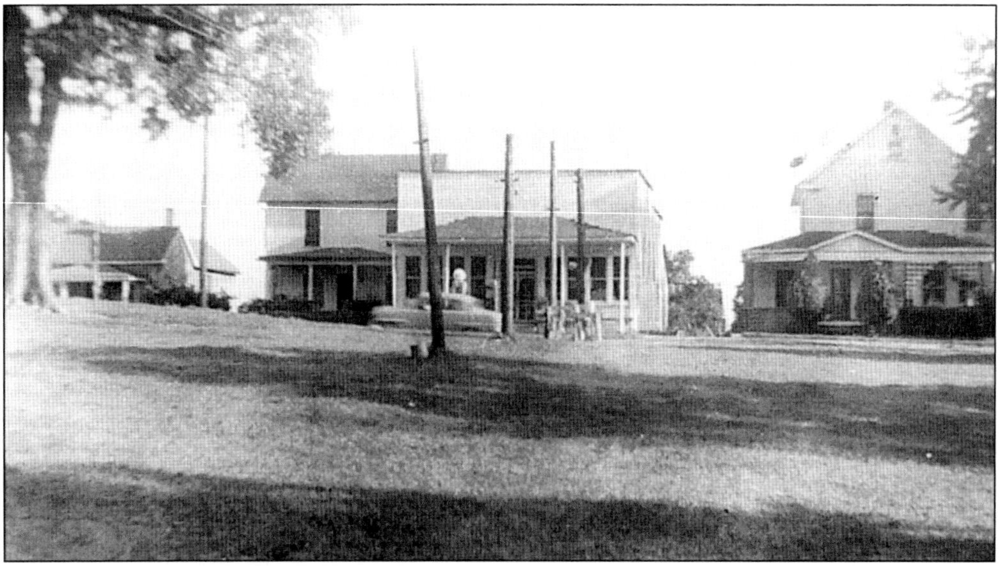

The community of Fairview was laid out in 1857, and came to be known by the name of the post office, Pleasant Mound. Taken in the 1950s, this photo shows Ralph Cheatham's home (left) and Wheatley's store (right), which was built in 1909 by James T. Harper. The home attached to the store was built in 1914 by C.J. Bauer when he ran the business. The large home on the right was built by Harper in 1914. All but the Cheatham home burned on November 26, 1970. (Courtesy Janice Baldwin.)

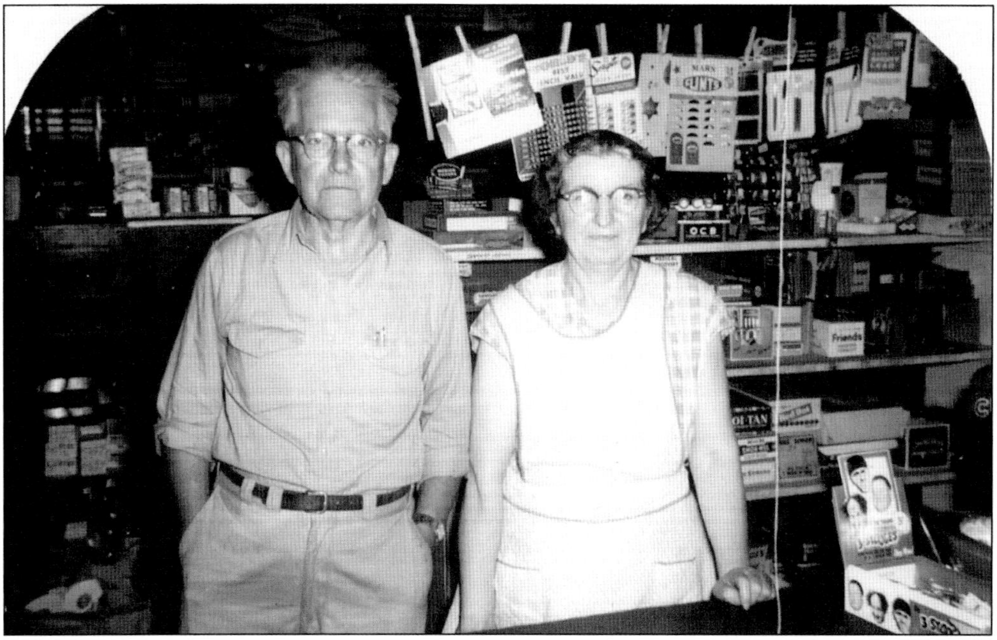

Douglas Wheatley, here with his wife, Lucinda, was the proprietor of the store in Pleasant Mound from 1940 to 1961. It housed the Pleasant Mound Post Office. Wheatley served as postmaster from 1932 until the post office was discontinued on January 31, 1954. Previously, the post office was housed in the old Harper store and in the old restaurant building just to its west. (Courtesy Vera Furry.)

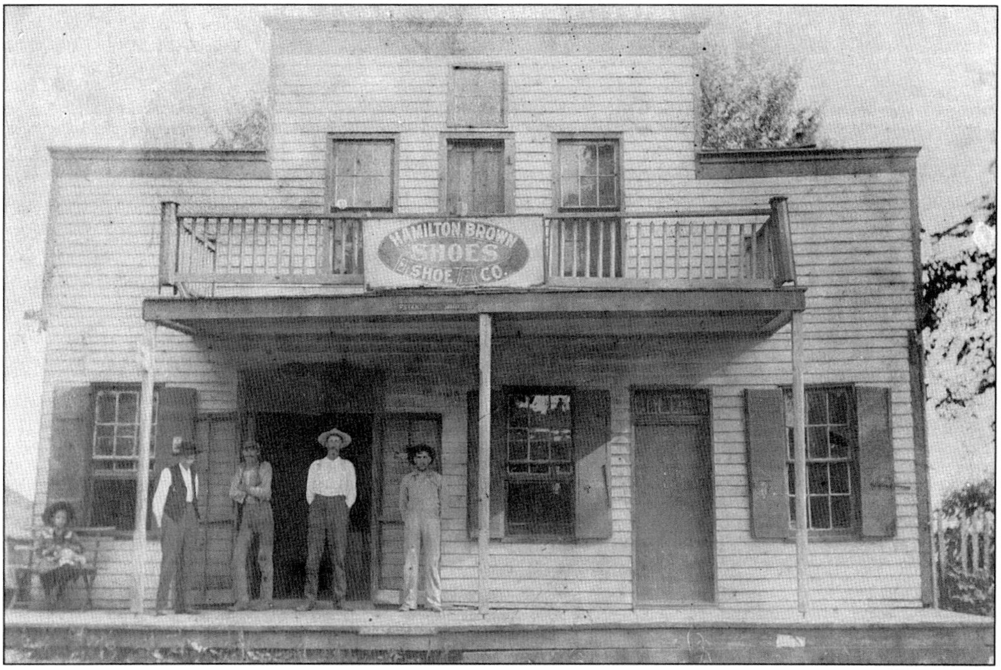

The first store in Fairview was built by brothers William C. and Ephraim Perkins in 1856. James T. Harper, the final owner, sold out its stock of goods to C.J. Bauer, who moved them to the new store building in 1913. In 1914, James Harper dismantled the old store and built a new home on the site. Identified above, *c.* 1900, are May Harper (Kuhn) on the bench at left, and James T. Harper in the white shirt, second from right. (Courtesy Lloyd Kuhn.)

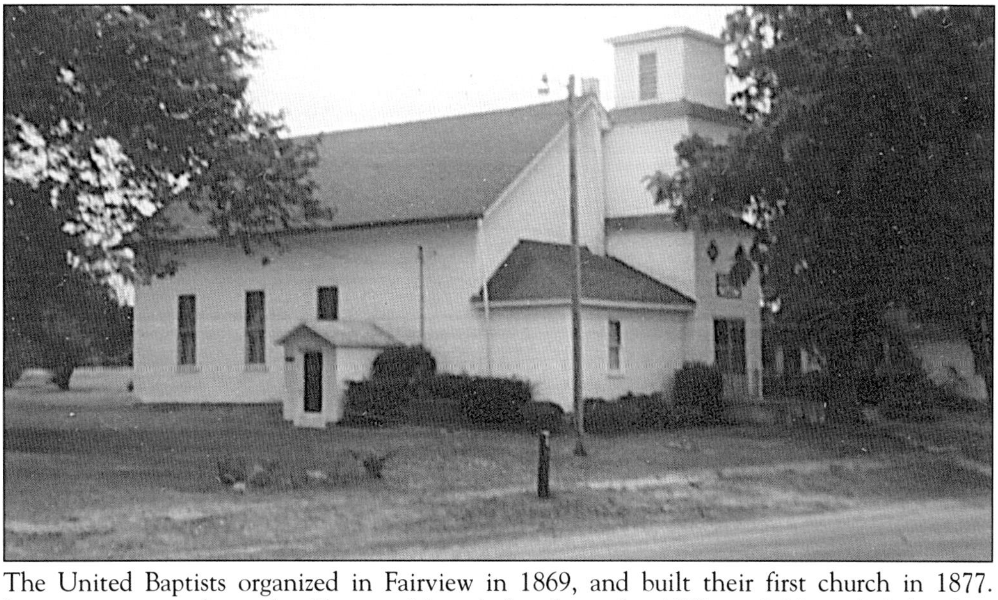

The United Baptists organized in Fairview in 1869, and built their first church in 1877. Improvements made to the Pleasant Mound church in the 1970s and 80s included indoor restrooms, a kitchen in the basement with running water, central air conditioning, and a handicapped access ramp on the southeast corner. The church serves a Southern Baptist congregation today. (Courtesy Kevin Kaegy.)

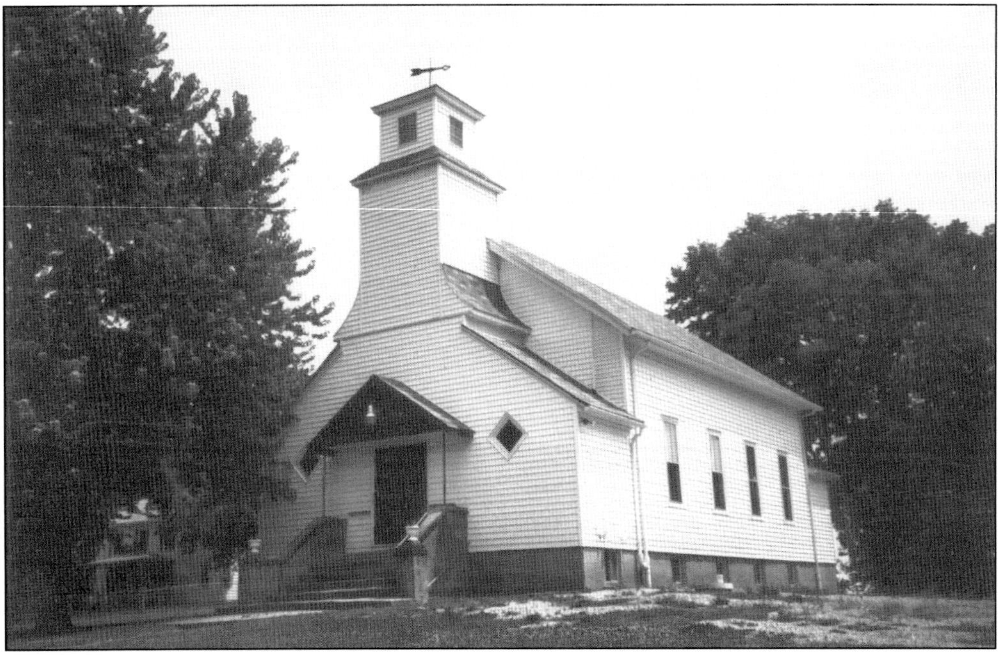

The Cumberland Presbyterian Church was built on land owned by John Reeves in 1849. Reorganization allowed a new church to be built in 1866. Due to dwindling membership, the church was sold in 1895 to the Methodists. A new front entrance and basement were dedicated in 1926. It continues to serve the community of Pleasant Mound as a United Methodist church. (Courtesy Janice Baldwin.)

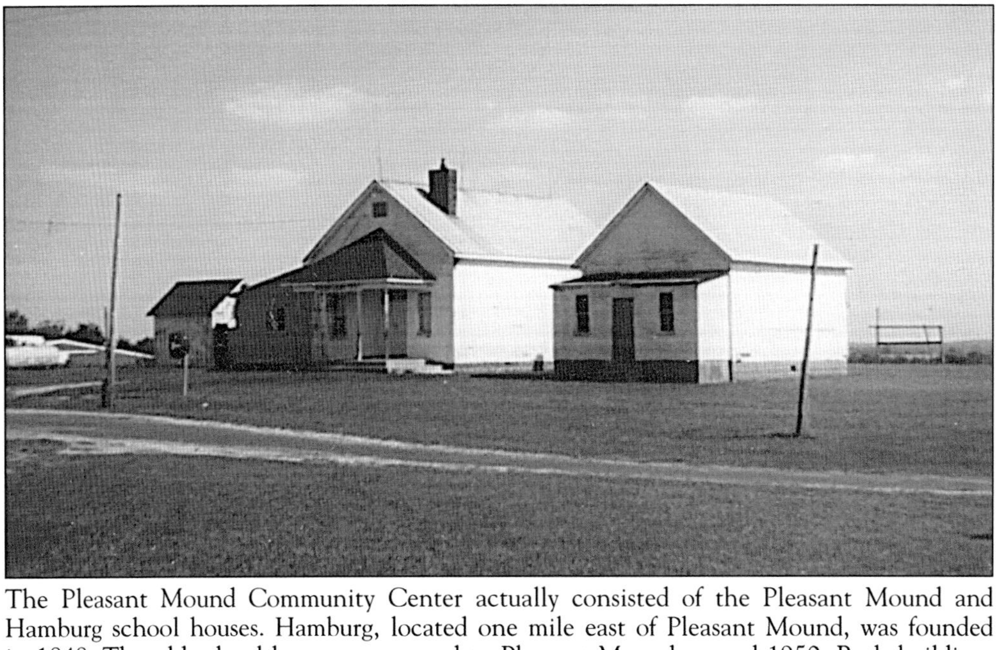

The Pleasant Mound Community Center actually consisted of the Pleasant Mound and Hamburg school houses. Hamburg, located one mile east of Pleasant Mound, was founded in 1848. The old school house was moved to Pleasant Mound around 1950. Both buildings served their community another 50 years, mostly as the site of the annual Maxey-Noffsinger Cemetery picnic. (Courtesy Kevin Kaegy.)

Five

Tamalco Township

If you combine three names: Taylor, MacLean, and Colwell, you might come up with a name like Tamalco. That's how Tamalco Township got its name, by combining the names of the three men who laid out the town. Tamalco came into being in 1884, as a result of the railroad. The township is located in the southeastern part of the county and was initially called Okaw Precinct, for the Kaskaskia River that flowed through the area. In the 1960s, the Kaskaskia was dammed by the U.S. Army Corps of Engineers, creating Carlyle Lake, which extends into this part of the county. The communities of Tamalco Township include Hookdale, Tamalco, and Keyesport. The town of Lehnsville was founded in 1883, and its name was changed to Hookdale in 1887. Keyesport was first settled around 1830, when a man named Martin had a ferry across the Kaskaskia. Thomas E. Keyes later bought the ferry and became the area postmaster. When the railroad passed through a half mile to the north, Keyesport doubled in size as businesses moved to the depot. The town of Keyesport was incorporated in 1887.

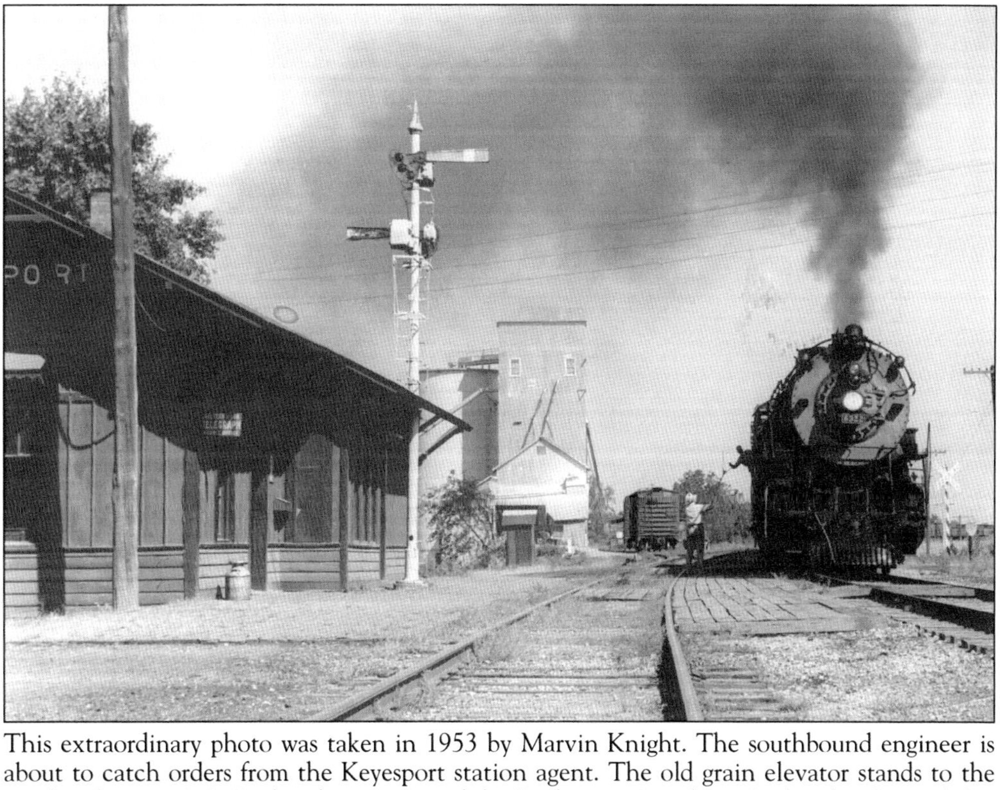

This extraordinary photo was taken in 1953 by Marvin Knight. The southbound engineer is about to catch orders from the Keyesport station agent. The old grain elevator stands to the north. The C.B.&Q. Railroad, now part of the Burlington Northern Railroad, relocated this section of track after Carlyle Lake was built in 1966. (Courtesy Marvin Knight.)

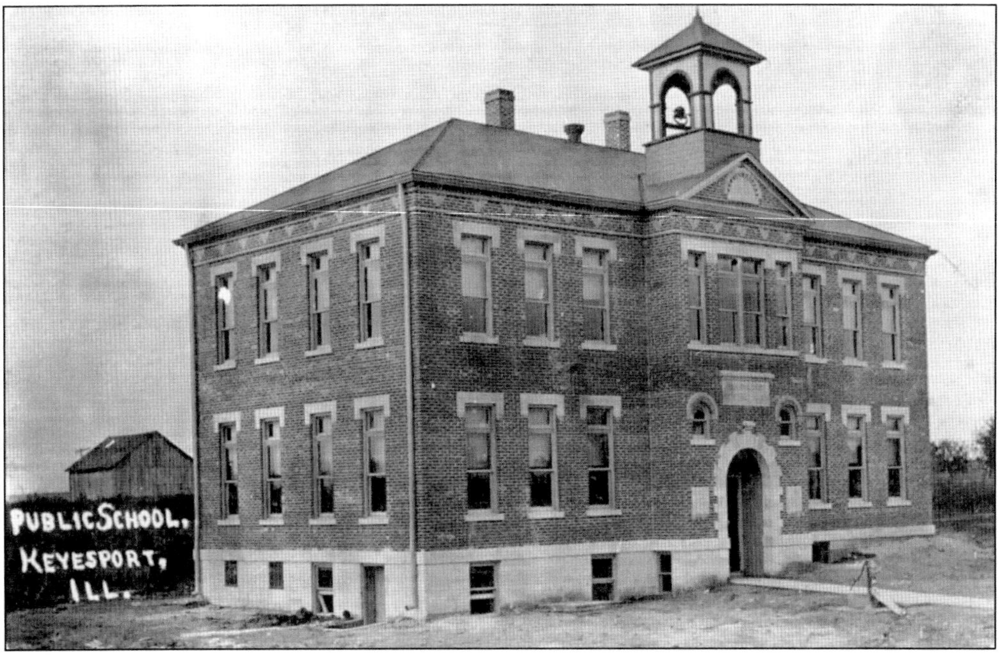

The old Keyesport Public School replaced a small frame building, and was built around 1907. It was a vast improvement over the smaller school, but by 1917, growing enrollment made it necessary to move some classes to another building. The building pictured here was destroyed by fire in 1934 and was replaced by a modern brick structure which served until 1985. (Courtesy David Meyer.)

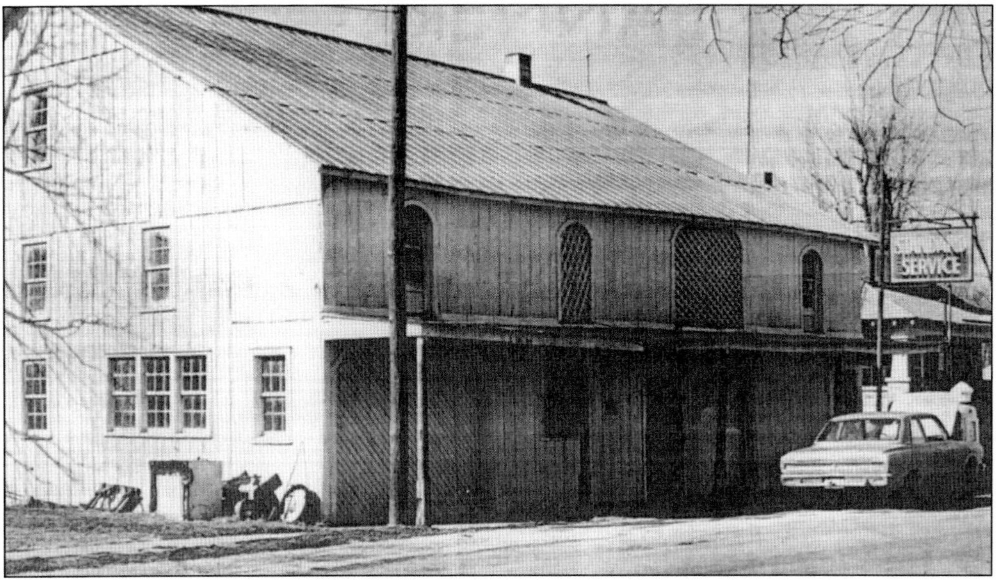

Fred Meyer's blacksmith shop in Keyesport was built in the 1880s. It faced the Mulberry-Keyesport Road and served many functions. It was a full-service blacksmith and repair shop with a line shaft to operate the machines while housing an opera house upstairs. It also served as the town's first gas station. It was torn down in 1998 to make room for the new bank. (Courtesy the *Carlyle Union Banner*.)

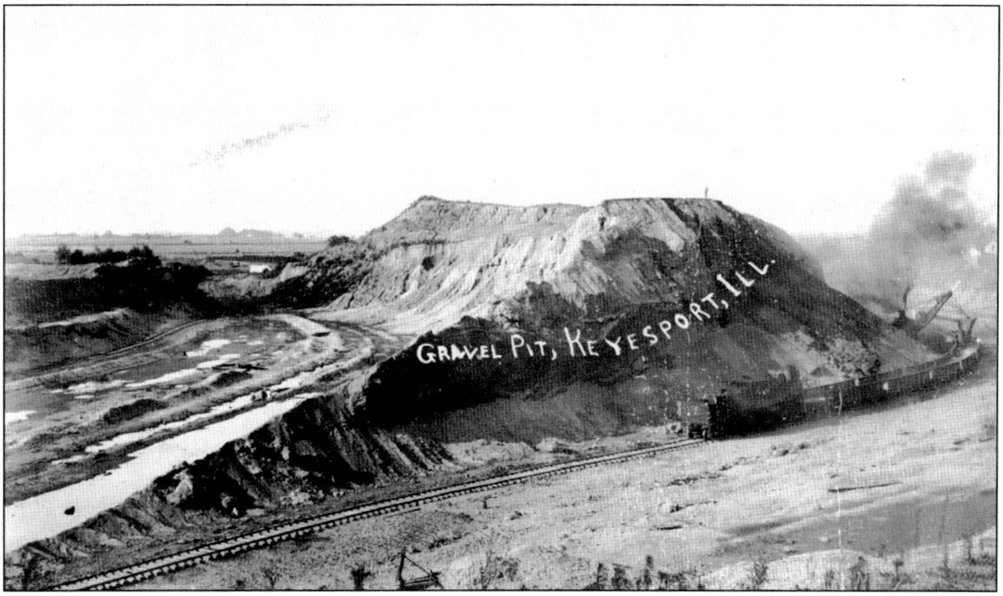

This gravel pit, located 1/4 mile west of the McKendree Chapel Cemetery, was in operation 100 years ago. Four teams of horses and wagons were driven in a continuous circle around the pit every day, all day, to receive gravel being excavated by the workmen. Filled wagons off-loaded onto train cars that ran on the "Y" railroad spur off the Jacksonville line out of Tamalco. (Courtesy Janice Baldwin.)

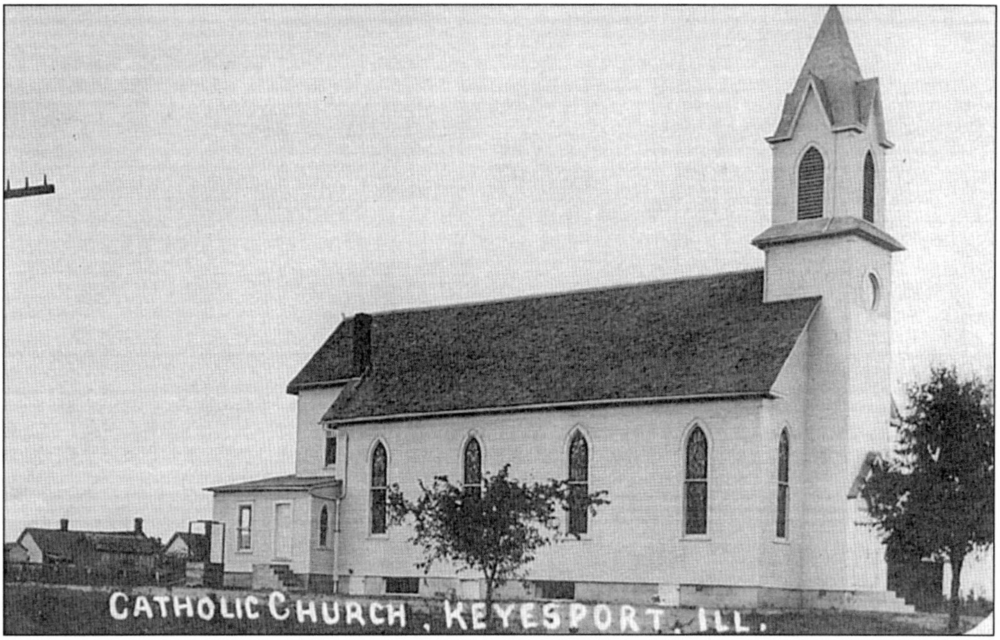

St. Edward's Catholic Church was organized in 1907 and held services in Meyer's Blacksmith Shop until building their own facility in 1909 on the County Line Road in Keyesport. In 1920, the church closed and the building was moved to Marydale in Clinton County where it became St. Theresa. This rural parish continues to thrive, serving southern Bond and northern Clinton Counties. (Courtesy Margaret VonHatton.)

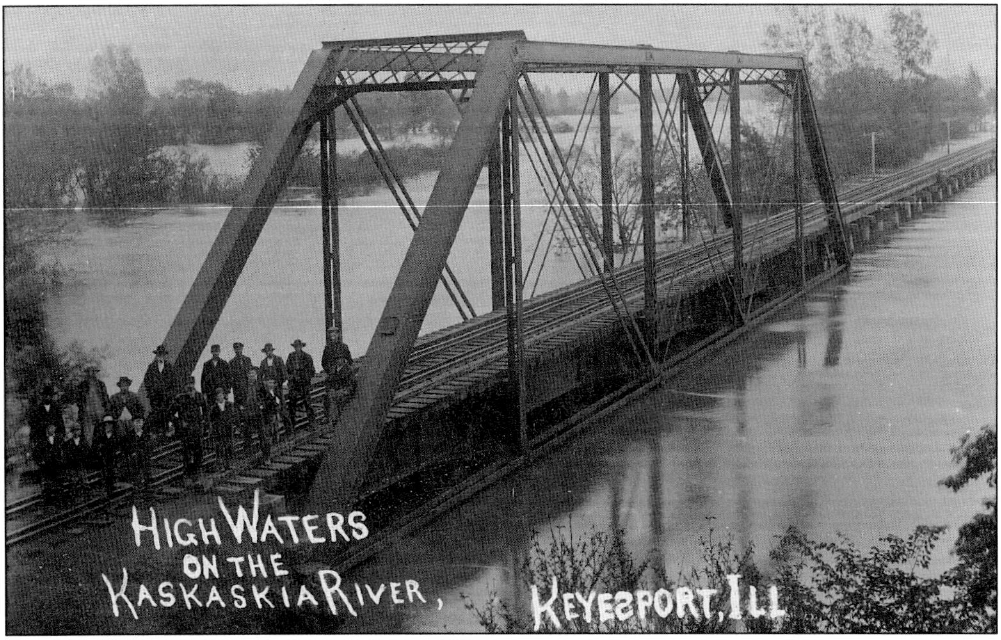

This flood on the Kaskaskia River in Keyesport occurred c. 1910. Among the men standing on the bridge are William Apple, Walter Essington, and his son, Walter Jr., and Mr. Ray. Later, in 1917, a passing train collapsed this bridge, and both the bridge and train fell into the river with the caboose protruding out of the water. (Courtesy J. Lloyd Elliot.)

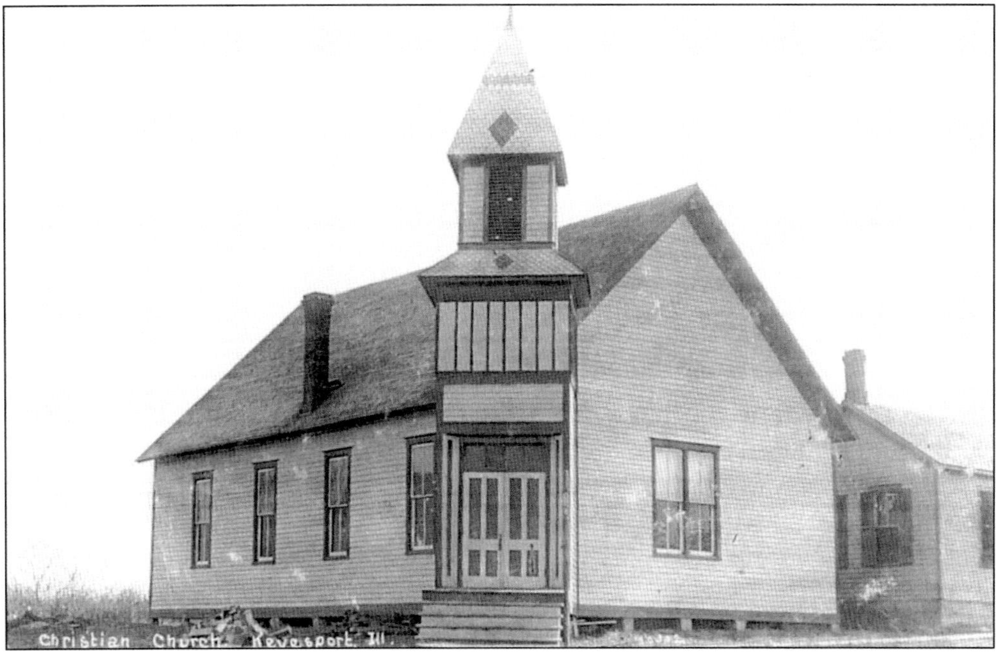

This photo of the Christian Church in Keyesport was taken c. 1910, and shows the corner entrance and steeple that was typical of most of the Christian Churches in the county at the time. This congregation remained active until the 1980s. The building, still standing, is privately owned and is used for storage. (Courtesy David Meyer.)

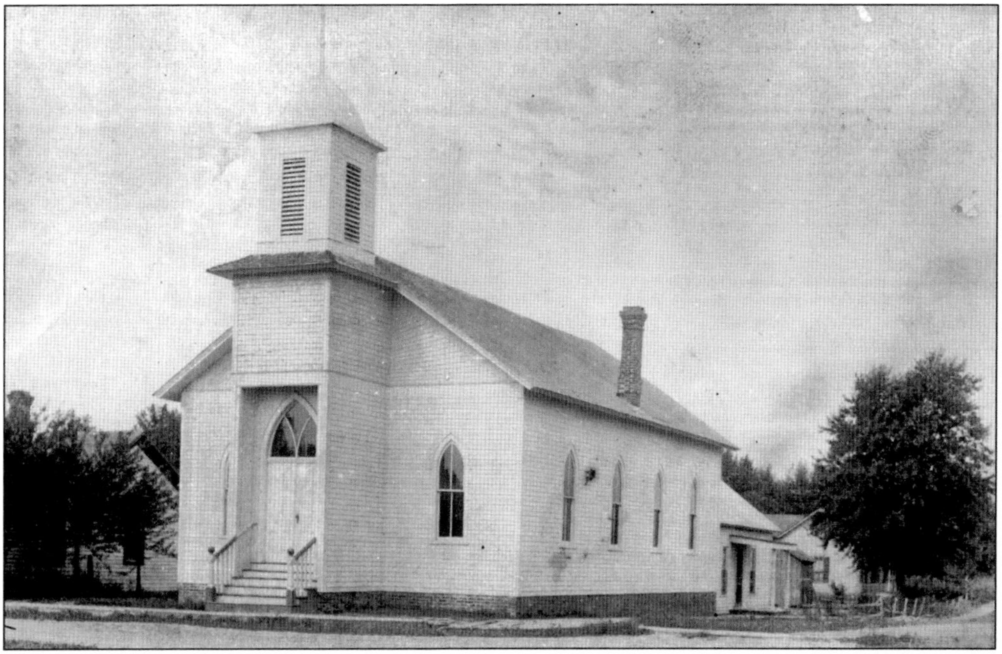

The Methodist Episcopal Church was built around 1900. Ben Lynch was contracted to construct the basement under the church in the early 1920s, and an addition was made to the back of the building in the 1980s. It is currently being remodeled and still serves a Methodist congregation. It is the last remaining of the five churches that were once in Keyesport. (Courtesy Janice Baldwin.)

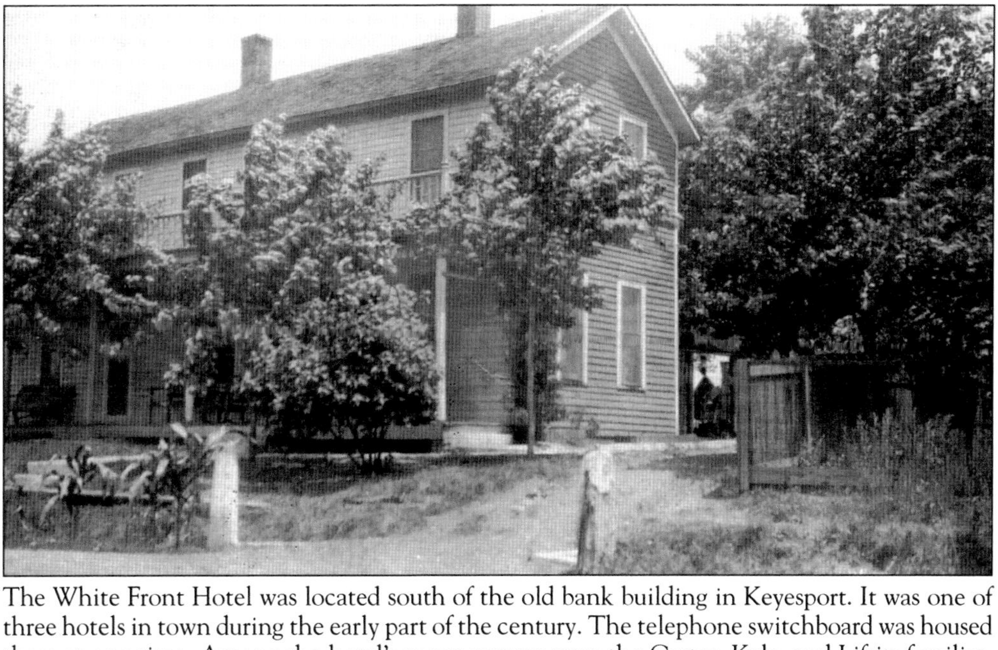

The White Front Hotel was located south of the old bank building in Keyesport. It was one of three hotels in town during the early part of the century. The telephone switchboard was housed there at one time. Among the hotel's many owners were the Carter, Kyle, and Lifritz families. (Courtesy Sue Wade.)

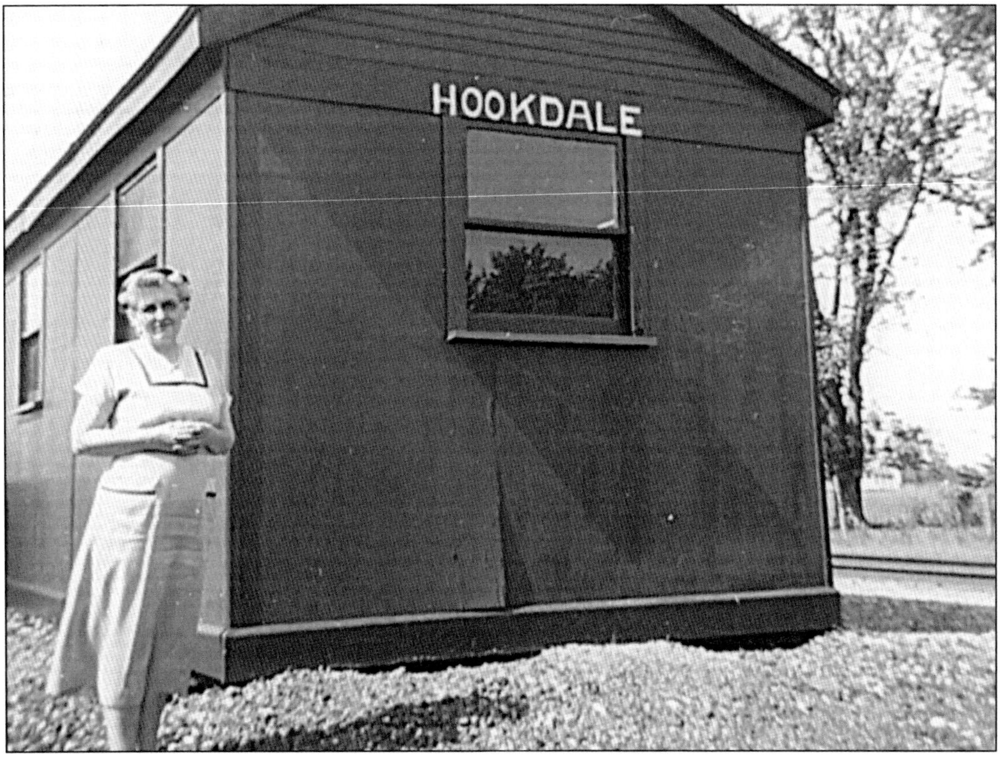

This small shed served as the last Hookdale Railroad station. Passengers could buy tickets here and the mail was received here. Several of these portable depots were located along the C.B.& Q. Mrs. Gib Clementz poses in this 1954 photo. (Courtesy Gib Clementz.)

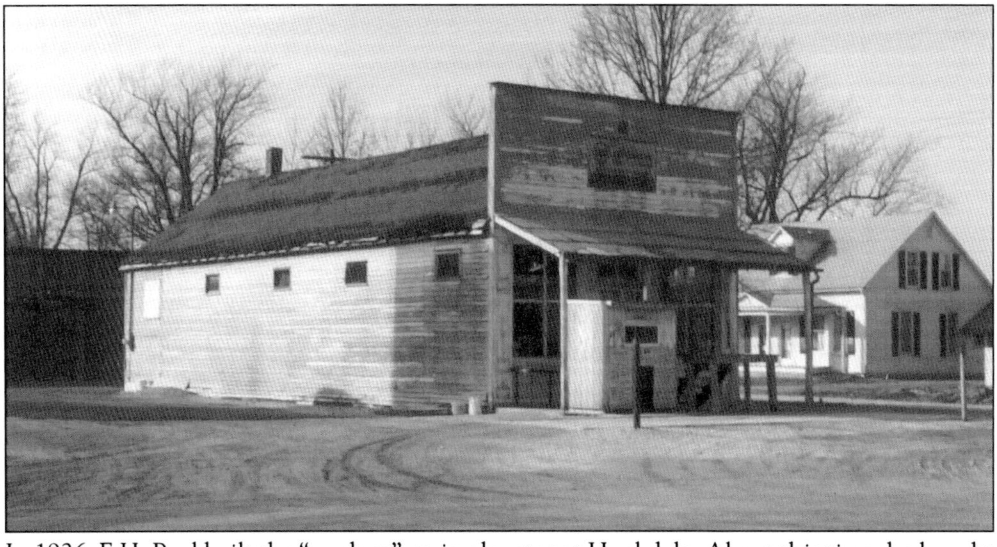
In 1926, E.H. Paul built the "modern" grain elevator at Hookdale. About this time, he bought this old store building. In 1932, he built the lumber sheds and operated a full-scale lumber and hardware business as well as his grain elevator. Frank Davis later ran the lumberyard and Metzgers ran the elevator. The store has been razed and South Central Farm Services owns the elevator. (Courtesy Kevin Kaegy.)

Lehnsville was laid out by Louis Lehn in 1883 after the Jacksonville Railroad came through the county. In 1886, the post office and town's name changed to Hookdale. This small store was built in 1918 by Albert Stern to be used as a tin shop. The post office was moved there by Postmaster Harold Roberts in 1936. He was the last Hookdale postmaster. He served 22 years until the office closed in 1958. It is now a home. (Courtesy Verna Lehn Roberts.)

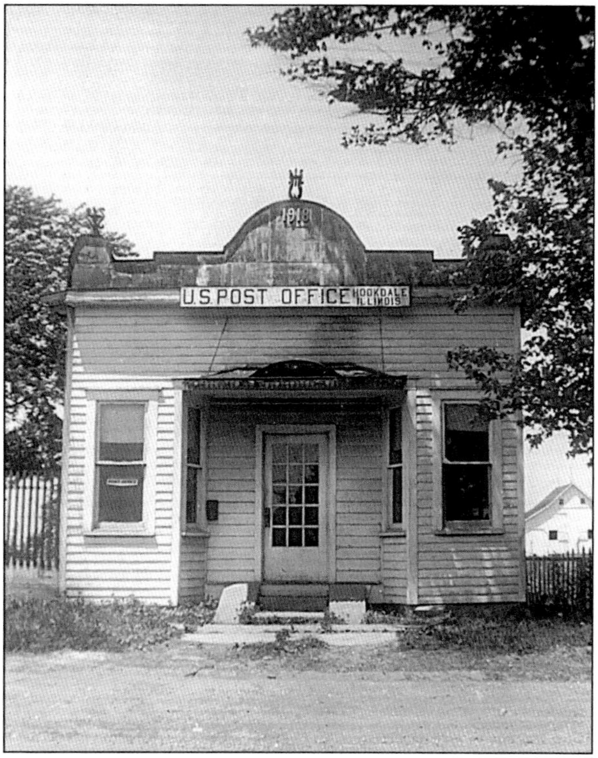

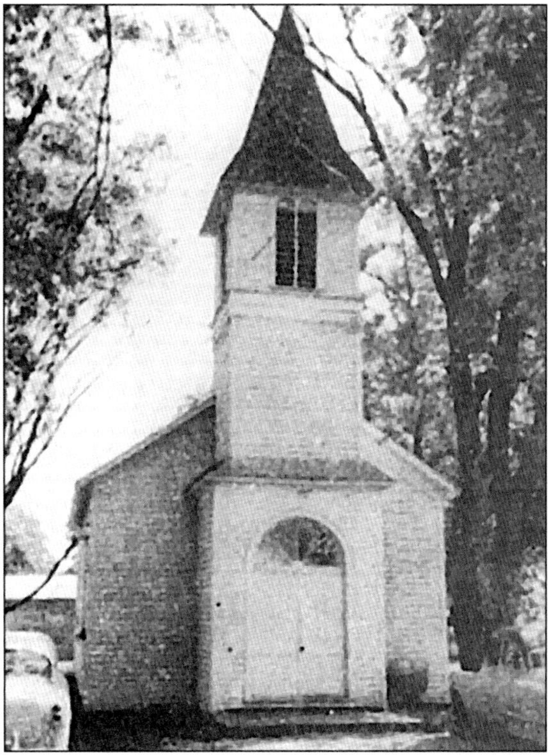

St. Peters United Church of Christ was founded in 1880, southeast of Hookdale. The Free Methodists built this building in 1889 and sold it to the St. Peters congregation in 1896. The congregation replaced the church, seen here with a modern brick structure in 1955. The church continues to serve the community. (Courtesy St. Peters United Church of Christ.)

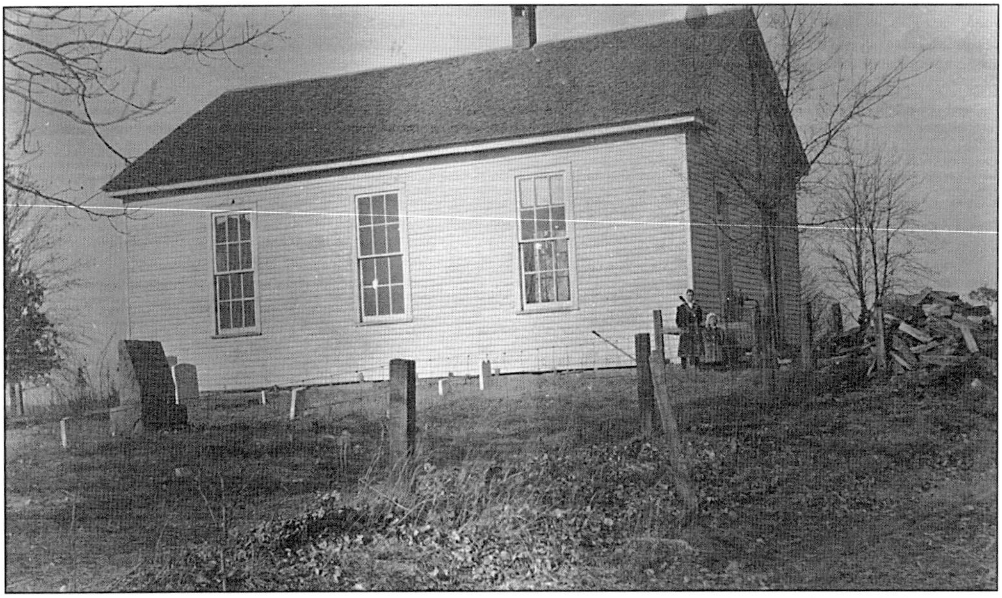

The McKendree Chaple Methodist Church was organized in 1842 by members of the Myatt family. This church was built in 1856 and served until the congregation disbanded in 1945. The McKendree Chaple Cemetery picnic has been held the last Saturday in August since 1901. It has become an area homecoming and the funds raised go to maintain the cemetery. (Courtesy Roberta Hoffman.)

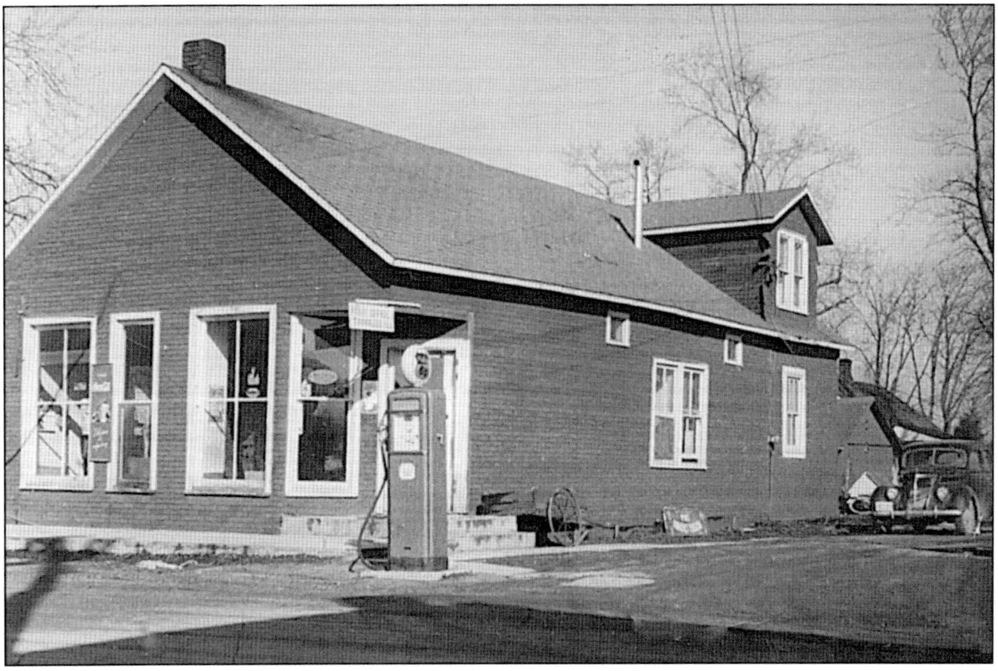

Dewey Hensley's General Store in Tamalco was located on the north side of the main street. It also served as the post office. This late 1940s photo shows the Phillips 66 gas pump in front. Across the street, about 20 feet away, were DX and Shell gas pumps at the Hallam Store. (Courtesy David Hensly.)

Perry and Caroline Hallam bought the Tamalco General Store in 1915 and operated it until their retirement. There was a Modern Woodman Lodge Hall upstairs where a dance was held every Saturday night. A dentist's office and post office were also located there at one time. Pictured here in 1941 are Caroline Hallam with grandson H.V. Clark. The store was dismantled in 1974, but their family home (in the background) still remains. (Courtesy Dr. H.V. Clark.)

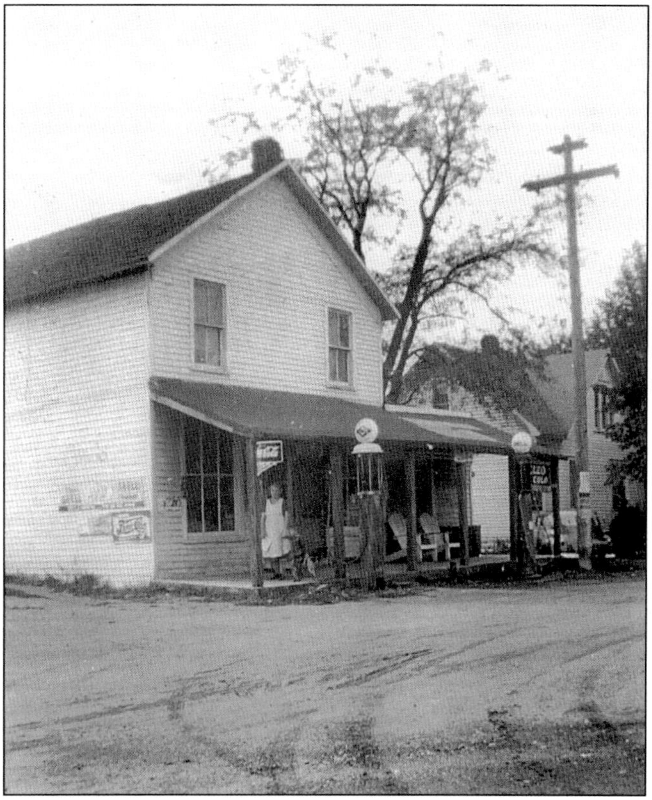

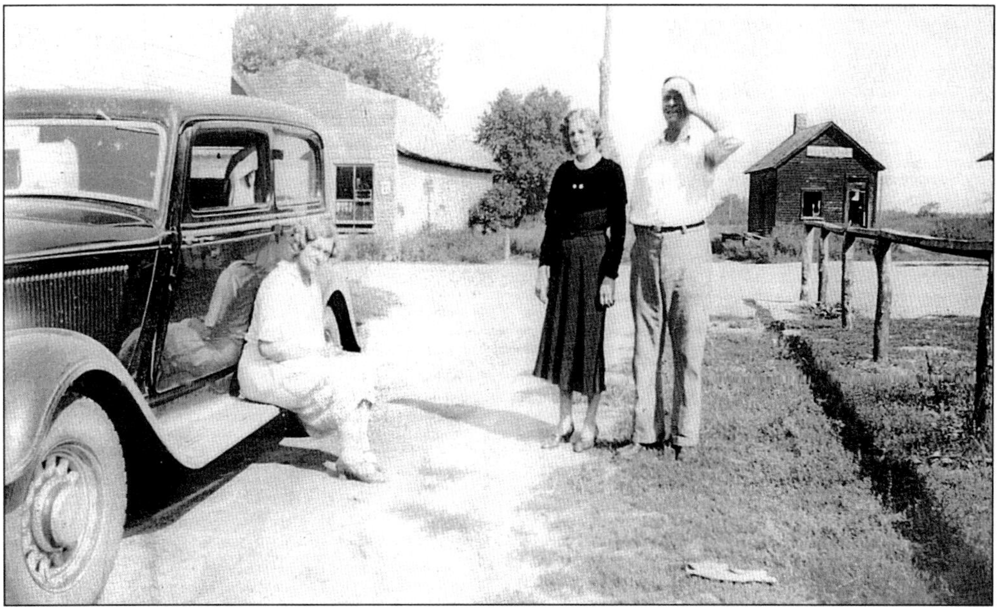

Mae, Caroline, and Perry Hallam pose on the east side of their store *c.* 1940. The Tamalco Village Hall and the old depot can be seen in the background. Tamalco was established along the railroad in 1884. Typical of most general stores, you could buy about anything there and even trade poultry and eggs for groceries. (Courtesy Mae Hallam Clark.)

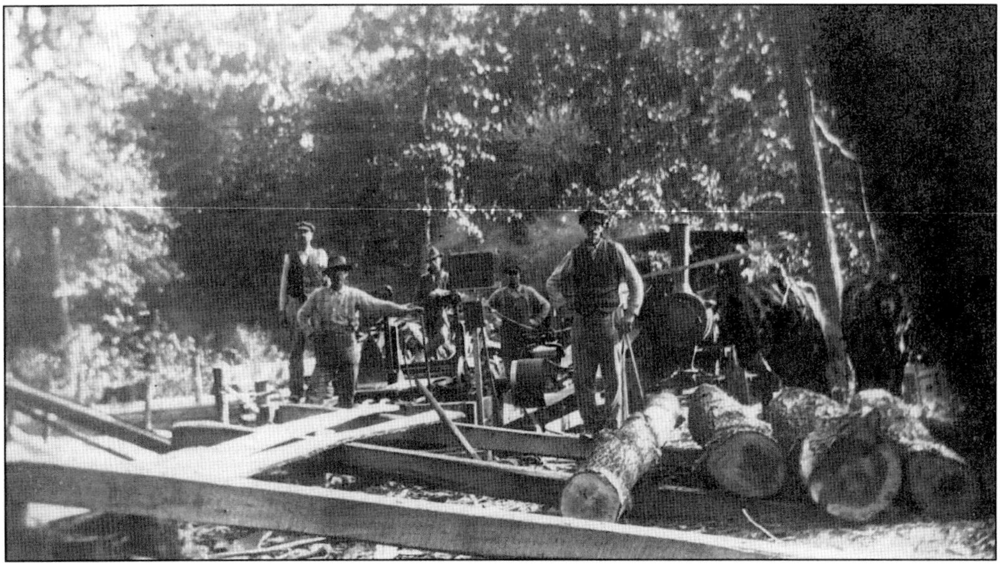

Louis Birkenstock operated a portable sawmill in the Kaskaskia River bottoms east of Tamalco from 1919 to 1920. Terrel Reavis was the log hauler, William Rench was the head sawyer, and Clarence Eller owned the steam engine. (Courtesy Caroline Birkenstock.)

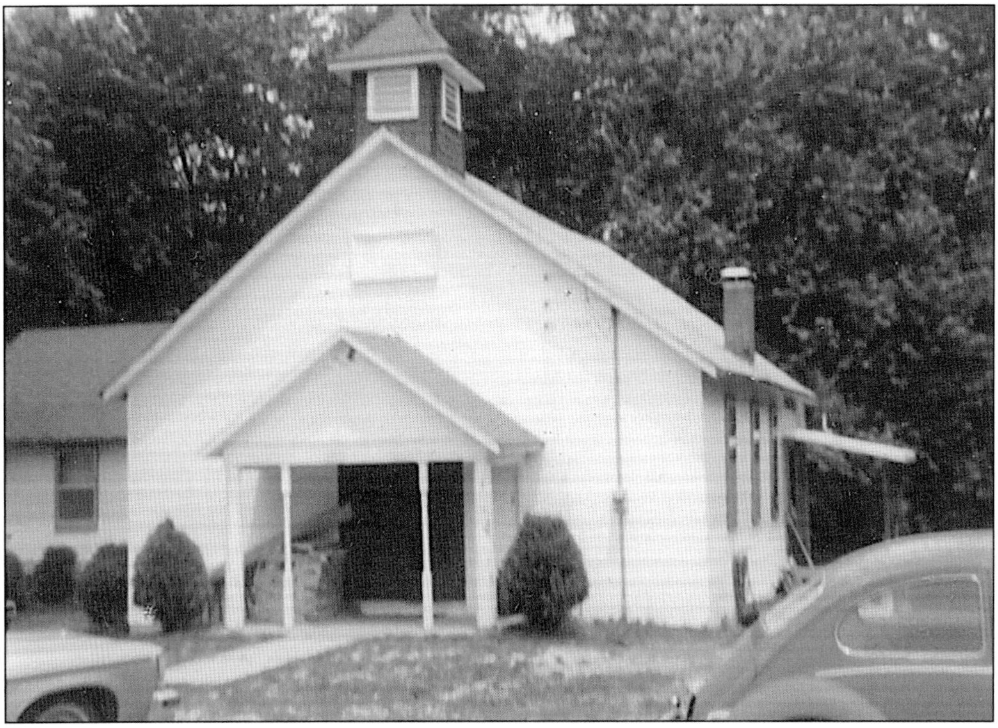

In 1941, Brother Leo Belcher and Brother Robert Hastings held a revival in the old Cart Hill School House. Eleven souls were saved and the Cart Hill Missionary Baptist Church was established. In 1944, they dismantled and relocated the old Kinmundy Baptist Church to their own lot on what is now Hookdale Avenue. The church disbanded in 1972 and the building is now a private home. (Courtesy Lena Trexler.)

Six

MILLS TOWNSHIP

Hill's Fort was the first settlement in Bond County, established in the northwest part of the township in 1809. It was named for Isaac Hill from Tennessee, who brought a surveying crew into the area. The fort was the site of a skirmish during the War of 1812. About 80 Indians ambushed 12 rangers as they left the fort on September 9, 1814. Another early settlement known as Jones Fort was located on the site of Greene Cemetery. The exact location of Hill's Fort, once lost to time and memory, was recently discovered by a young archeology student. Mills Township was named for Andrew Gibbs Mills, an early settler of the area whose family came in 1827. The three communities of the township include Gathton, Dudleyville, and Wisetown, also called Beaver Creek. Gathton, although never platted, at one time had several homes, a post office, and a blacksmith shop, though only one home remains today. Dudleyville was founded by John Dudley in 1857 and laid out by R.K. Dewey. Its post office operated from 1861 to 1902. Beaver Creek was established first as a post office in 1838. In 1860, R.K. Dewey laid out a town for David Wise, who had a store in the area. The town became commonly known as Wisetown.

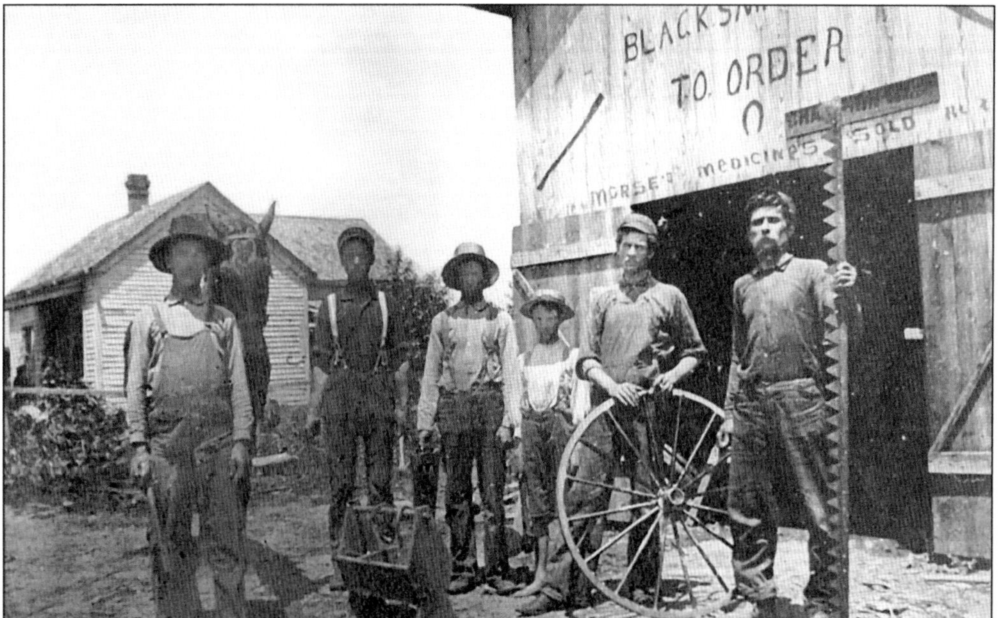

Dudleyville had two different blacksmith shops. This one was located east of the old Methodist Church and was operated by the Chapman Brothers, and then A.W. Reed. Pictured here in 1891 from left to right, are unidentified, Harvey Allen, unidentified, Floyd Harlan, William St. Clair Harlan, and Fred Plant. In the 1920s, the house was moved east of town and the shop was taken down. (Courtesy Roberta Hoffman.)

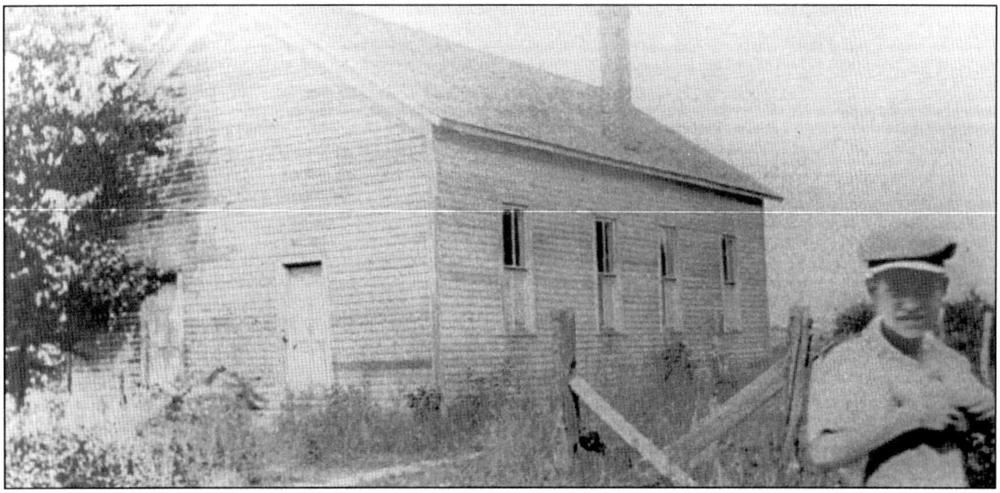

The Dudleyville Free Methodist Church was organized in 1880 and the building was constructed during the summer of 1881. Over 25 pastors filled the pulpit until it closed in 1936. The structure was dismantled and the lumber used to build two cabins at Durley Camp. Bill Harlan is the young man in this 1920 photo. (Courtesy Edna Sparlin.)

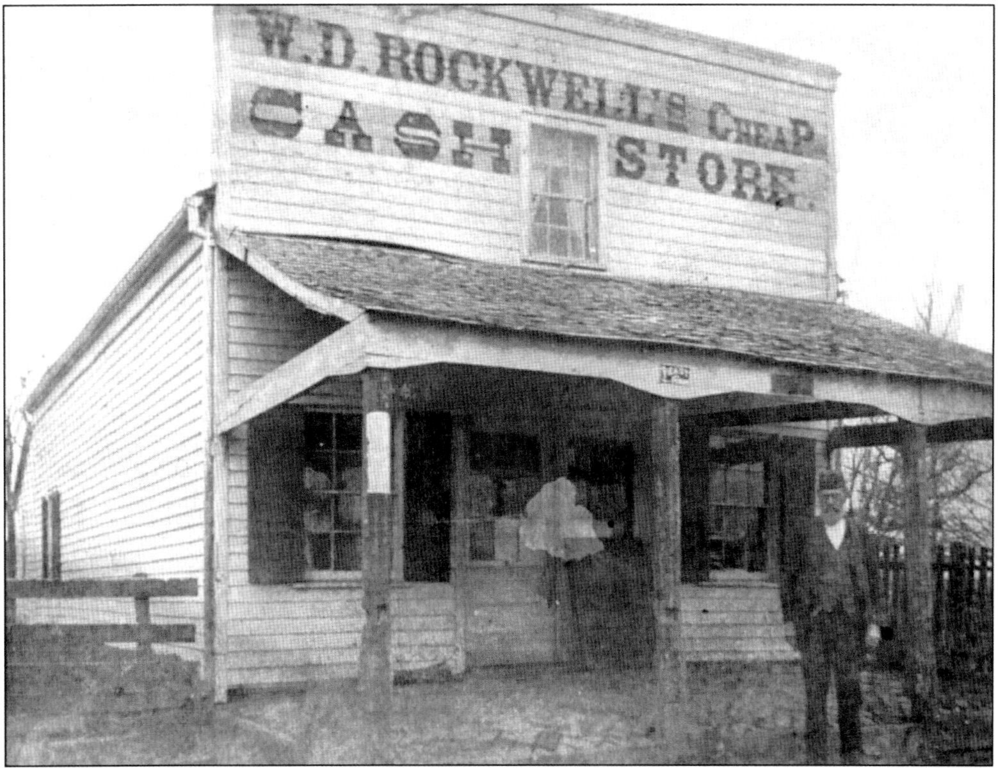

John Dudley, founder and namesake of Dudleyville, opened the first store, which he sold to Fredrich Thraner. Thraner built the store building, pictured above, and later sold out to W.D. Rockwell, who operated it for many years as W.D. Rockwell's Cheap Cash Store. It was also a post office from February 1861 to July 1902. Mr. Rockwell stands in front of his store in this c. 1890 photo. (Courtesy Helen Upton.)

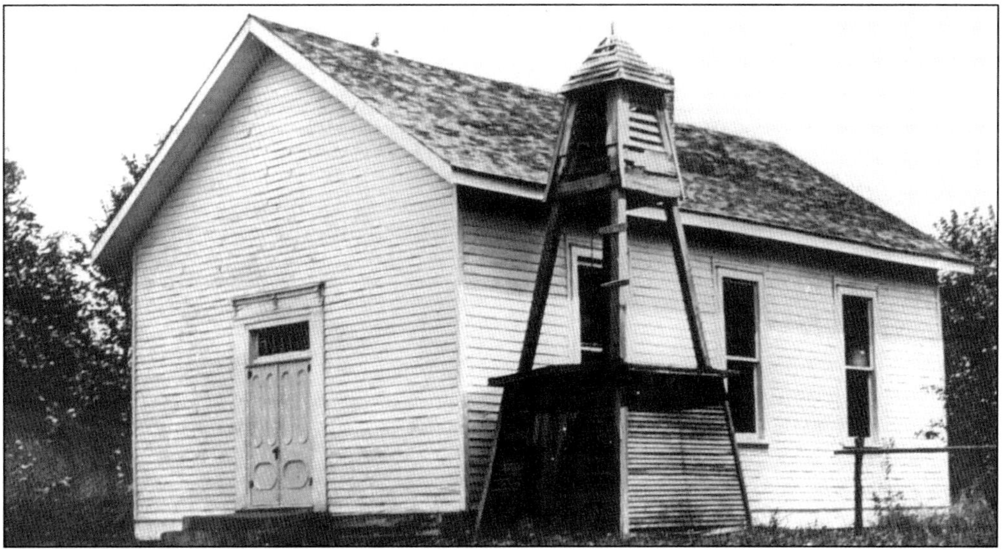

The Dudleyville Methodist Church was organized about 1820 by Rev. Simeon Walker. The congregation met in members' homes until John Dudley laid out Dudleyville in 1857. He donated the lot for the church and the building was constructed the same year. It closed in 1954 and was dismantled in 1964. The bell tower stands above a coal shed in this *c.* 1930 photo. (Courtesy Ruth Dieckmeyer.)

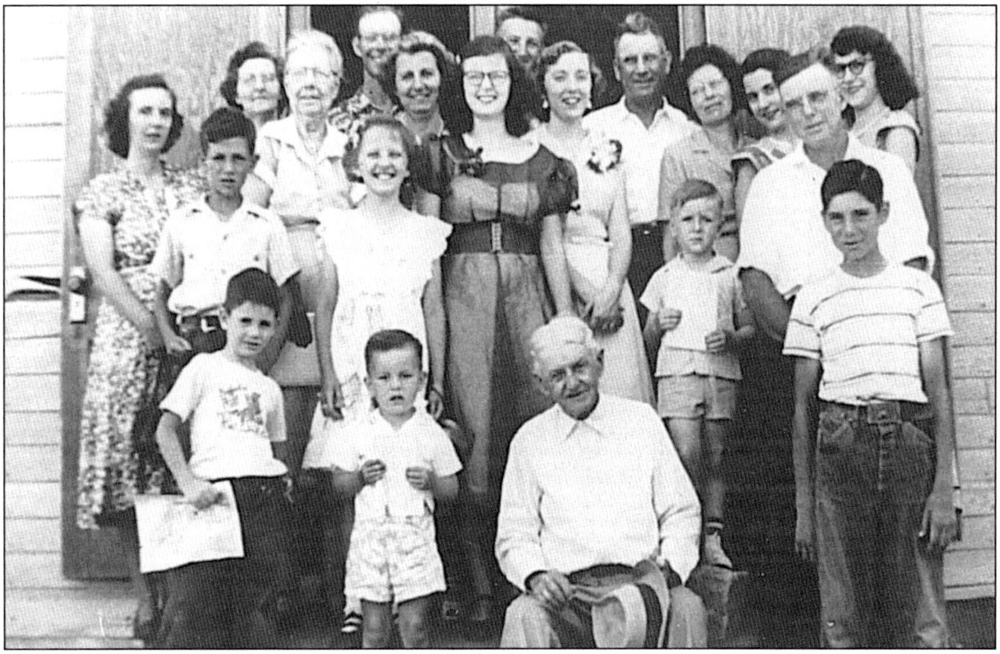

This photo of the Dudleyville Methodist Church congregation was taken in 1953. "Grandpa" Ed Gaffner is seated in front. The children, pictured here from left to right, are the following: Lloyd and Bill Walker, Sharon and Dan Kaegy, Lynn Kaegy, and Hope Walker Jr. The adults, pictured here from left to right, are as follows: Bessie Kaegy, Lena Kaegy, Nora Gaffner, Lloyd Alexander, Edna Sylvia, Max and Merle Kaegy; Hope, Elsie, and Jeannine Walker; Howard Kaegy and Mable Walker. (Courtesy Lena Kaegy.)

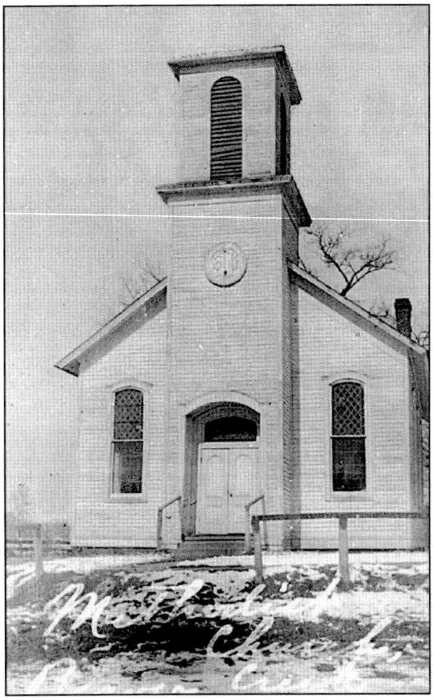

Built in 1878, the Wisetown Methodist Church was actually used as a Union Church and served the Methodists, Baptists, and Cumberland Presbyterians. Eventually, they each built their own buildings. Before it closed in the 1950s, it was part of the Beaver Creek Methodist circuit made up of three churches: Wisetown, Dudleyville, and Hopewell. All shared one minister, who visited each on a rotation of Sundays. (Courtesy Amy Hentz.)

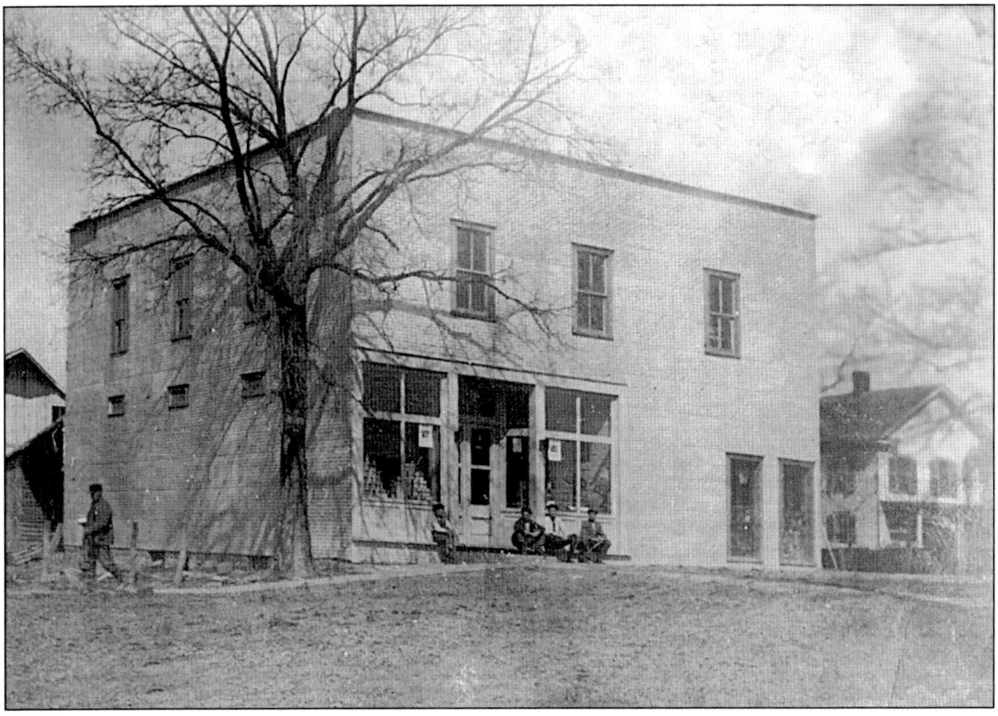

Wisetown was laid out in March of 1860 by David Wise, who ran the first store in town. The post office, named Beaver Creek, was established in 1838, before the town existed. Martin Berreis built the store pictured above in 1915, after Joe Harnetiaux's store burnt. In 1942, Nick Basler took over the store. Later owners were John Basler, Al Clark, Irving Cordonnier, David Wade, Earnest Jackson, and Lee Bryant. It closed in 1968 and was torn down in 1980. (Courtesy Lucy Henry.)

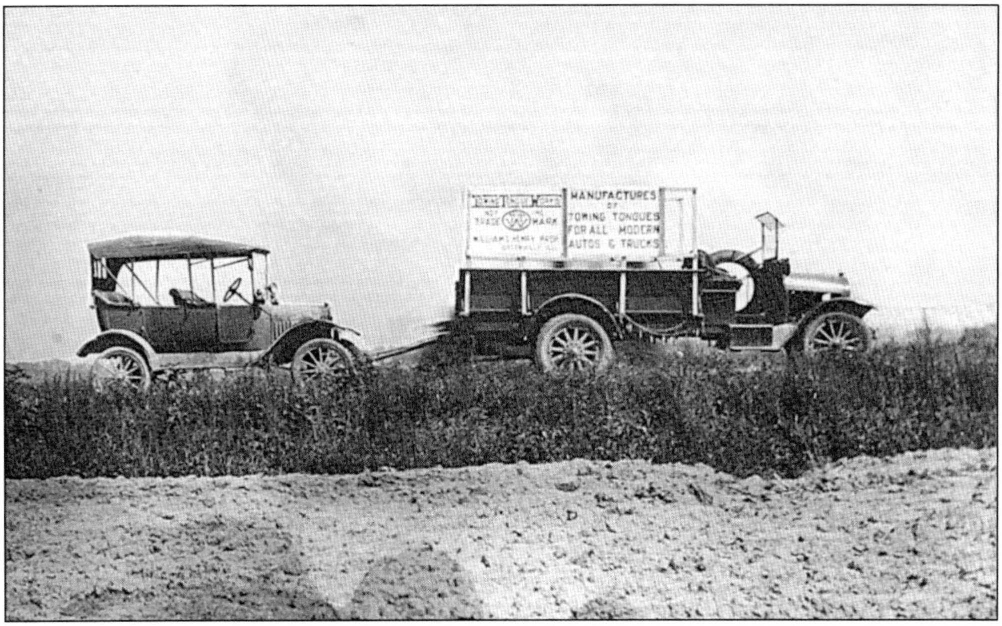

A Wisetown area farmer, William D. Henry, was also an inventor. Around 1920, he patented, manufactured, and sold a Model T towing bar. To demonstrate it, he and his neighbor Dean Wade drove the rig (pictured above) to Springfield for the State Fair. The banner says "For All Modern Autos and Trucks." (Courtesy Marlin Wade.)

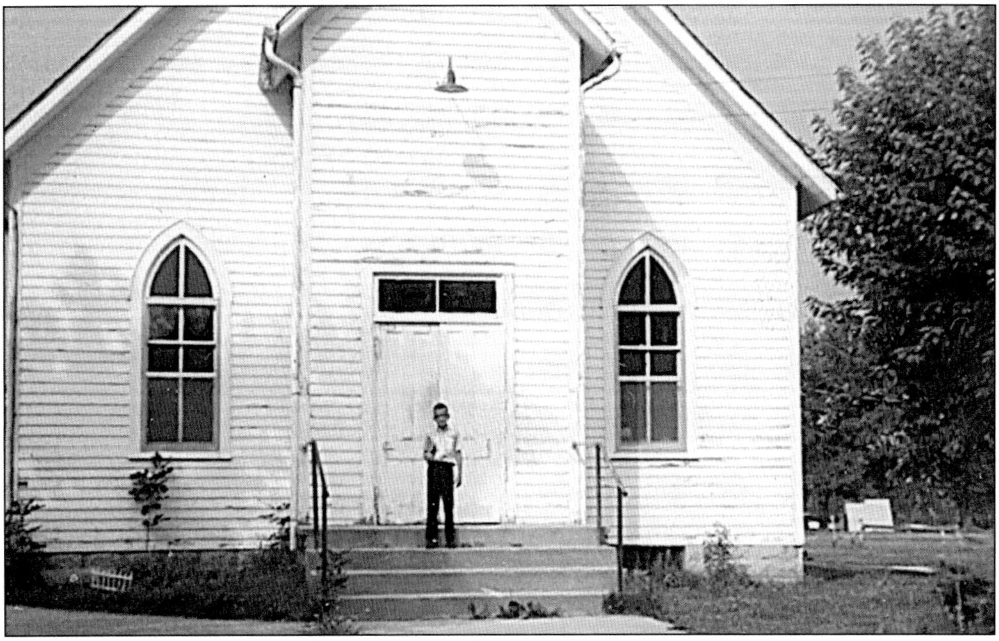

The Wisetown Baptist Church was organized in August of 1881 and met in the Union Church. They sold their share in that church to the Methodists and built their own building in 1893. This thriving congregation built a new facility in 1969 and since then has built an addition and a parsonage. Young Lynn Zobrist stands on the front steps of the old church in this photo, taken shortly before it was torn down. (Courtesy Shirla Zobrist.)

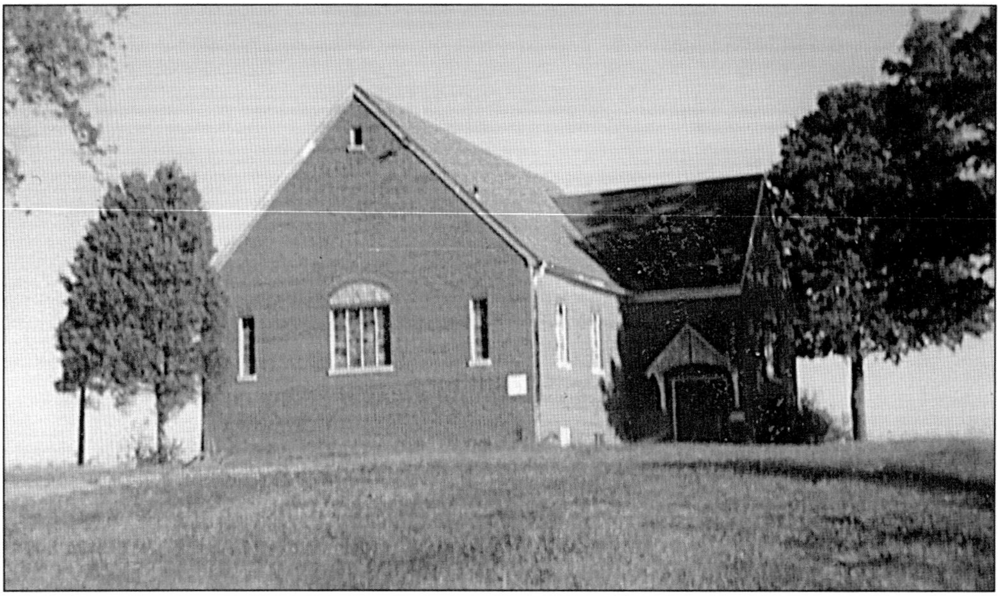

The Mount Carmel Methodist Church was founded in 1862 by Simeon Walker. The congregation built a small brick church in 1866, which served them for over 80 years. The present church was built in 1947. Even though it closed in 1969, the "brick church," as it is known to most, remains a well-cared for landmark at the corner of Route 143 and Millersburg Road. (Courtesy Kevin Kaegy.)

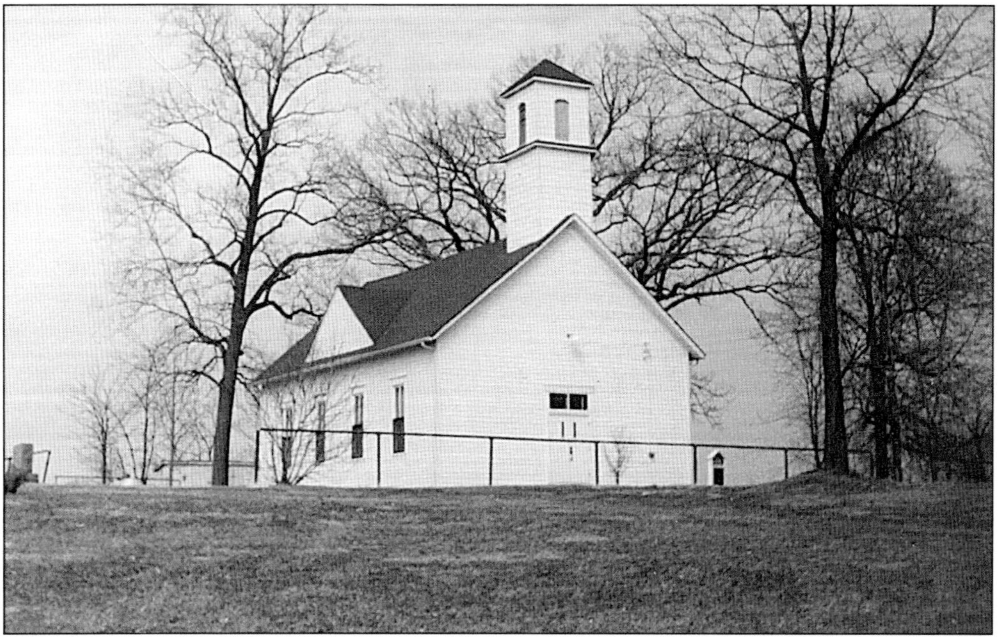

The Campground Cumberland Presbyterian Church was organized about 1826. At first, camp meetings were held on this site for days at a time. A strong spring across the road provided the water. The first church was built in 1835, and was replaced by the present structure in 1892. Although modernized with a kitchen and restrooms, the old horse hitching rack remains out in front. (Courtesy Kevin Kaegy.)

Seven

Burgess Township

Burgess Township in the southwestern portion of the county was named for William Burgess, an early surveyor and ranger who was part of the group that defended Hill's Fort during the War of 1812. Formerly called Pocahontas Precinct, Burgess Township has three main communities: Pocahontas, Millersburg, and Pierron.

Benjamin Johnson founded a town and named it Hickory Grove, after the row of hickory trees that surrounded his home. The Hickory Grove Post Office opened in 1831. After a time, the town was nicknamed Amity, after the name of a National Road hotel there. In 1850, the village changed its name to Pocahontas.

Millersburg was named for Charles Miller, who built a grist mill in the area in the late 1840s. Also known as Baden Baden, Millersburg was primarily a German settlement. A legal necessity arose when Millersburg hooked into Pierron's water line in the late 1970s. As a result, Millersburg became part of Pierron, which was ironic, because originally, Pierron had been established to be part of Millersburg. Pierron straddles the Bond-Madison county line and was one time known as Oakdale. It was laid out in 1868 by Jacques Pierron and his son August was the first postmaster. The post office was established in 1870, and the village was incorporated as Pierron in 1893.

This photo, taken *c.* 1910, shows the steam powered mill that was located a few blocks southeast of the Pocahontas village square. The mill was built by William S. Wait around 1858 and sat at the corner of Kavanaugh and Union Streets. It was both a grist mill and a sawmill, and eventually proved to be more reliable than the water mill east of town on Shoal Creek. All that remains of this mill is a ravine where the mill pond once stood. (Courtesy Jerry Nance.)

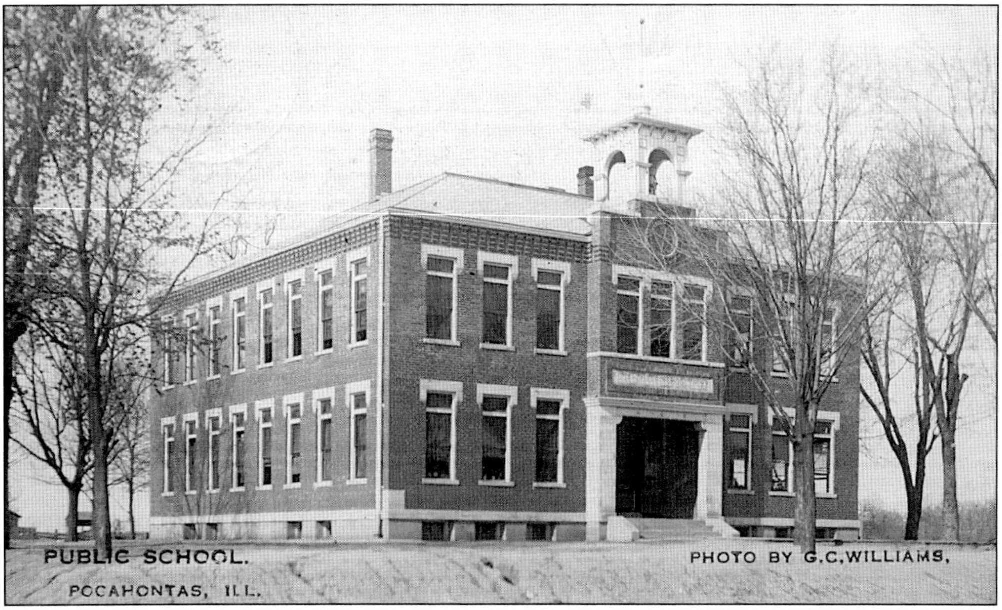

The Pocahontas Public School was built in 1910 and served all grades. In 1936, the WPA built a gymnasium and classrooms were later added to connect the two buildings. In 1956, the high school students were transferred to Greenville when the rural school districts were consolidated. The old two-story portion of the school was taken down in 1969. (Courtesy Jerry Nance.)

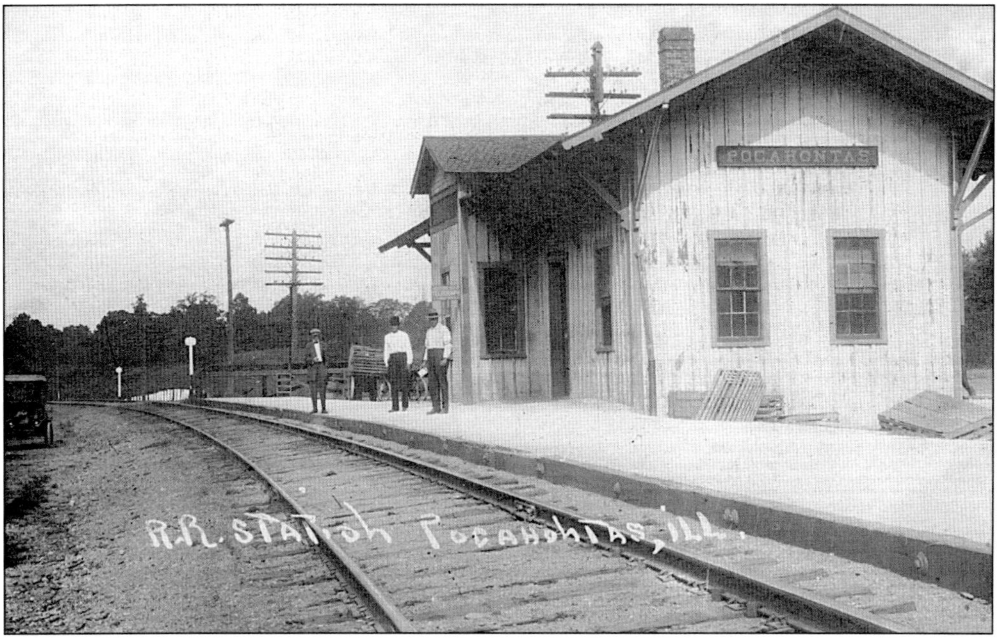

The St. Louis, Vandalia & Terre Haute Railroad was built just south of the village of Pocahontas in 1868. The depot stood at the intersection of Academy and Union Streets. Pocahontas started to thrive after the arrival of the railroad. A railroad spur was built to accommodate the coal mine just southeast of the depot. (Courtesy Jerry Nance.)

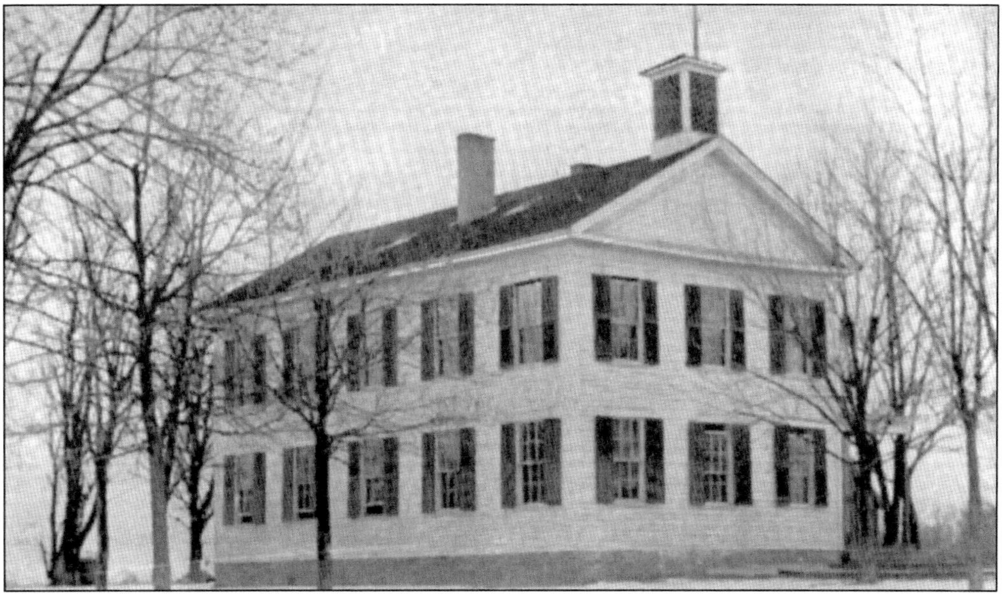

The Pocahontas Academy, the first formal public school building in Pocahontas, was built in 1851 on a plot of ground north of the National Road (now State Street), in the vicinity of where the present school stands. It served the community for over 50 years. In 1909, the Pocahontas Academy was moved across the street and bricked over. It became the National Hotel. (Courtesy Dr. Charles Johnson.)

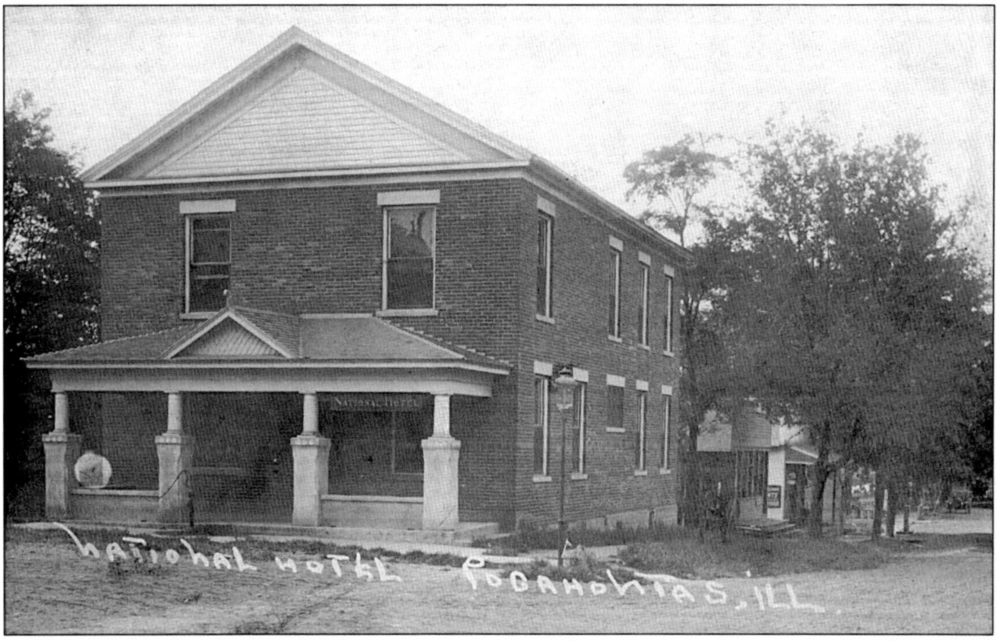

The National Hotel on the northeast corner of the village square replaced an earlier hotel that had stood on the same site. Given its proximity to the National Road, it had a small restaurant and serviced three generations of travelers along what later became U.S. Route 40. The building still exists, one of the earliest in Pocahontas. It continues to serve as an apartment house, cafe, and other business ventures. (Courtesy Jerry Nance.)

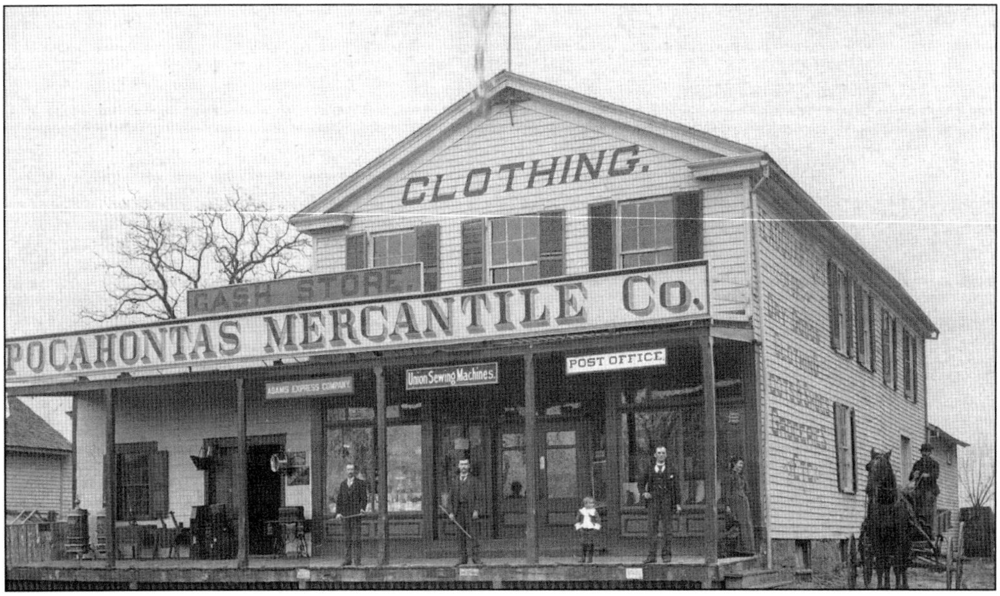

Simon S. Brown, born in Old Ripley Township in 1862, purchased the Pocahontas Mercantile Co. cash store on the north side of the square in 1905. For a while, the post office was located there. He sold everything from clothing and footwear to groceries, dry goods, and sewing machines. He operated the business, later named the S.S. Brown Hardware Store, for 20 years. (Courtesy Margaret Brown.)

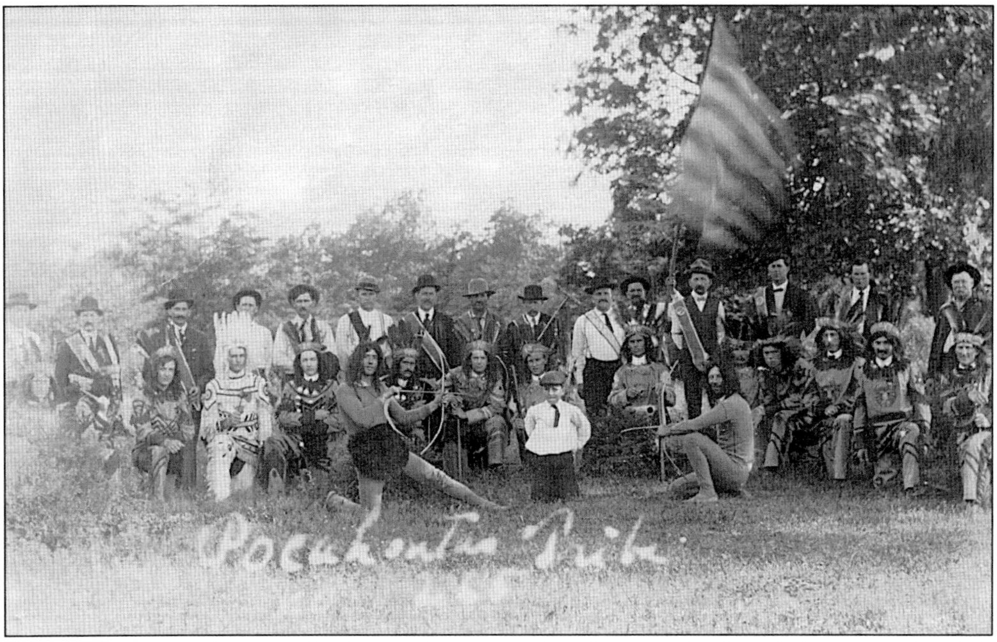

Among the more colorful of the fraternal societies that flourished in Bond County in the 19th century was the Improved Order of Redmen, a patriotic, fraternal, and charitable organization. This "Pocahontas Tribe," c. 1900, appears to be dressed for a Fourth of July celebration. DeMoulin Bros. in Greenville, who made regalia for many fraternal orders, including the Redmen, very likely made these costumes and accoutrements. (Courtesy Jerry Nance.)

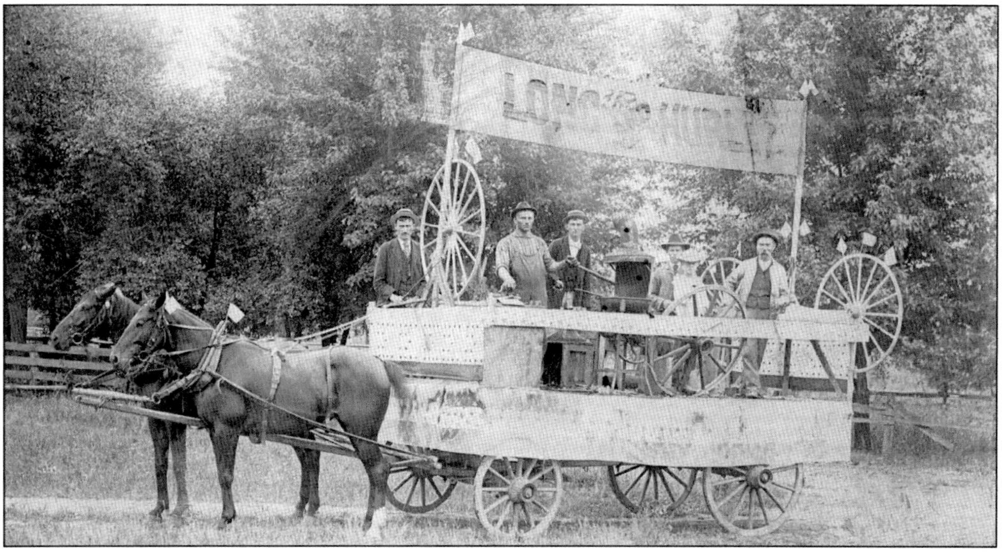

This Long and Hurley float was made for a Fourth of July parade in the 1890s. J.W. Long and Mr. Hurley were partners for a time in the Long Blacksmith Shop. Note the small flags on the horse collar hames, wagon wheels, and banner. J.W. Long is believed to be the one wearing overalls, standing by the forge, which came from the blacksmith shop. (Courtesy George Gobberdiel.)

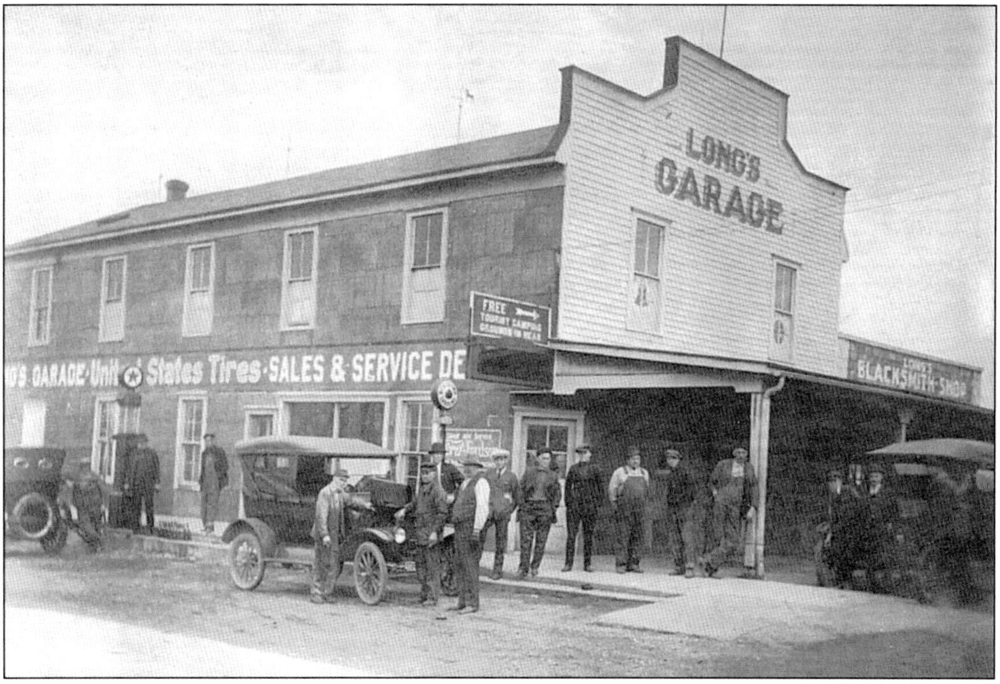

Long's Garage and Blacksmith Shop, shown here *c.* 1920s, was located on the Old National Road in Pocahontas. It later became a Ford Auto Agency under Mr. Long's son-in-law, George U. Gobberdiel. The automobiles came by rail partially disassembled. A freight elevator was installed to take the auto sections to and from the second floor for storage and assembly. Today, this building is Village Square Antiques. (Courtesy George Gobberdiel.)

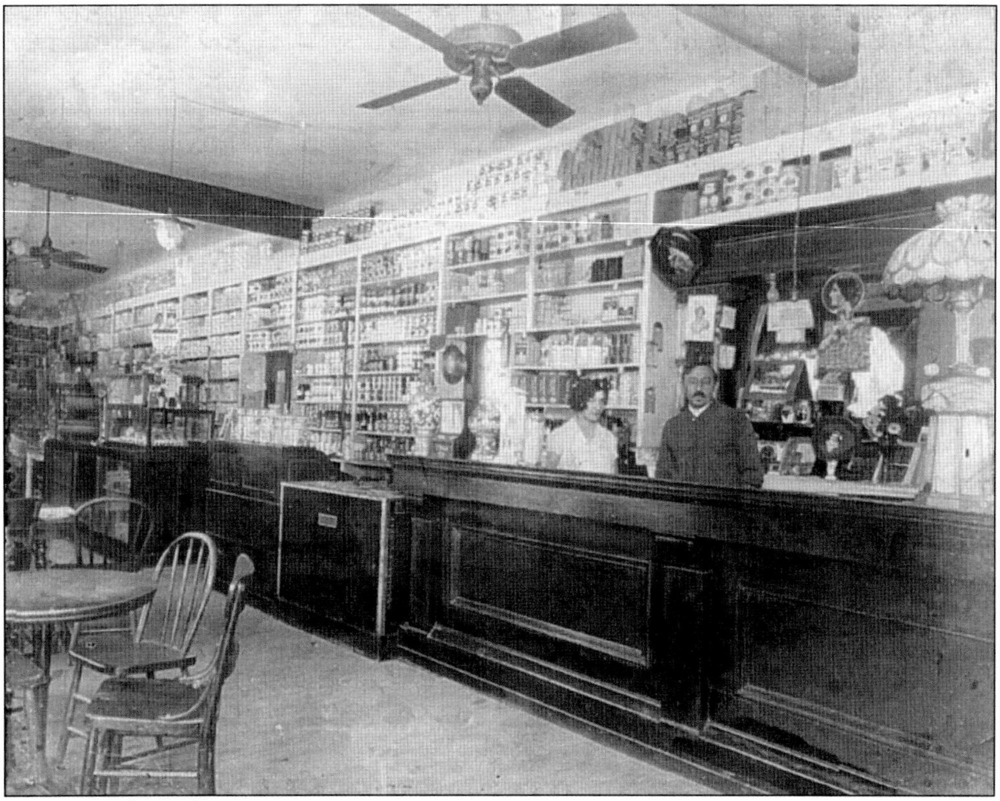

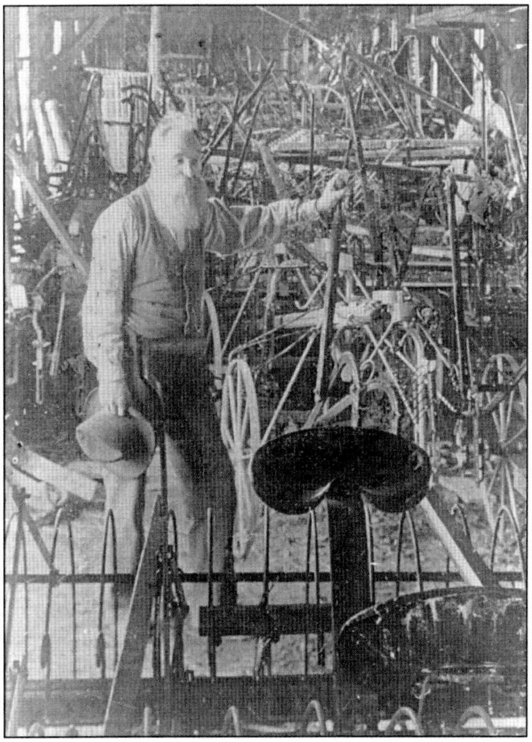

John DeLaurenti, an Italian immigrant, came with his family to Pocahontas sometime after 1911. After an injury working in the mine, John, with his wife, Mary, built a general store in Pocahontas, shown in this *c.* 1920s photo. The store carried a complete line of groceries, clothes, shoes, patent medicines, ammunition, and miners' accessories. Since the family lived in rooms behind the store, it was always open for "emergency" supplies. (Courtesy Judge John DeLaurenti.)

Henry Jenner came to Bond County from England in 1882. For a while he operated the old grist mill on Shoal Creek just west of Nuby's Steakhouse. He opened the Henry Jenner Lumber Co. in Pocahontas in 1887, located where the current lumber yard is now. This photo, *c.* 1900, shows Henry among the many farm implements he also sold. (Courtesy Gerald Jenner.)

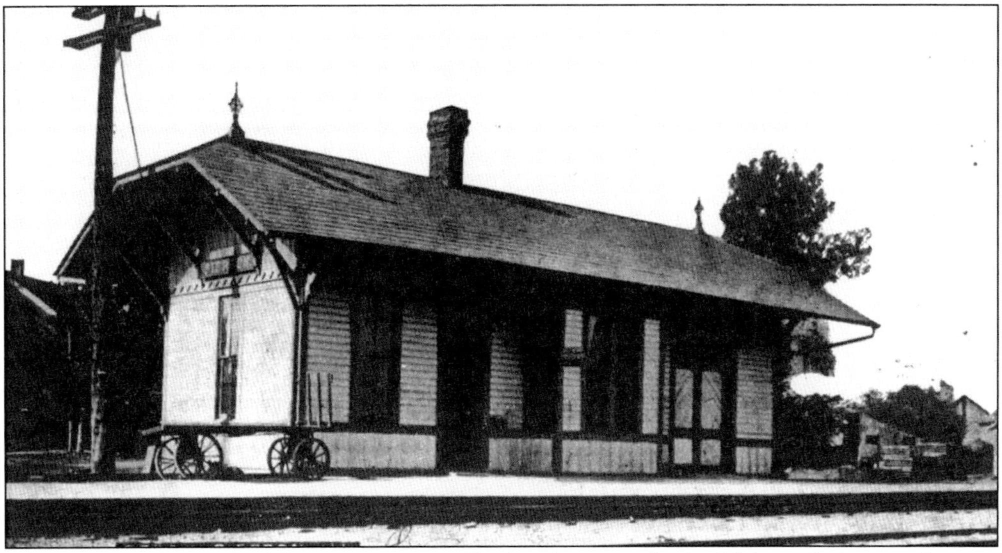

When the St. Louis, Vandalia & Terre Haute Railroad proposed to build through the area, Jacques Pierron donated the right of way through the entire length of his farmland and contributed funds for a depot. Originally called Oakdale, Pierron was founded in 1869 by Jacques Pierron, a native of Lorraine, France. The Pennsylvania Depot, pictured here, was built around 1870 and was situated in the center of town. (Courtesy Willie Knebel.)

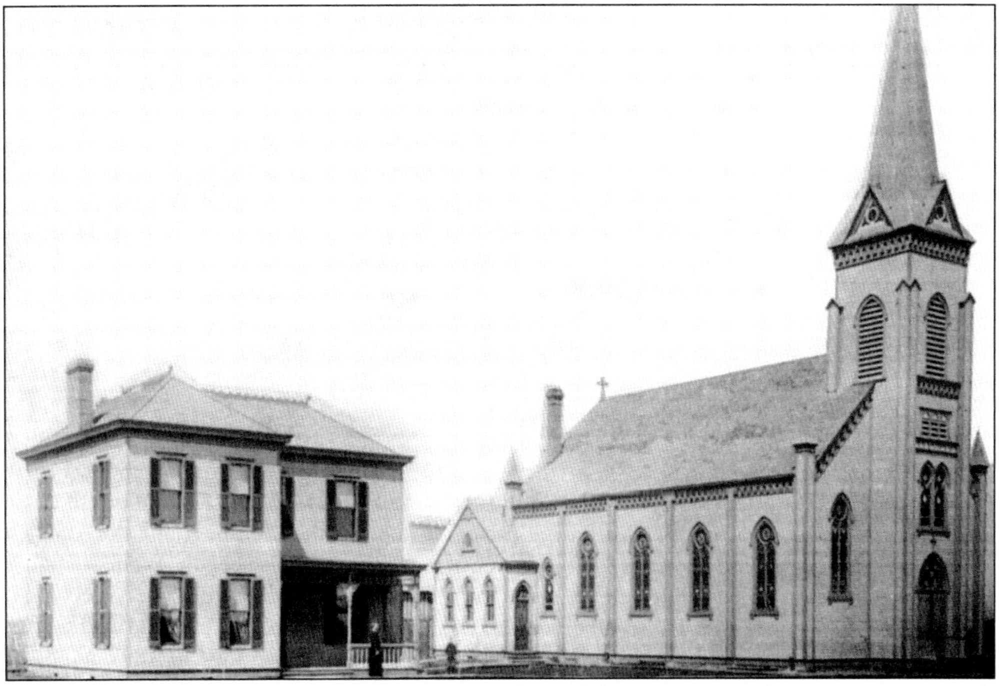

In the 1880s, Catholic families residing in Pierron formed the new Immaculate Conception Parish under Rev. William Futterer from Pocahontas and Grantfork. The Immaculate Conception Church was started in 1892. The new rectory next door was completed in 1893, and this photo was taken soon after. In 1972, the congregation built a new facility on the same site. (Courtesy Immaculate Conception Parish.)

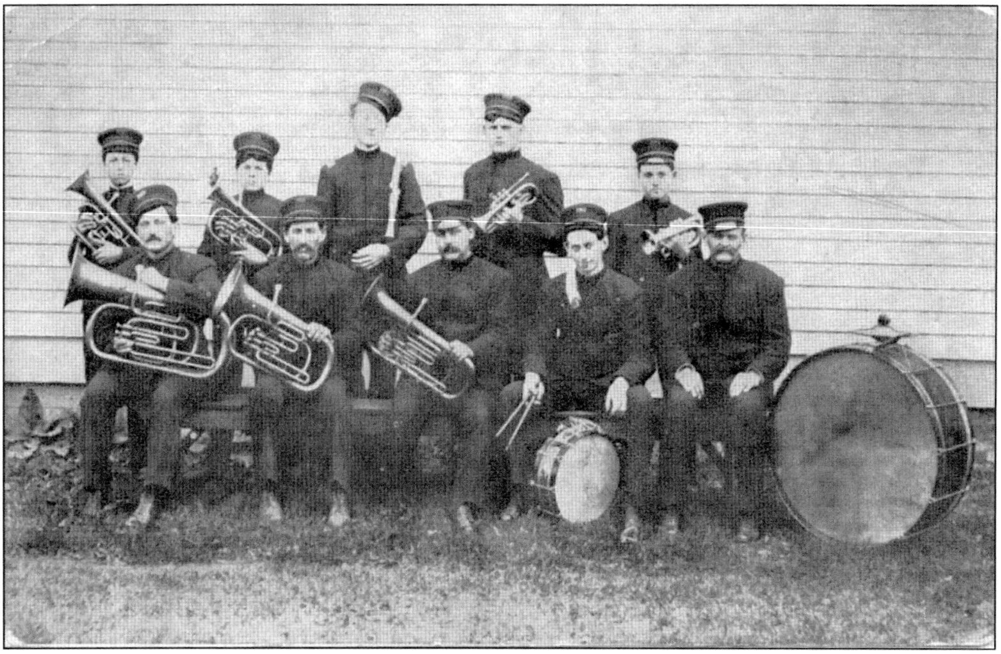

The Pierron Military Brass Band takes time away from their performance to pose for a picture in the early 1900s. Those known to be in the photo are, pictured here from left to right, Bill Hirsch, Rudy Charmilean, Robert Hoffman, Edgar Hartlieb, and Tom Leiling (back center). (Courtesy Jeff Leidel.)

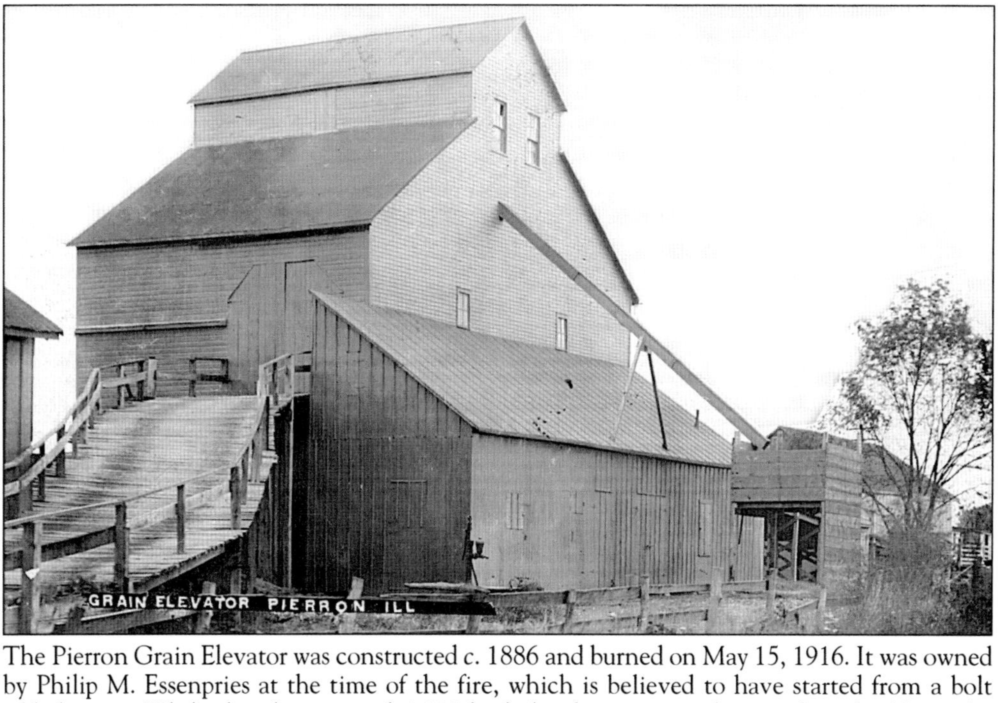

The Pierron Grain Elevator was constructed *c.* 1886 and burned on May 15, 1916. It was owned by Philip M. Essenpries at the time of the fire, which is believed to have started from a bolt of lightning. While the elevator and 6,000 bushels of grain were destroyed in the blaze, the warehouse and other nearby buildings were saved by the firemen. (Courtesy Jeff Leidel.)

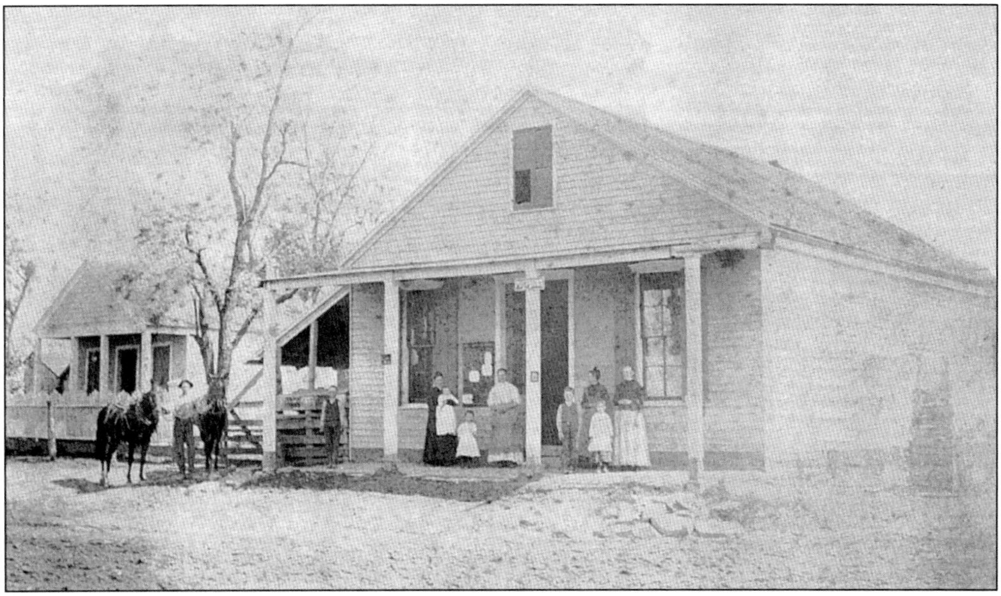

The Millersburg Store was established in 1852 by Peter Minges. Millersburg at this time was also known as Baden Baden, the name of the post office. This *c.* 1887 photo includes the following, pictured from left to right, Adam Fifer, Edward Leaher, Emma Minges, Matilda Minges, Louis Minges, Josephine Minges, and Dice Fifer. As it was in all villages, the store served as both a commercial and social hub. (Courtesy Carlos Hawley.)

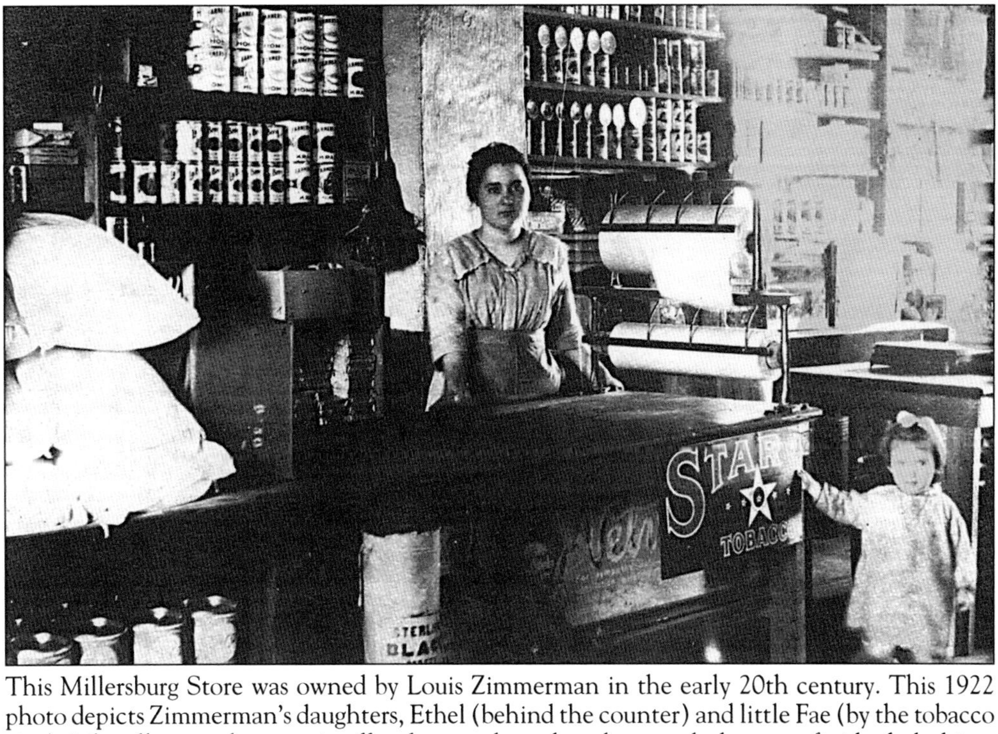

This Millersburg Store was owned by Louis Zimmerman in the early 20th century. This 1922 photo depicts Zimmerman's daughters, Ethel (behind the counter) and little Fae (by the tobacco sign). Like all general stores, it offered canned goods, tobacco, cloth, some finished clothing, tools, sacks of flour, and other essentials. (Courtesy Dee Zanchetti Pollinger.)

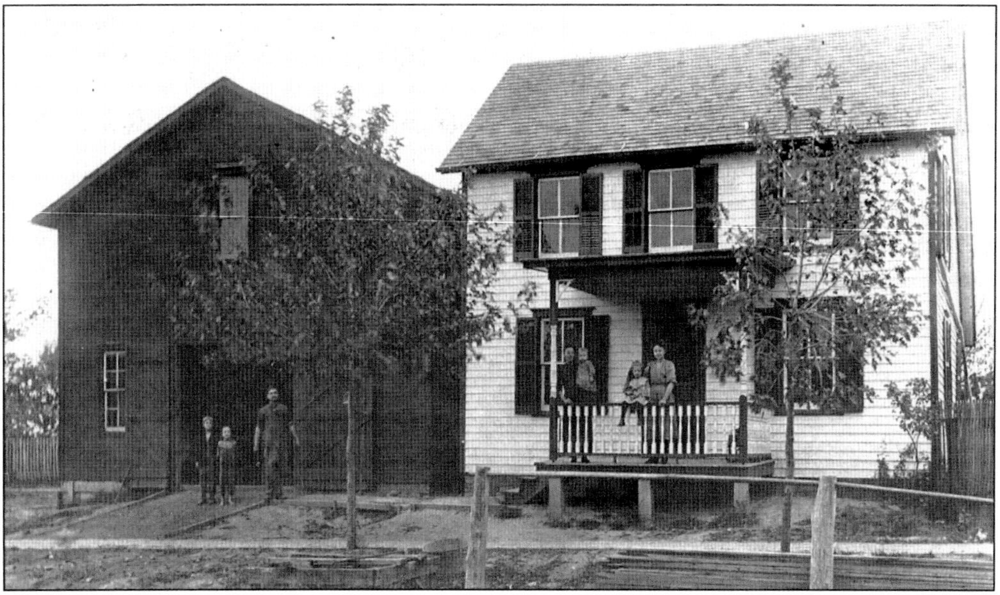

Louis Minges operated a blacksmith shop in Millersburg. The Minges shop and residence were located on what is now Route 143. This c. 1890 photo shows the following Minges family members, from left to right; Louis' sons, Ernie and Olin, Louis, his Aunt Josephine holding his daughter Ruth, daughter Grace and wife, Emma. Millersburg is now officially part of Pierron after joining to Pierron's water line in the late 1970s. (Courtesy Carlos Hawley.)

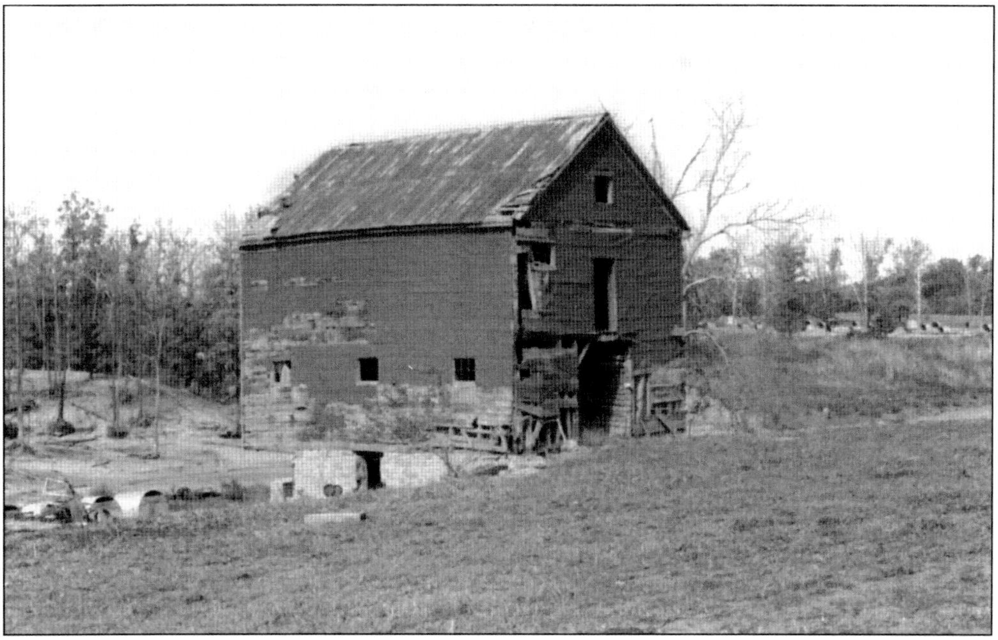

In the late 1840s, Charles Miller built this grist mill. A neighbor, William Burgess, laid out the town in 1851 and named it Millersburg for Charles Miller. By the 1880s, the Peter Streiff family owned and operated the mill. The last operator was John Streiff, whose sawmill helped keep the business going into the 1920s. The mill was used as a granary and storage building until it collapsed in 1999. (Courtesy Kevin Kaegy.)

Eight

Old Ripley Township

Old Ripley Township is in the west central section of the county and was formerly called Ripley precinct. Back in 1812, Elezarum Ripley Wheelock and his brother laid out a settlement not far from the Shoal Creek location of Brown's Mill. On the old maps, the ones where Bond County runs north all the way to Lake Superior, Ripley is often the only town shown in the entire county. At one time, it bid to be the site of the capital of the new state of Illinois. It had a post office from 1819 to 1823. Sometime shortly after that, Ripley was abandoned and New Berlin was established by Charles Plog on higher ground to the southwest. A post office named Old Ripley was established there in 1850, and closed in 1903. New Berlin took the name of the post office, and Old Ripley was incorporated as a village in 1906. It was and is the only community in the township. To the northeast, Terrapin Ridge, a neighborhood made up of mostly related farm families, developed a community club in 1921 that lasted until 1975, mainly for the benefit of the otherwise isolated farm mothers and wives. They held picnics, celebrations, and quilting bees.

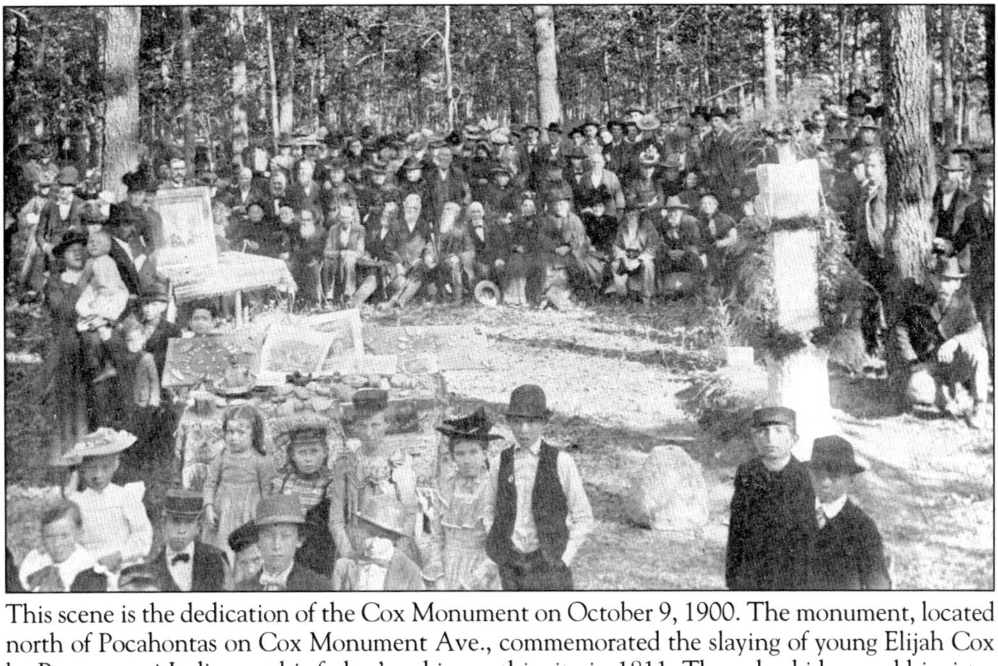

This scene is the dedication of the Cox Monument on October 9, 1900. The monument, located north of Pocahontas on Cox Monument Ave., commemorated the slaying of young Elijah Cox by Potawatomi Indians at his father's cabin on this site in 1811. They also kidnapped his sister Rebecca, who was later found by way of a trail of apron pieces she tore off and left behind as she was carried off. (Courtesy Historical Souvenir of Greenville, Illinois, 1905.)

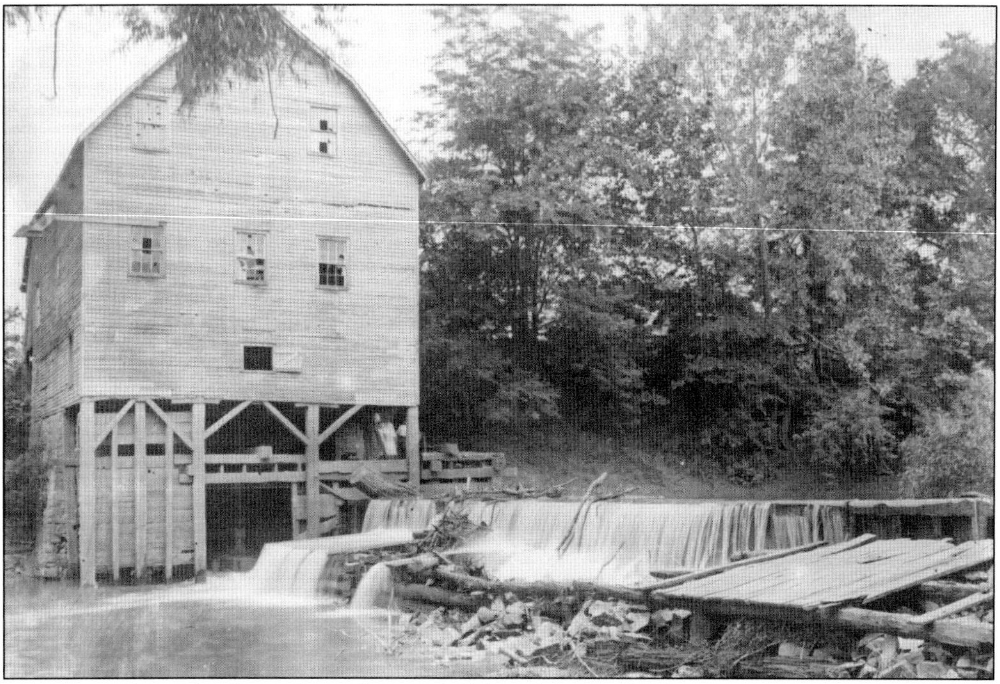

Brown's Mill on Shoal Creek northeast of Old Ripley was the first water powered mill built in Bond County. A settler named Lee built a grist mill on the site in 1817. Around 1840, the mill was acquired by the Brown family, who owned it for almost 90 years, except for the year 1866–67 during which time George Patterson ran it. This shot was taken in 1909 by H.R. Collman. The mill was dismantled in 1929. (Courtesy C. Jeff Brewer.)

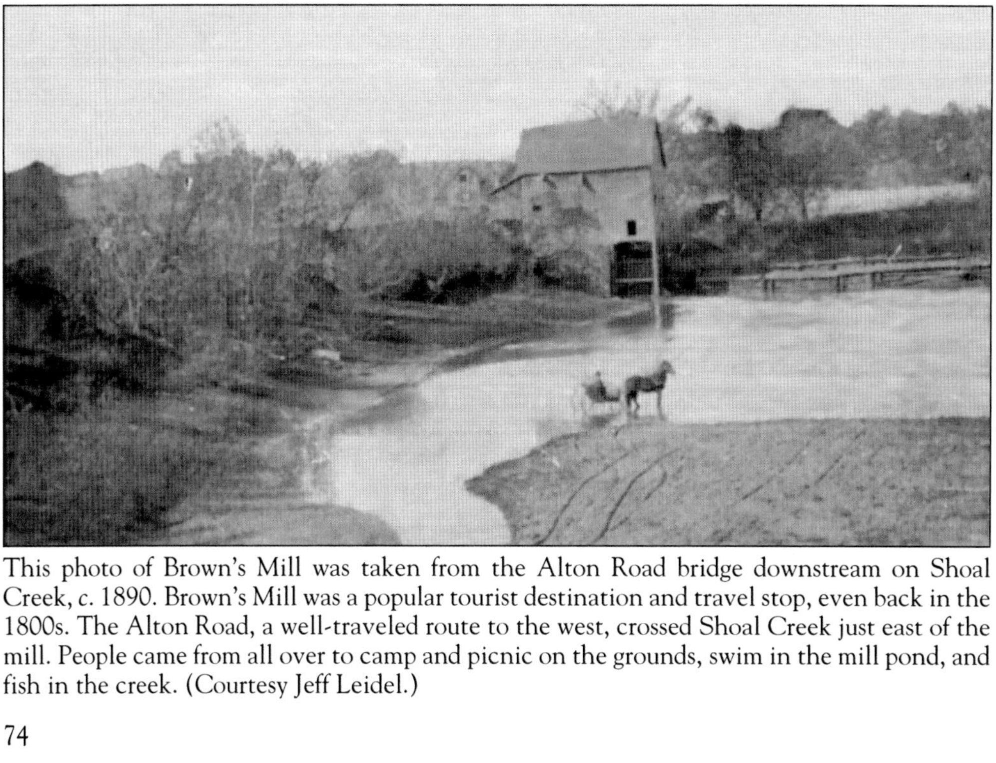

This photo of Brown's Mill was taken from the Alton Road bridge downstream on Shoal Creek, c. 1890. Brown's Mill was a popular tourist destination and travel stop, even back in the 1800s. The Alton Road, a well-traveled route to the west, crossed Shoal Creek just east of the mill. People came from all over to camp and picnic on the grounds, swim in the mill pond, and fish in the creek. (Courtesy Jeff Leidel.)

The first oil well in Bond County was located a short distance west and south of Brown's Mill. When it was drilled *c.* 1910, there were great hopes for an oil boom in the region. The last large crowd of people who gathered near the mill was when the well was "shot." The result was disappointing, and the oil boom waned, although small pumps can still be seen here and there in farm fields of the western townships. (Courtesy Tom Paine.)

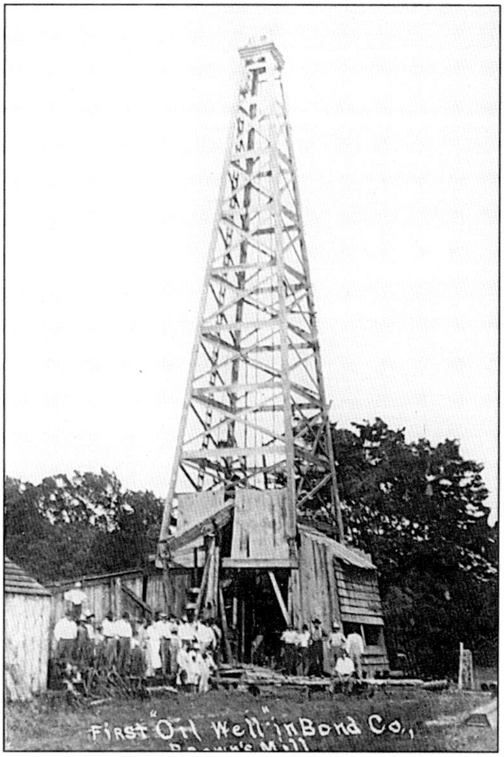

This unusual atmospheric view of Brown's Mill was taken in the early 1900s from the top of the oil well rig west and south of the mill. Before its demise, Brown's Mill was a popular subject for local painters and photographers. The Alton Road and the bridge over Shoal Creek appear as a pale ribbon in the upper right of the photograph. (Courtesy C. Jeff Brewer.)

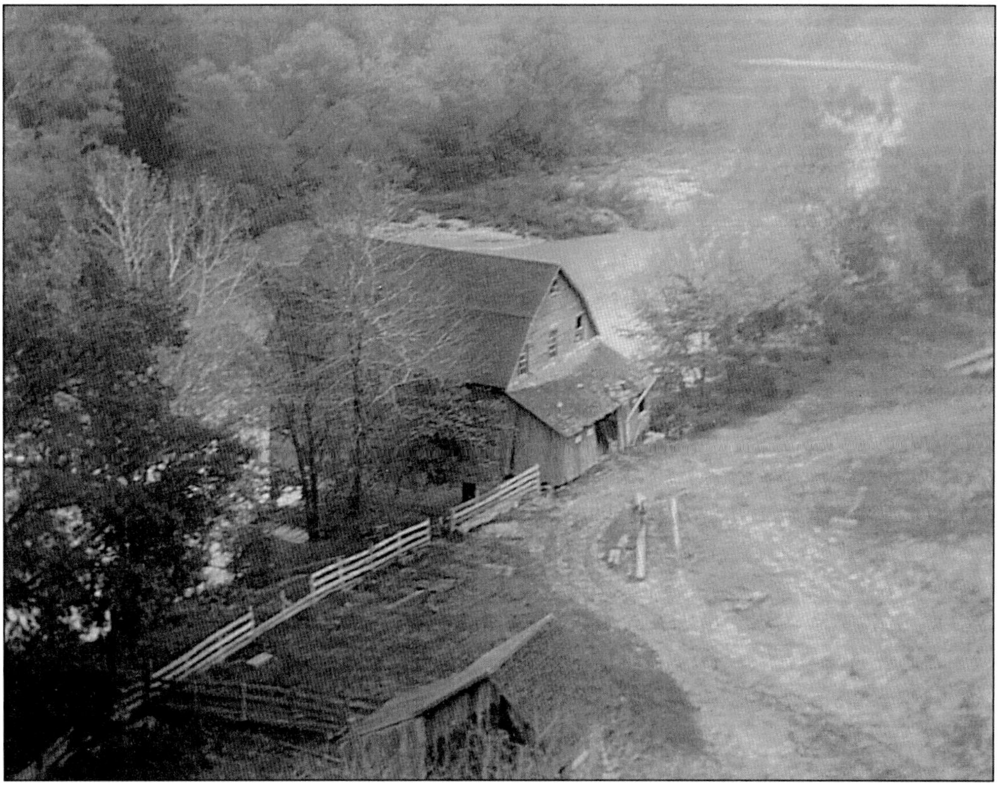

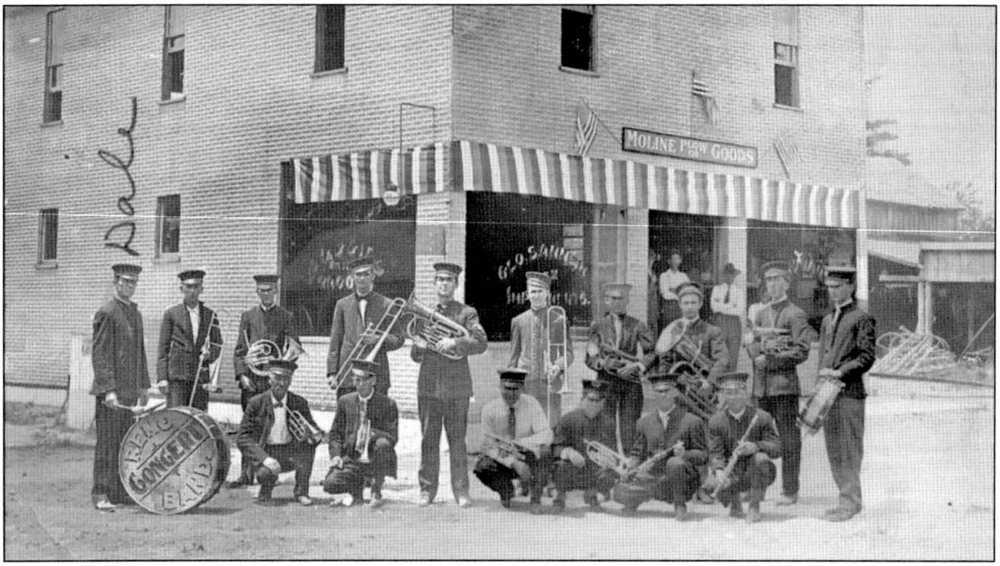

At Old Ripley on July 4, 1911, the Reno Concert Band poses in front of George Sanner's hardware store on the corner of Main and St. Louis Streets. The band members, pictured from left to right, are: (kneeling) Harry J. Miller, Clarence Brewer, Eugene Ferguson, Emmet McAliney, William Stanton, and William E. Miller; (standing) Walter Smith, Charlie Jones, Roy Herndon, Dale Shultz, Julian Herndon, Ralph File, George Weber, Henry Collman, and Willis Willeford. (Courtesy Bond County Historical Society.)

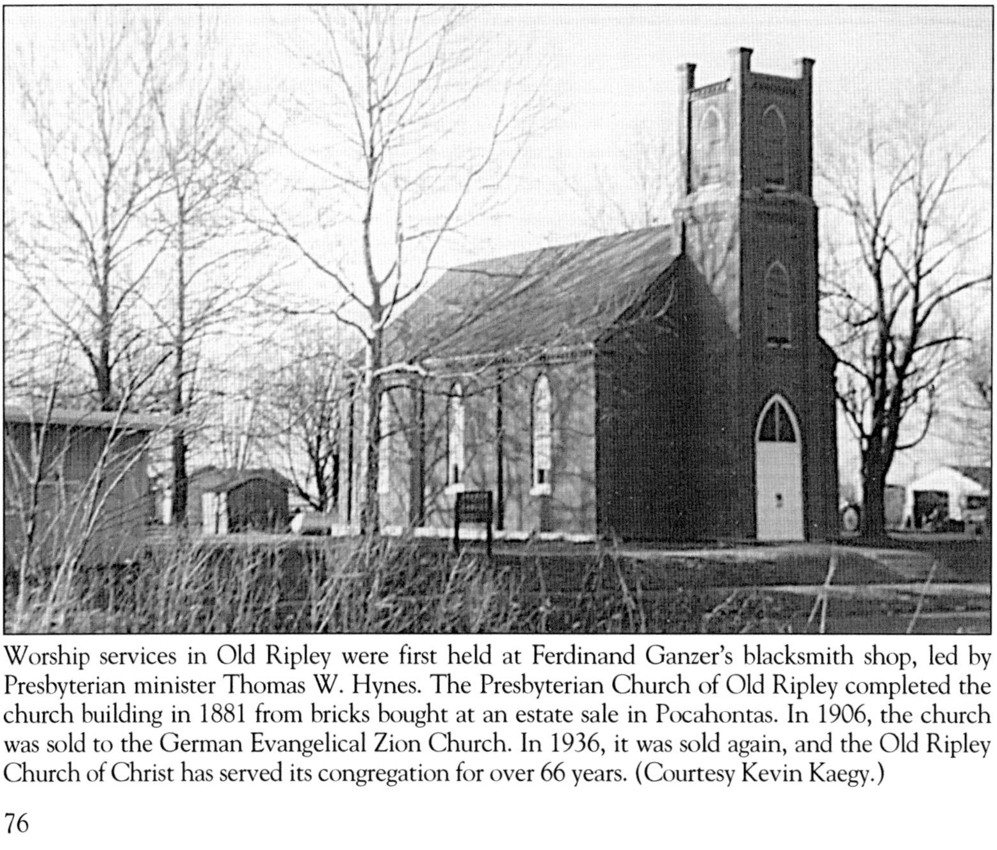

Worship services in Old Ripley were first held at Ferdinand Ganzer's blacksmith shop, led by Presbyterian minister Thomas W. Hynes. The Presbyterian Church of Old Ripley completed the church building in 1881 from bricks bought at an estate sale in Pocahontas. In 1906, the church was sold to the German Evangelical Zion Church. In 1936, it was sold again, and the Old Ripley Church of Christ has served its congregation for over 66 years. (Courtesy Kevin Kaegy.)

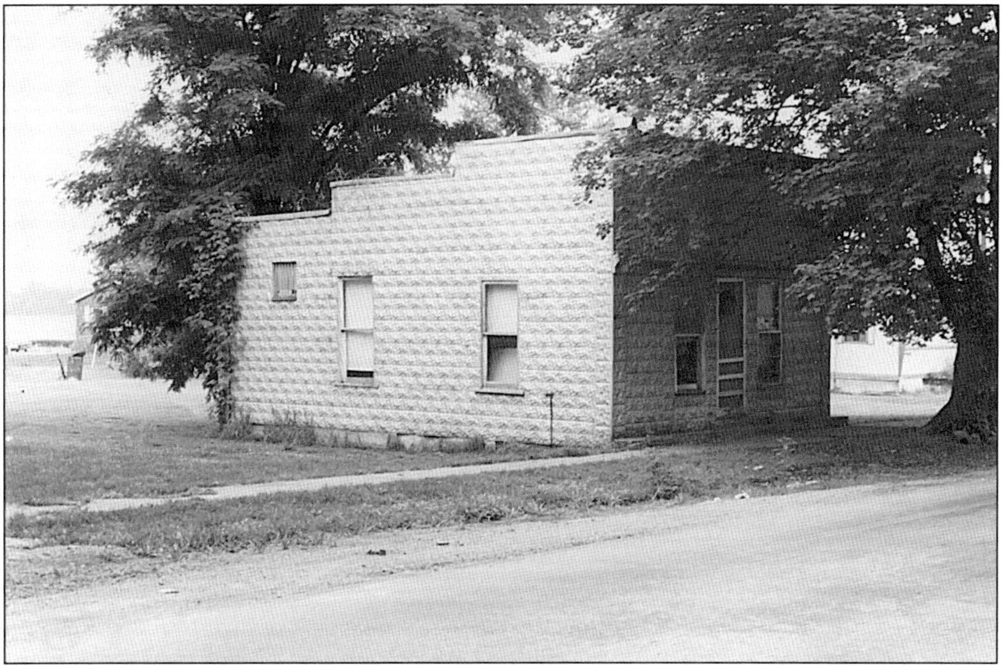

After weekend sprees and community celebrations, the Old Ripley Jail was more a holding pen for the drunk and disorderly than an actual penal institution. During World War II, the steel cells were sold for the scrap drive. For a number of years after that, it served as the polling place and the village hall, where town meetings were held. After being sold in the 1990s, it was eventually demolished. (Courtesy Kevin Kaegy.)

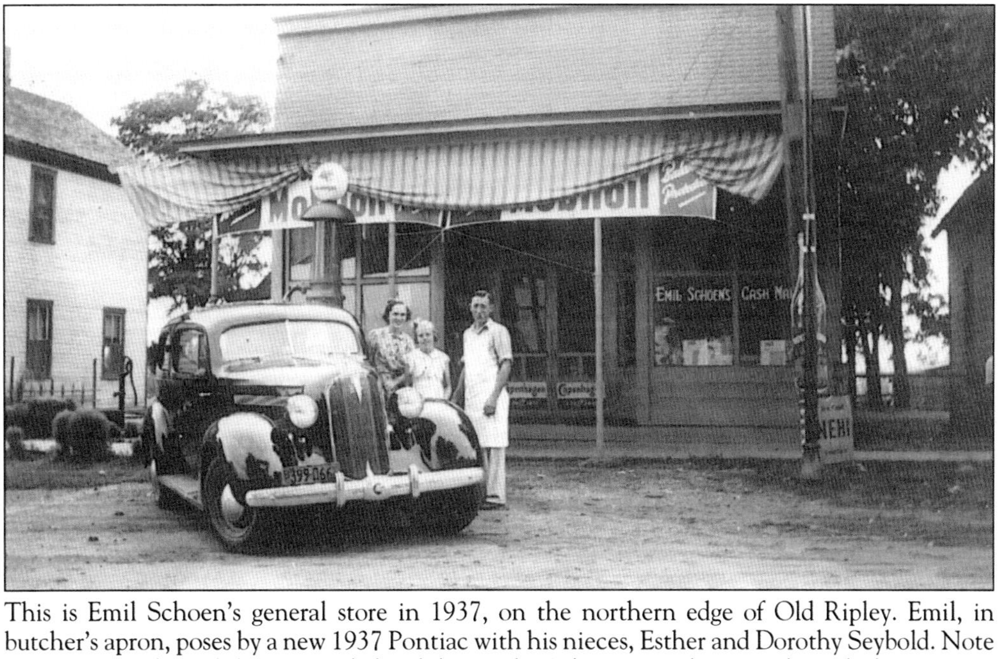

This is Emil Schoen's general store in 1937, on the northern edge of Old Ripley. Emil, in butcher's apron, poses by a new 1937 Pontiac with his nieces, Esther and Dorothy Seybold. Note the gravity-style Mobil gas pump behind them. The Schoens ran the store through the 1970s. It closed and was dismantled in 1987. (Courtesy Ruth Schoen Govaia.)

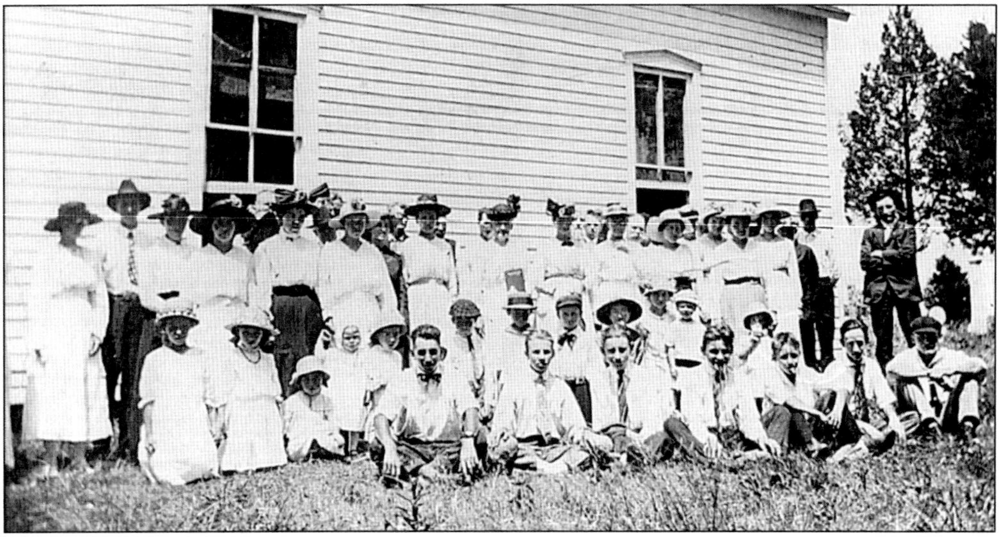

The original Mt. Nebo United Baptist Church (Old Nebo) was organized in 1833 by Elder Peter Long, who served as pastor for over 40 years. A log meeting house was built in 1835 and later, several frame churches were built on the same site. The congregation split in 1868 over doctrine, creating two Mt. Nebo churches. This photo, c. 1920, shows a sizable congregation, but by the 1950s Old Nebo had disbanded and the church was removed in the late 1970s. (Courtesy Martha Jenner.)

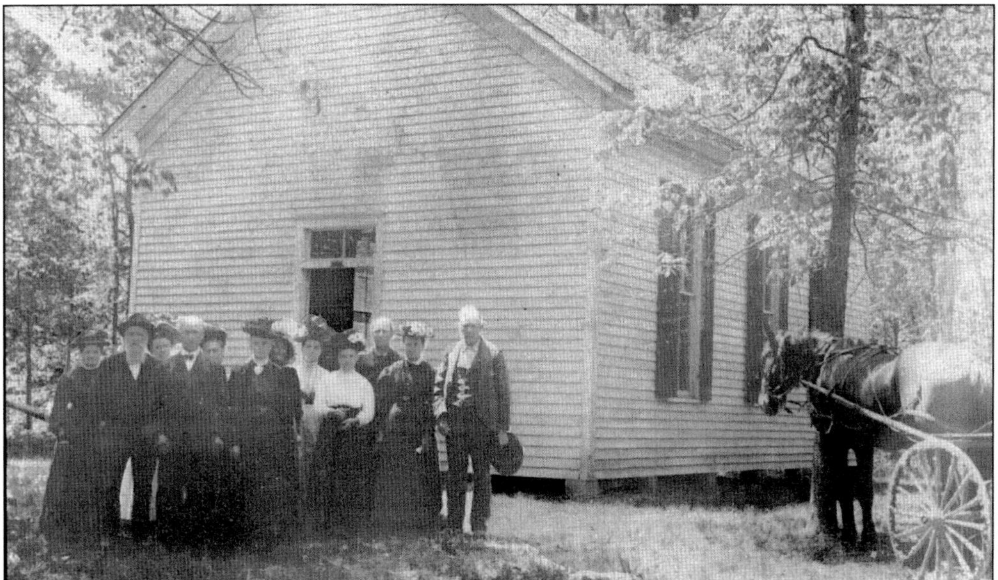

The reorganized Mt. Nebo Primitive Baptist Church (New Nebo) built this frame meeting house in 1881 in the Terrapin Ridge neighborhood. The church thrives to this day with descendants of the original founders as members. This photo, c. 1910, shows the following congregation members from left to right: Julia Clanton Willeford, Willis Willeford, Katie Frueh, Elder John H. Willeford, Martha File Clanton, Sarah Hunter Willeford, Narcissa Webster Coyle, Rose Tabor Willeford, Mary Jane Willeford File, William Willis Willeford, Amanda and Peter Coyle. (Courtesy Martha Jenner.)

Nine

Central Township

Central Township is in the center of Bond County and was formerly Greenville Precinct. Central's major community is the county seat, Greenville, founded in 1815. Settled early on, Central Township was the site of Lindley's Fort, which was probably just a fortified blockhouse during the War of 1812. It was located southwest of present Greenville. One of the earliest inhabitants of the area was "old" Benjamin Henson, who lived in a large hollow sycamore tree as early as 1806. When the Indian troubles came, which all but emptied the entire county during the War of 1812, he never left or stayed in a fort. He was found just as hale and hearty as ever when the settlers returned. He ferried travelers across Shoal Creek southwest of Greenville near where Nuby's Steak House is now. Just southwest of Greenville, Moody Campground was an early Methodist meeting ground, dating from around 1820.

Another community is Stubblefield, of which only a few homes remain, and the Smith Grove neighborhood, best known for its Baptist Church. Greenville, besides being the county seat, was the crossroads of the county. It acted as a hub for the National Road from the east and the Alton Road to the west, the Red Ball Trail to the northeast, and the Black Diamond Trail (now Route 127) that went north. The St. Louis, Vandalia, & Terre Haute Railroad (later Pennsylvania RR) had a major station in Greenville and Stubblefield.

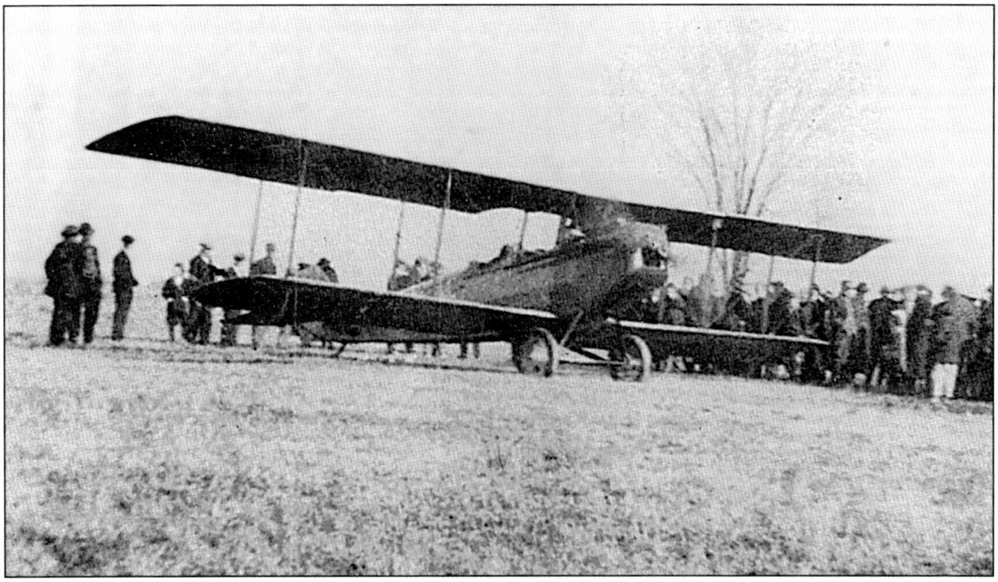

This photo of Charles Lindberg's mail plane was taken in the mid-1920s on Bud Chestnut's farm near Sorento. Before his historic nonstop flight to Paris, Lucky Lindy flew mail routes in the Midwest and was a sometime visitor to Bond County. Greenville's first airport was established along the Old Hillsboro Road (Route 127) to the west of Ayers Road. The first flight from there was on May 19, 1938. (Courtesy Velma Enloe.)

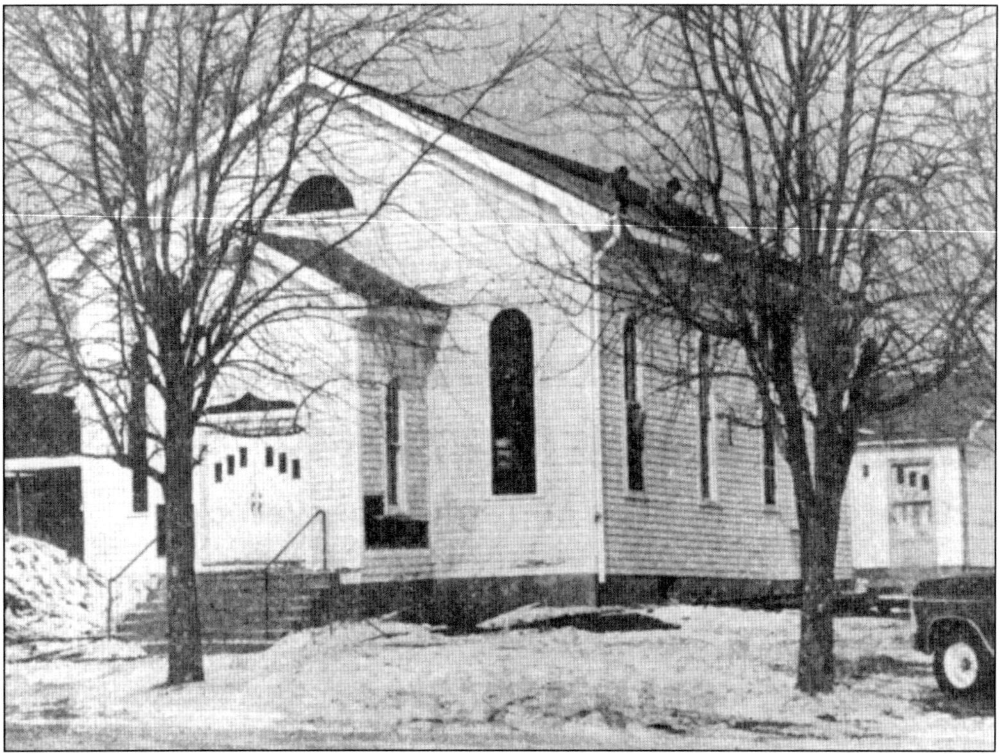

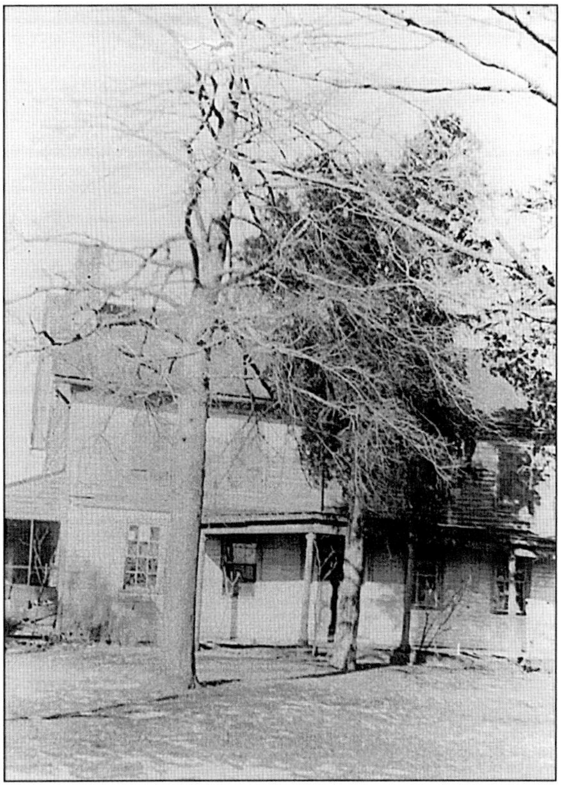

The Smith Grove Baptist Church was organized in 1869 by members of Old Mt. Nebo Church. They worshipped in the brick Smith Grove School until they built their own church west of the schoolhouse in 1880. They built a new large church building in 1977 and, as a Southern Baptist congregation, are the most active rural church in Bond County. (Courtesy the *Greenville Advocate*.)

The John Leaverton Home stood on the west side of Millersburg Road just south of Smith Grove School. In December 1864, Leaverton, an ardent unionist, was attacked by armed pro-Southern sympathizers who broke into his house to rob him. On December 8, 1864, Capt. Samuel McAdams was killed while trying to arrest Jacob Sanner in connection with the Leaverton robbery. This was just one instance of the unrest throughout Bond County during the Civil War. (Courtesy Eddie Ulmer.)

The St. Louis, Vandalia & Terre Haute Railroad was built through Bond County in 1868. Shown here is the old Stubblefield switch tower, which was moved to the Schmollinger farm about 1940. The Pennsylvania Railroad straightened the right-of-way and eliminated the old track where this switch tower once stood. The village of Stubblefield was laid out around 1870 and was a convenient shipping point for farm produce. The post office operated out of a general store from 1872 to 1918. (Courtesy Kevin Kaegy.)

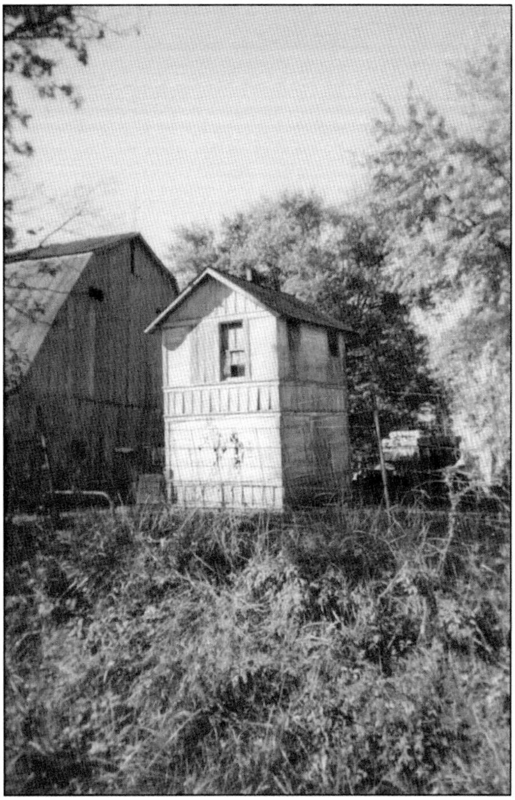

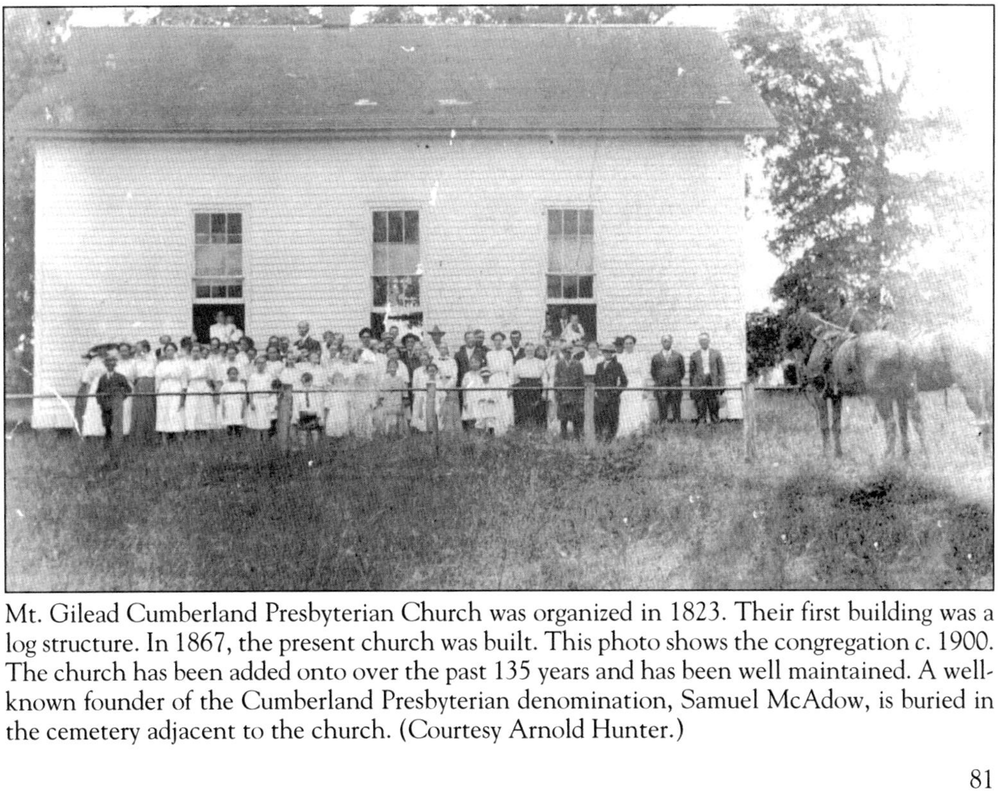

Mt. Gilead Cumberland Presbyterian Church was organized in 1823. Their first building was a log structure. In 1867, the present church was built. This photo shows the congregation c. 1900. The church has been added onto over the past 135 years and has been well maintained. A well-known founder of the Cumberland Presbyterian denomination, Samuel McAdow, is buried in the cemetery adjacent to the church. (Courtesy Arnold Hunter.)

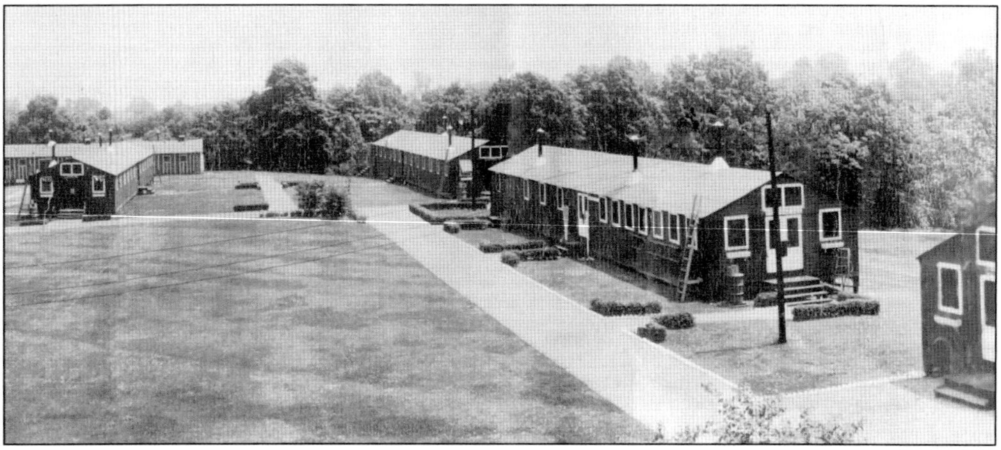

During the Depression, the Civilian Conservation Corps (CCC) opened a camp north of Greenville on land owned by Ulysses S. DeMoulin. Among the 200 men who served in Company 1621 was future Cardinal Hall-of-Famer, Red Schoendienst. Their construction projects included several county schoolhouses, three gyms, the Greenville Sewage Plant, and the City Park. The camp closed in 1941, and Utlaut Memorial Hospital now occupies the camp site. (Courtesy James O. Stever.)

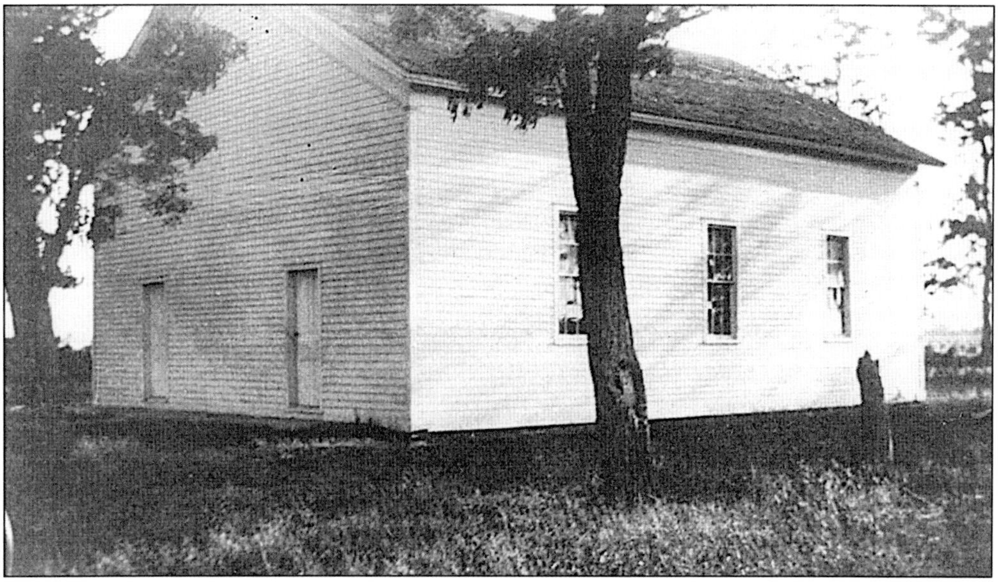

The Centenary Methodist Church Society formed around 1820 from the Horeb and Sinai Societies. Their first church was built in 1825, the centennial year of Methodism. It was located on Alton Road (later Route 140) approximately four miles west of Greenville. In the old days, services were held every other Sunday and the members worshipped with the nearby Mt. Gilead Church every other week. Centenary Church closed *c.* 1950 and was taken down. (Courtesy Kevin Kaegy.)

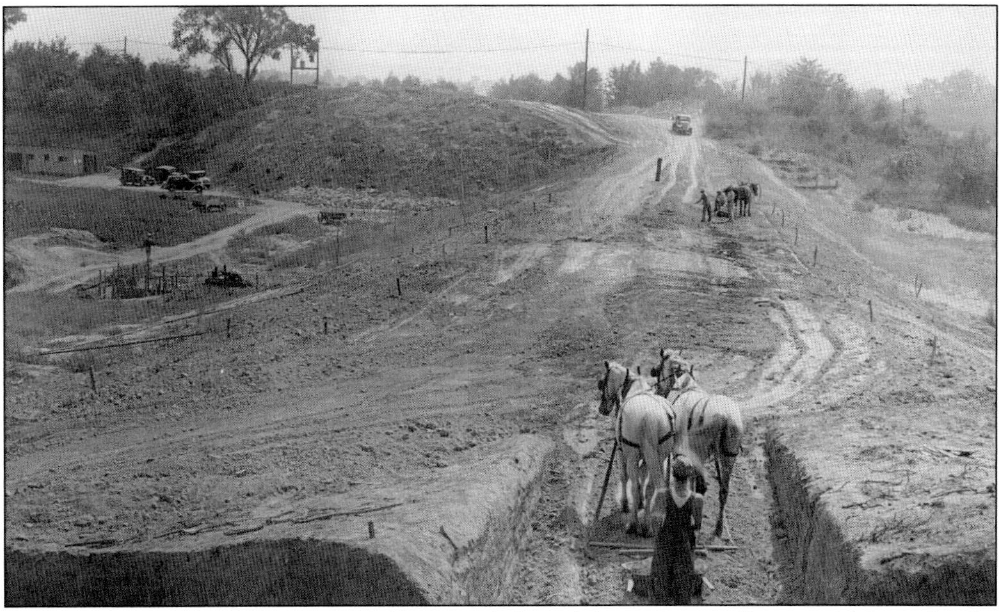

In 1935, the Federate Club, one of the many ladies' clubs in Greenville, raised $5,000 for the purchase of property for a city park west of town, which was donated to the City of Greenville. Alice Baumberger Hoiles and a few other ladies personally bought and donated additional acreage to the northeast to create a lake. Work on the lake commenced in 1936 with horses and slips (above). (Courtesy Doug Marti.)

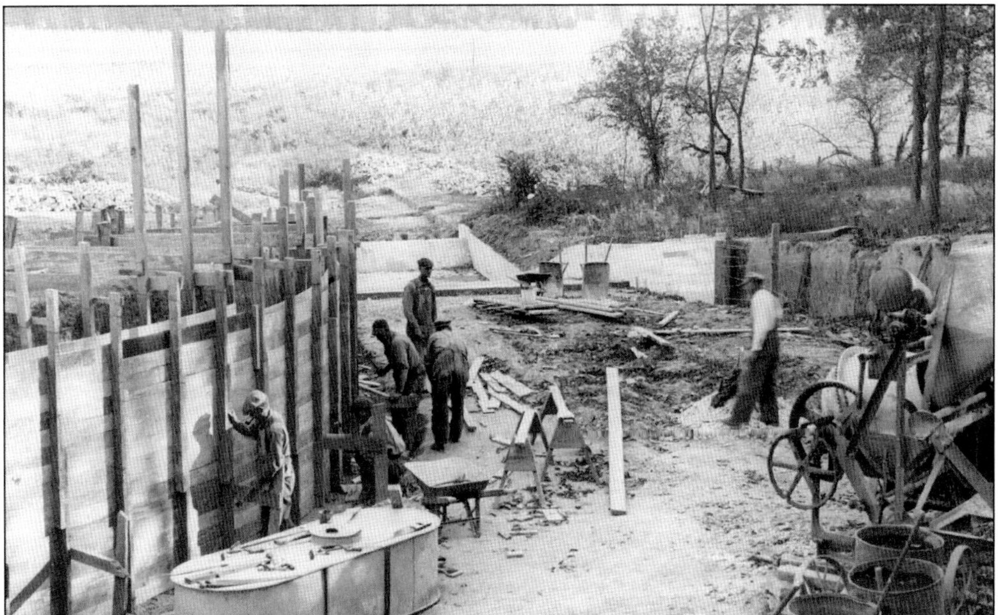

Robert Baumberger was responsible for the design and engineering of the lake and supervised its construction. This photo shows the building of the dam spillway in 1936, which was a WPA project. The old City Park, now known as Patriot's Park, was a popular recreation spot. Many generations learned how to swim in the city lake. (Courtesy Doug Marti.)

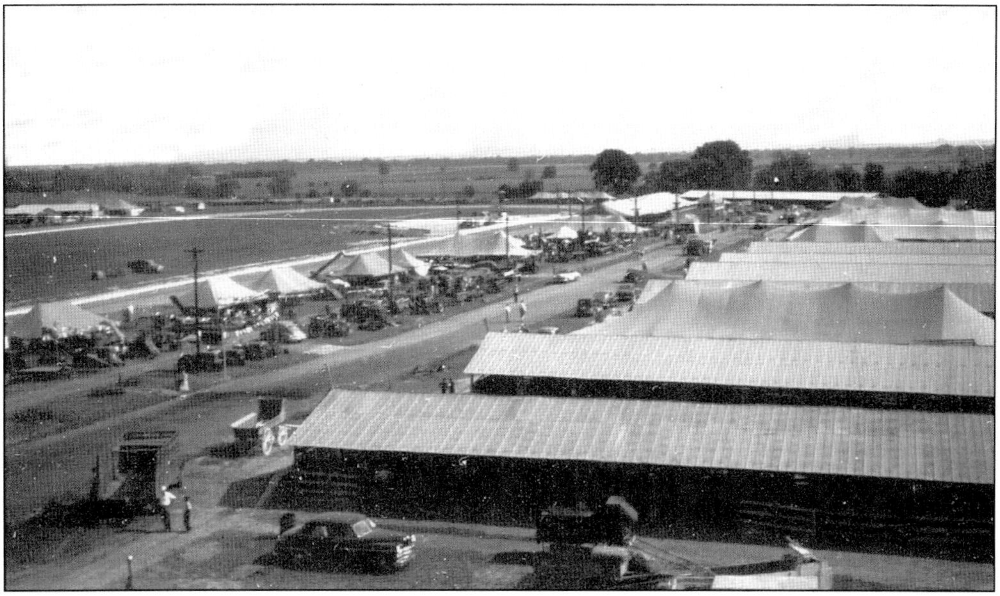

This view of the Bond County Fair was taken from the top of the Ferris wheel by Marvin Knight in 1951. He was looking south down the midway and the carnival was set up north of the livestock barns. The fair was formally organized in 1948. Louis Ledbetter, Tally DeFrees, and Harold Gaffner were the early leaders of the fair board. Prior to World War II, the Farmer's Institute, founded by John Hartley in 1901, was held every fall in Greenville. (Courtesy Marvin Knight.)

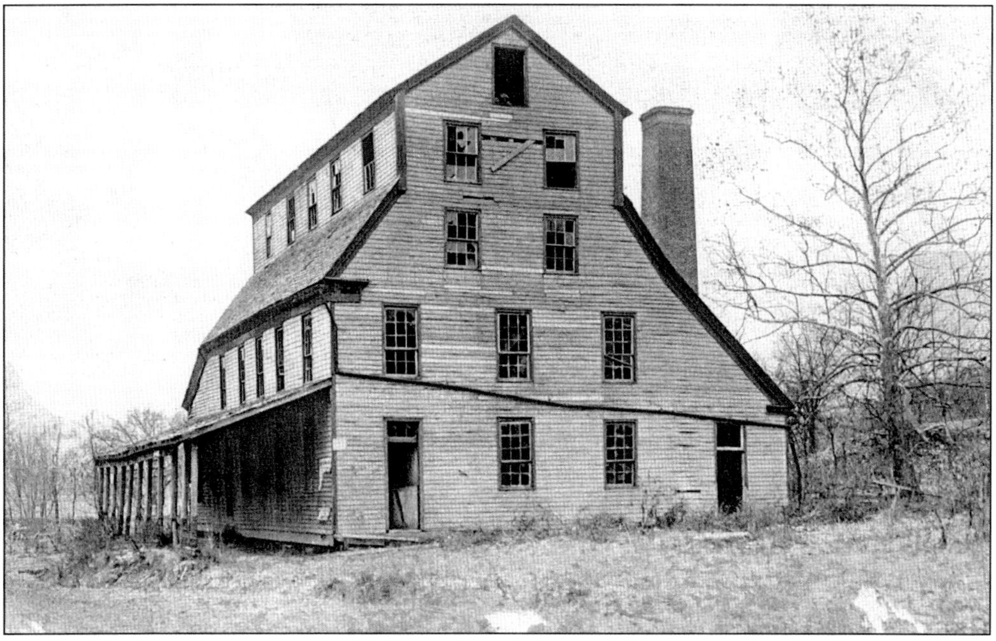

Steuber's Mill was located on the Hillsboro Road (Route 127) just south of Little Shoal Creek bridge, giving the area its common name, Mill Hill. When built in 1854, W.S. Smith was one of the owners. It was then called the Phoenix Mills. It was operated by steam, and the boilers were brought to Greenville from Alton by ox cart. It was closed and dismantled around 1913. (Courtesy Jeff Leidel.)

Ten

City of Greenville

Greenville was founded in 1815 by George Davidson. Later, around 1817, Davidson built a tavern on the southwest corner of what is now Main and Sixth Streets to service travelers on the National Road, which then ran along the present Sixth Street.

Situated on high ground in the center of the area, Greenville was chosen for the county seat in 1821. It was incorporated as a town in 1855 and as a city in 1872. Several historic neighborhoods within Greenville include the following: Cobtown, south of the railroad tracks near the grain elevators, was named because families heated their homes by burning corn cobs; Piety Hill, just north of downtown, was named for the ministers that lived there; New Jerusalem, just east of Greenville College, so-named for several religion professors who lived in that neighborhood, and last, but not least, Buzzard's Roost, on the southwest corner of town, named for the old men who sat on their front porches, watching travelers pass on the National Road.

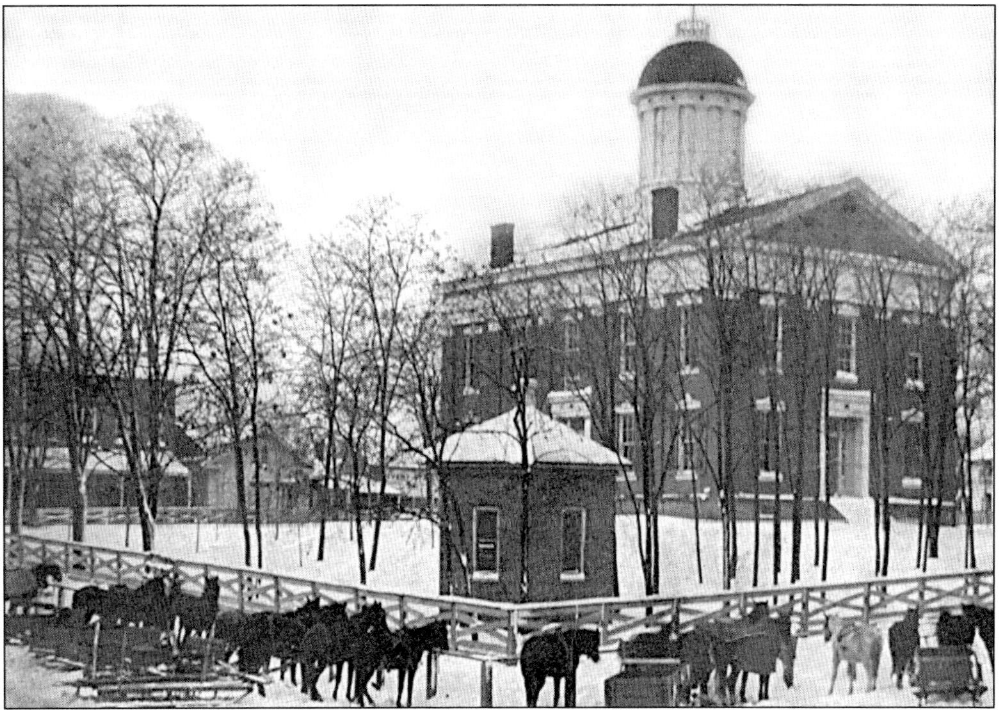

This graceful Greek Revival building, the third Bond County Courthouse to stand on the Greenville Square, was built in 1853. Horses with sleds line up around the southeast corner in this winter photo, taken prior to 1880. In the foreground is a six-sided building used as an arsenal for weapons during the Civil War. It was later used as a holding cell for those awaiting trial. (Courtesy Bill Donnell.)

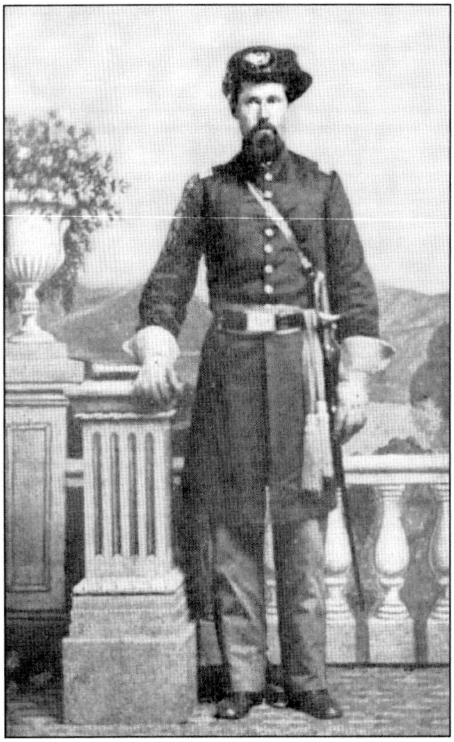

During the Civil War, Captain William Colby of Company F 130th Illinois Volunteers, was one of 200 Bond County men to serve in that unit. He died during the siege of Vicksburg in 1863 and was sent back home for proper burial. A full scale military funeral was held in the old courthouse and 34 pall bearers escorted his and Lt. Ives' remains to the old City Cemetery. Colby post G.A.R. was named in his honor. (Courtesy Dr. Denny Donnell.)

This shows the old courthouse after being remodeled and painted in 1880. Built in 1853, it burned down 30 years later, after chimney sparks set the roof on fire. State's Attorney W.A. Northcott led a bucket brigade to the attic and put down the flames long enough for the county records to be saved. He later served as lieutenant governor of Illinois. (Courtesy Kevin Kaegy.)

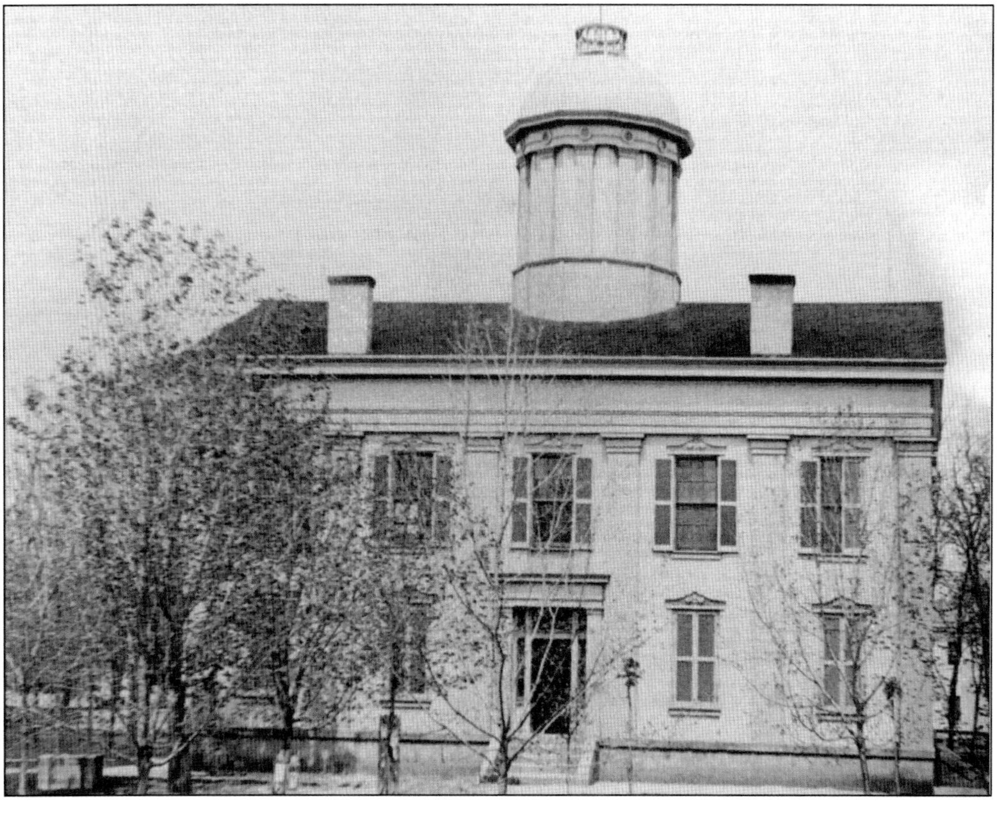

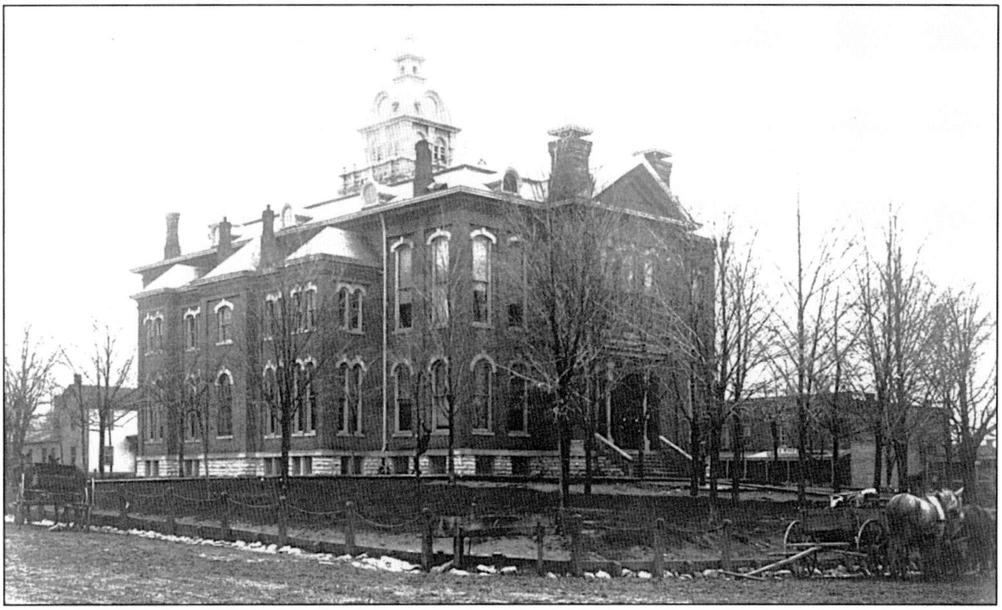

The cornerstone for the present Bond County Courthouse was laid June 4, 1884. The building, designed by W.R. Parsons of Quincy, cost $20,000 to build. The dormer windows, cupola, and chimney caps were removed for maintenance reasons. Although many remodeling projects have taken place since the 1940s, much care has been taken to preserve the original trims, woodwork, and Victorian details of the structure. (Courtesy Kevin Kaegy.)

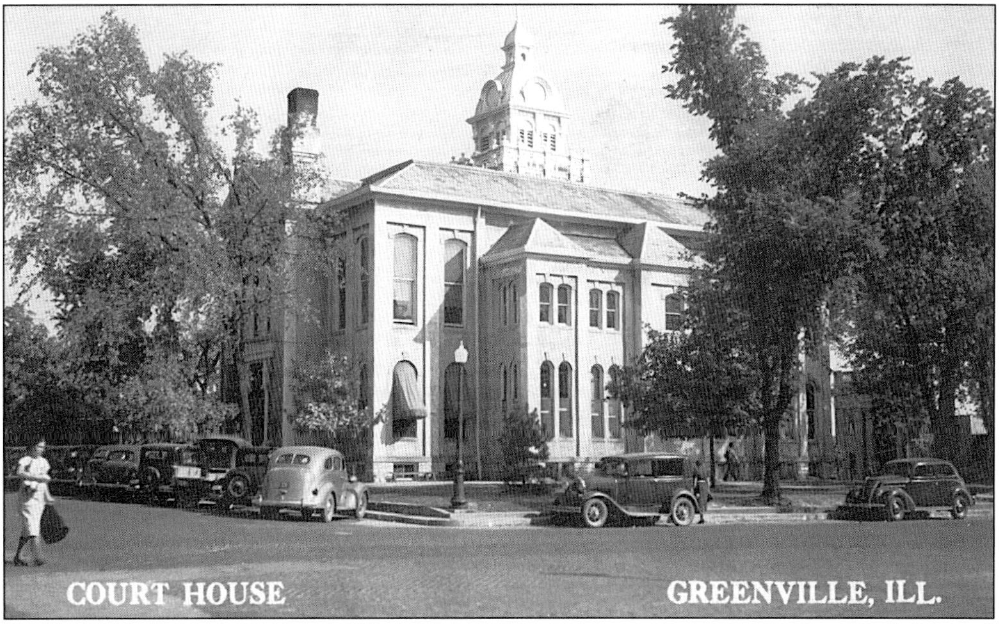

This photo of the Bond County Courthouse in the 1930s gives a better view of the elaborate cupola that surmounted the building at the time. In 1948, the flagpole was struck by lightening, which also damaged a corner of the cupola. Both were removed in August of that year for a cost of $175. During the 1930s and 40s, the courthouse was covered with gray stucco. Fortunately, it was of such poor quality that it was all removed. (Courtesy Jeff Leidel.)

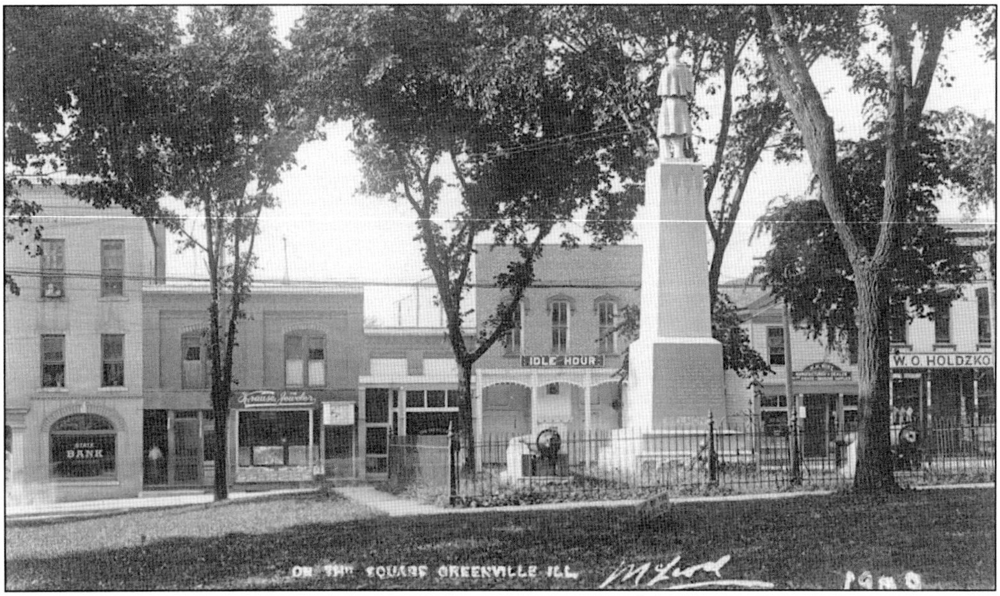

The south side of the Greenville Square in 1909 is depicted here from left to right: the State Bank, founded in 1869 by Charles Hoiles; A.H. Krause Jewelers; the Idle Hour silent movie house; the Wirz Cigar Store; and W.O. Holdzkom's Red Front Notion Store. Watson's Drug Store and the grocery store would have finished out the block. The Idle Hour preceded the Lyric, Bond, and Globe Theatres. (Courtesy Nelda Anthony.)

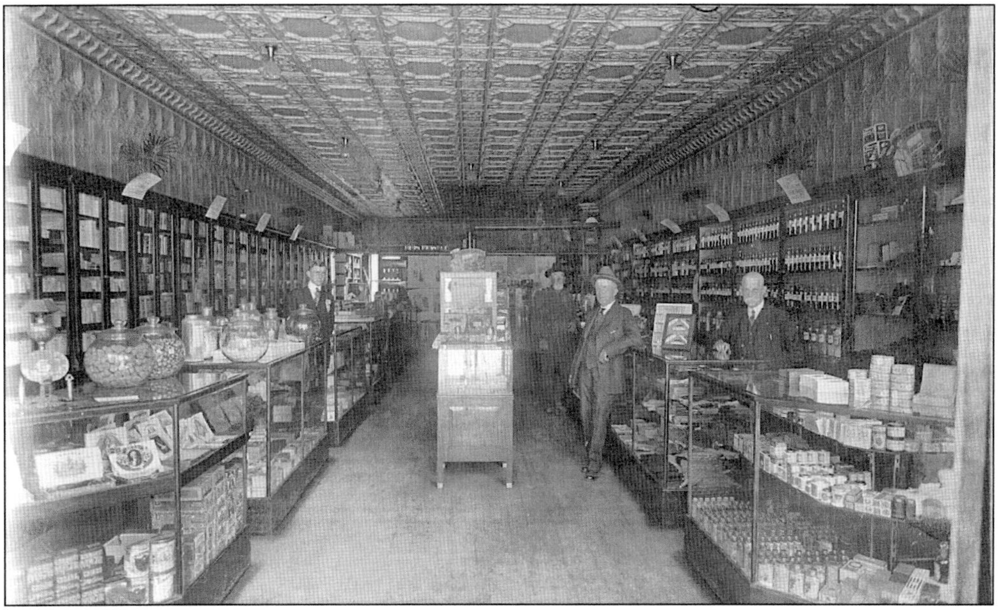

Watson's Drug Store was first opened in 1881 by Charles W. Watson on the south side of the courthouse square. His nephew Frank E. bought the business in 1902 from which period the above photo is taken. Note the magnificent pressed metal ceiling above the narrow, well-stocked aisles. Frank's son, Charles I, continued as owner in 1940, and current pharmacist and State Senator Frank C. took over from his father in 1972, expanding the store to include all three Miller Block buildings. (Courtesy Frank Watson.)

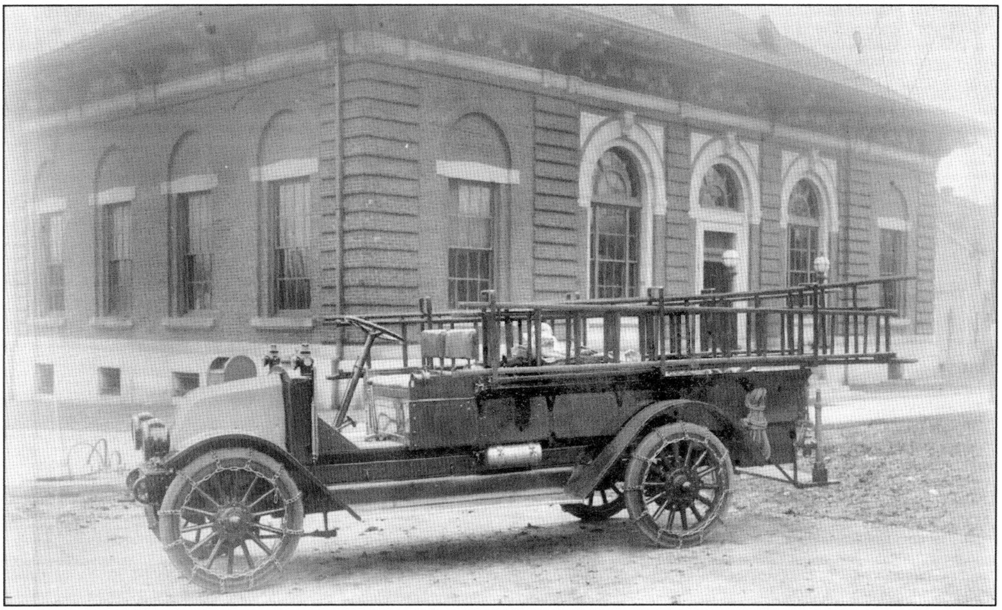

With the newly constructed post office in the background, this *c.* 1912 photo shows the Greenville Fire Department's first gas engine truck. Ironically, the truck was destroyed by fire at the firehouse, which was located on North Third Street in the old city hall (now Rainbow House). Fireman "Dutch" Bauer tried to rescue the truck, but burned his hands on the steel wheel and was not able to drive it out of the building. (Courtesy the Greenville Fire Protection District.)

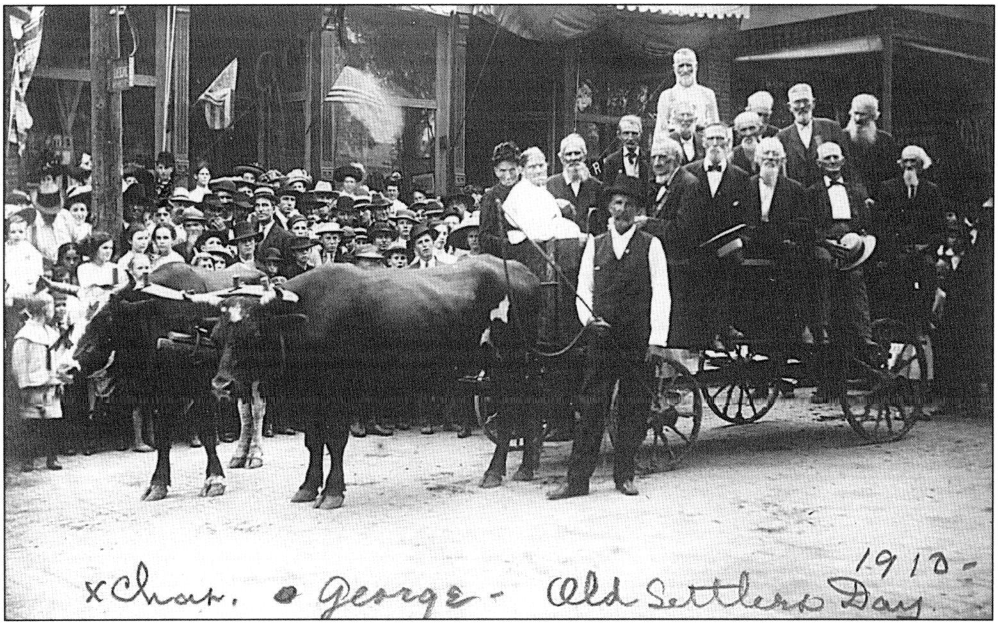

On Old Settler's Day in 1910, some of the earliest inhabitants of Greenville rode in an ox-pulled wagon down Third Street on the west side of the courthouse square. Behind them, the DeMoulin Building, which burned down in 1913, was located where the Baumberger-Whitlock Insurance Agency is now. (Courtesy Frank Watson.)

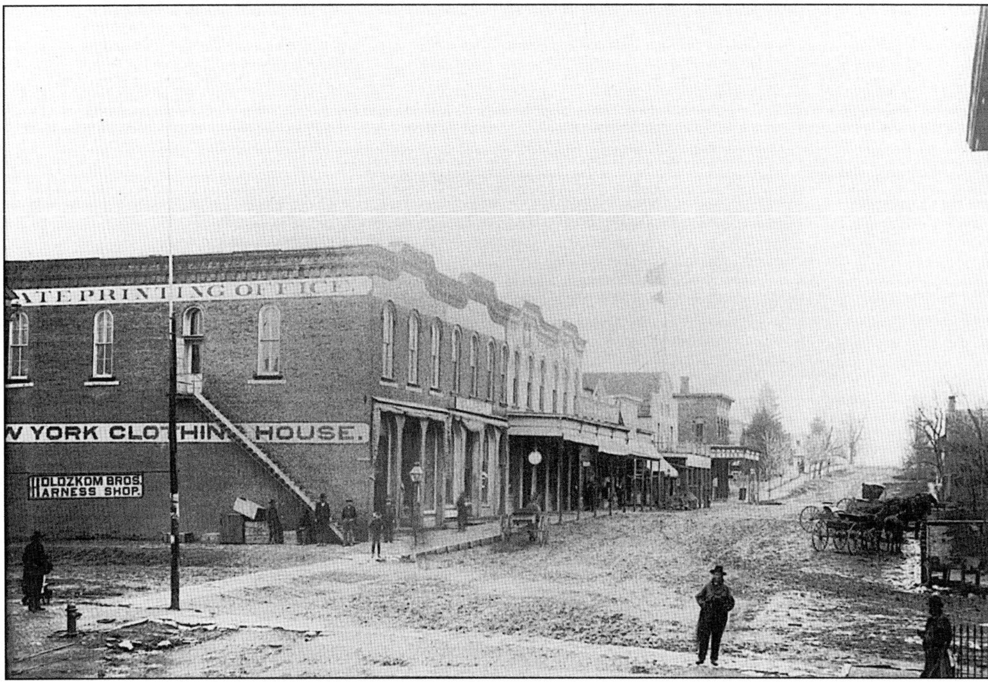

The Morse Building was built in 1869 and covered the south half of the west side of the square. When Ed DeMoulin took this photo in 1892, businesses in this building were the *Greenville Advocate*, above the Heuter Brothers Grocery Store, a millinery shop, and Weise & Bradford's clothing store. The Morse building burned down on October 27, 1904. (Courtesy Kevin Kaegy.)

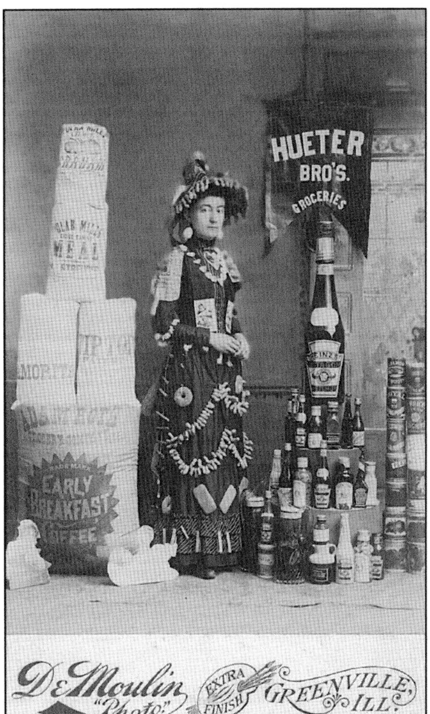

Decked out with peanuts, donuts, and assorted comestibles, this unidentified lady posed amid brand-name products to create an imaginative advertising card for Heuter Brothers Grocery Store, which was located in the Morse Building. Ed DeMoulin took this photo in the 1890s. Although most products have changed since then, the Heinz label is still easily recognized. (Courtesy Bond County Historical Society.)

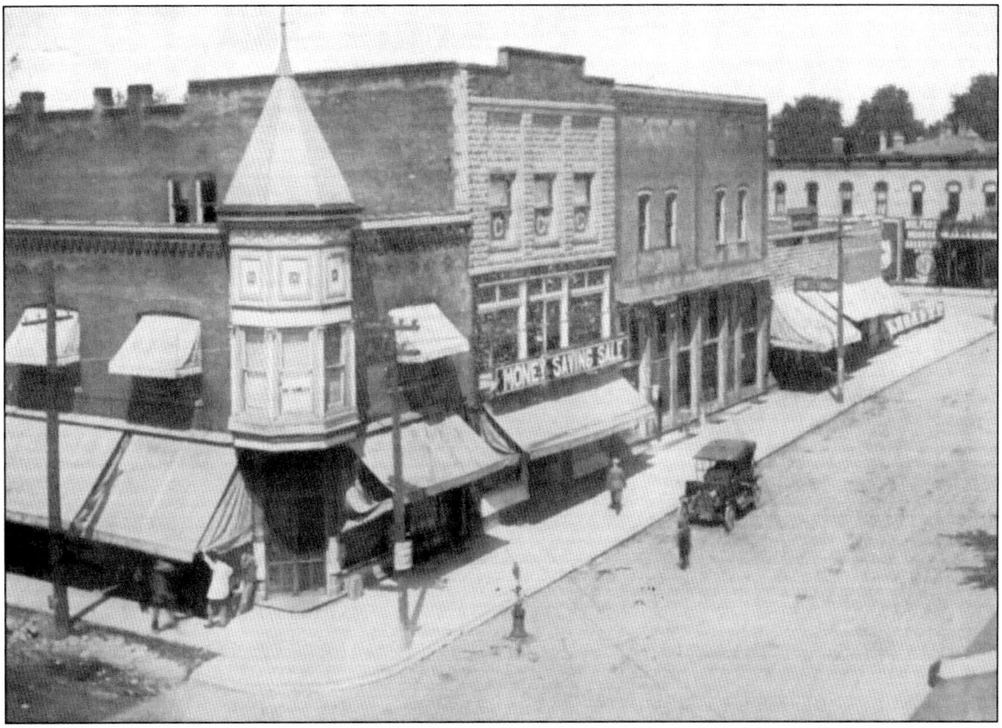

After the great fire of 1904, the present three buildings were built on the south half of the west side of the square. The Turret Building at the end of the block was occupied by four small shops. The middle building was a hardware store for many years and is currently owned by WGEL Radio. The third building was an implement dealership until it was converted into the Bond Theatre in the 1930s. (Courtesy the *Greenville Advocate*.)

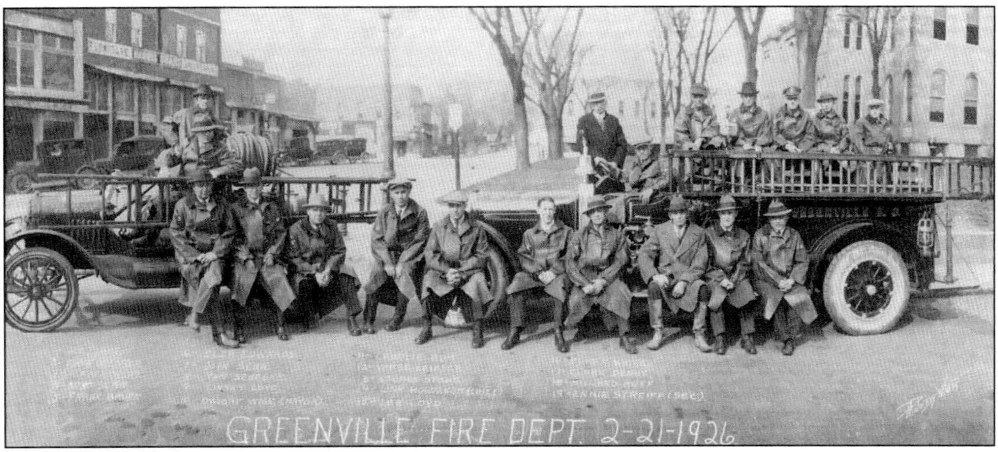

The Greenville Fire Department poses on the square in 1926. The Model T truck on the left had a small compartment for adding chemicals to water that created fire suppression foam. The Dodge hose truck on the right had a 100-gallon water tank. When a fire call was received, the hose truck was driven from behind the station and around front so the firemen could jump on board. (Courtesy Greenville Fire Protection District.)

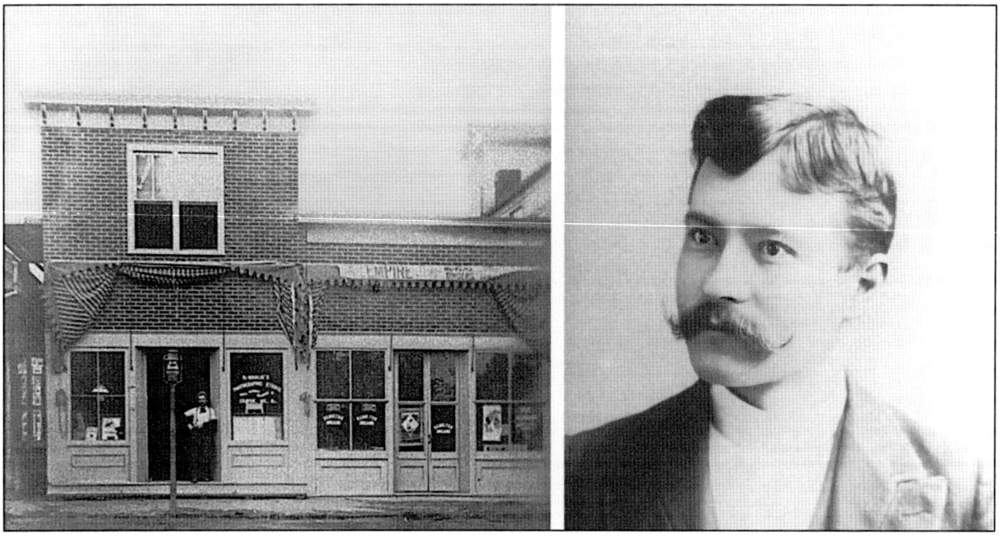

Ed DeMoulin established a photo studio in Greenville in 1886. He and his wife, Constance, operated this successful business on the west side of the square where Baumberger-Whitlock now stands. He published a pictorial album of Greenville in 1892 and several of those photos are used in this book. He was successful at many things and founded the DeMoulin Bros. Factory and also served as mayor of Greenville for seven years. (Courtesy Kevin Kaegy.)

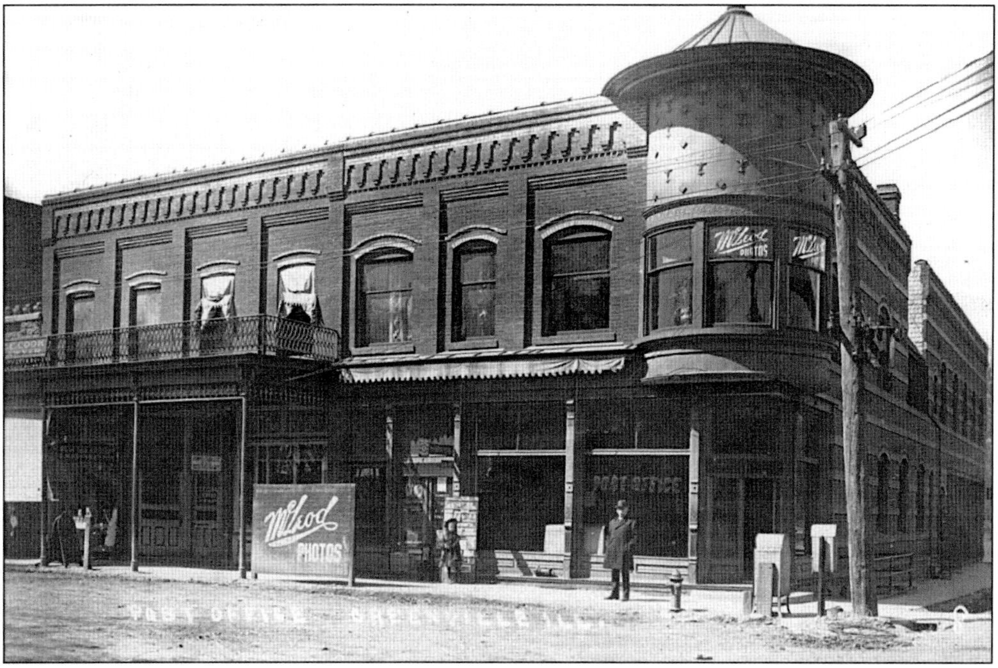

The DeMoulin Building was built in 1900 on the north half of the west side of the square. It housed the post office, a confectionary, a restaurant, the Cook Law Office, and West Side Grocery. The McLeod Photo Studio was above the post office. The west side of the square had turret buildings on both ends for only eight years. This building with the north turret burned in 1913. The south turret, built in 1905, still marks the corner of Third and Main Streets. (Courtesy Jeff Leidel.)

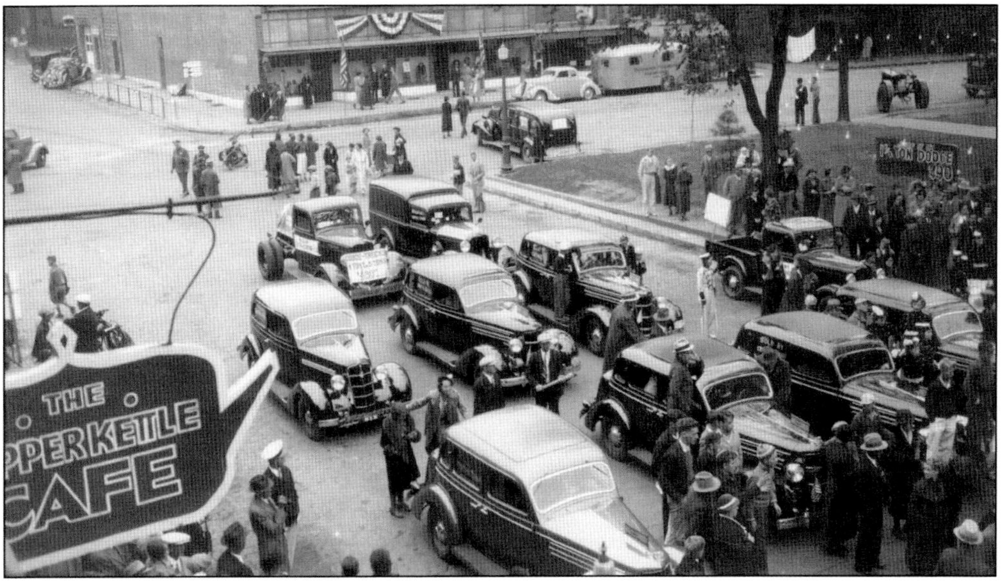

First introduced to Greenville in 1901, the "horseless carriage" by the 1930s had become a necessity rather than a luxury. Even in the Depression's hard times, this Dodge dealership display on the west side of the courthouse square attracted much attention during the *c.* 1938 Farmer's Institute. The cars were parked in front of the Copper Kettle Cafe, which was operated by George Lamb and his wife. (Courtesy Bill Donnell.)

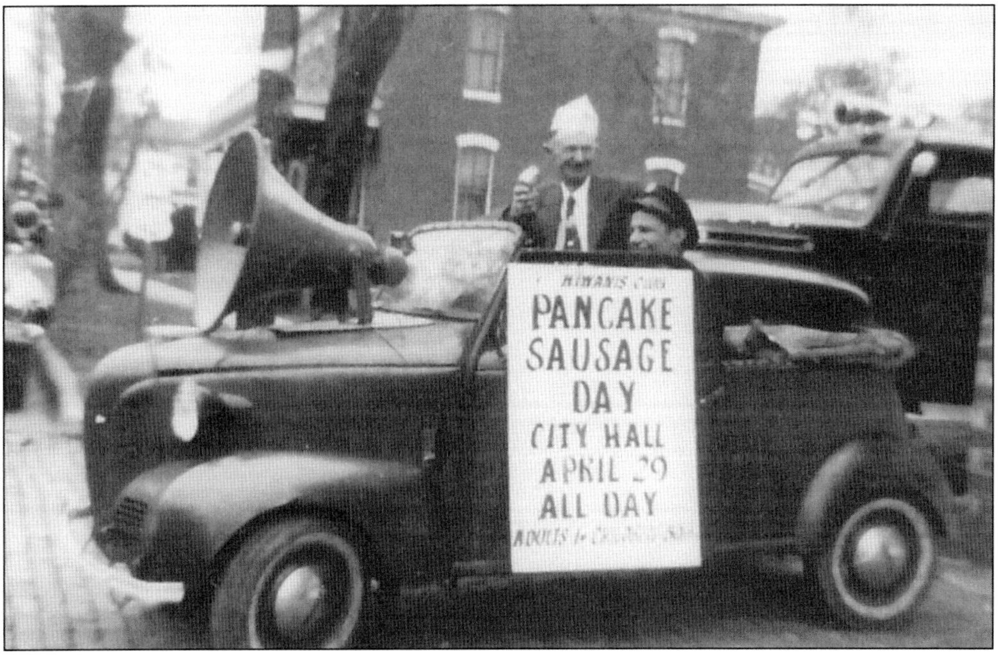

It is spring of 1951 and George Bauer Sr. takes the microphone to announce the Kiwanis Club's Pancake and Sausage Day. Harold Gaffener wired up a megaphone to his old 1937 Crosley for the event. The driver in uniform is Maurice Mauer, home on furlough from the Korean War. They are at the old city hall on North Third Street, with the Leisch home visible behind them. (Courtesy Bob Gaffner.)

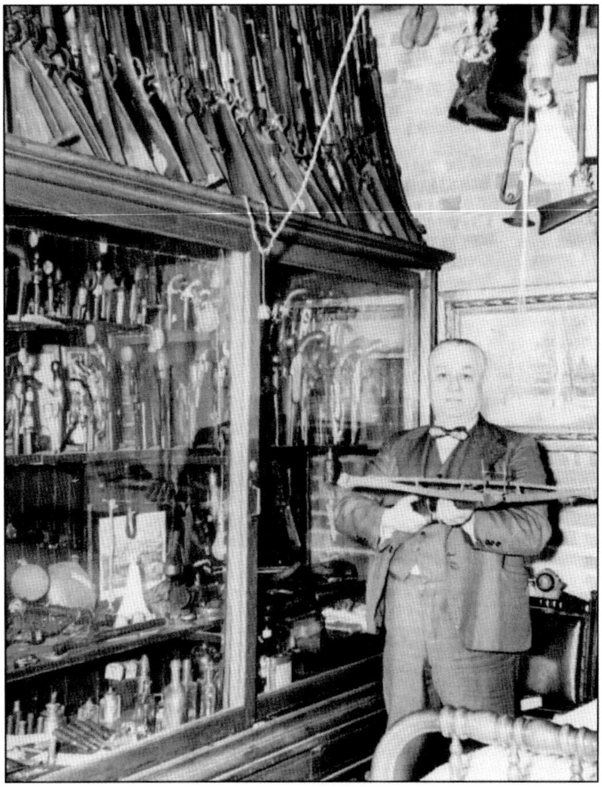

Mayor Paul Zeeb holds a crossbow in his gun room at the old Bennett mansion on N. Third Street. After serving overseas during World War I, he opened the Greenville Machine Shop, which he operated until 1947. Devoting the rest of his life to civil service, he served as Greenville mayor from 1953 to 1957, was head of the Red Cross, and was a very active member of the Methodist Church. He married Della Smith and their home became a veritable museum of antique firearms, Indian relics, coin glass, and Greenville memorabilia. (Courtesy Bill Donnell.)

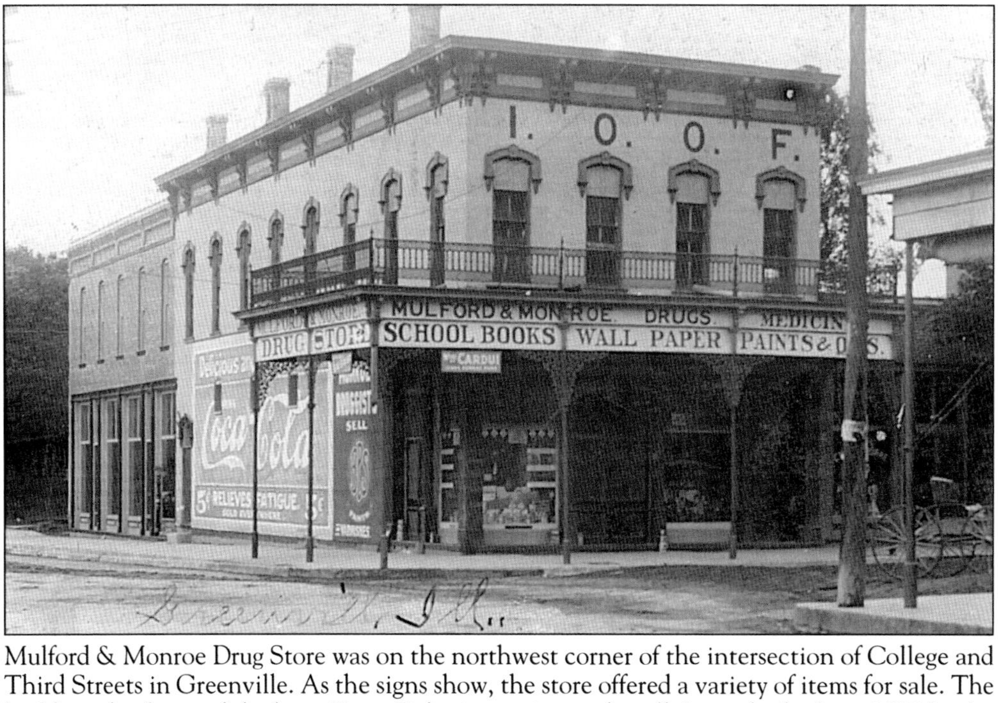

Mulford & Monroe Drug Store was on the northwest corner of the intersection of College and Third Streets in Greenville. As the signs show, the store offered a variety of items for sale. The building also featured the large Coca-Cola sign on its south wall. It was built about 1870 by the Bennett family. (Courtesy Jeff Leidel.)

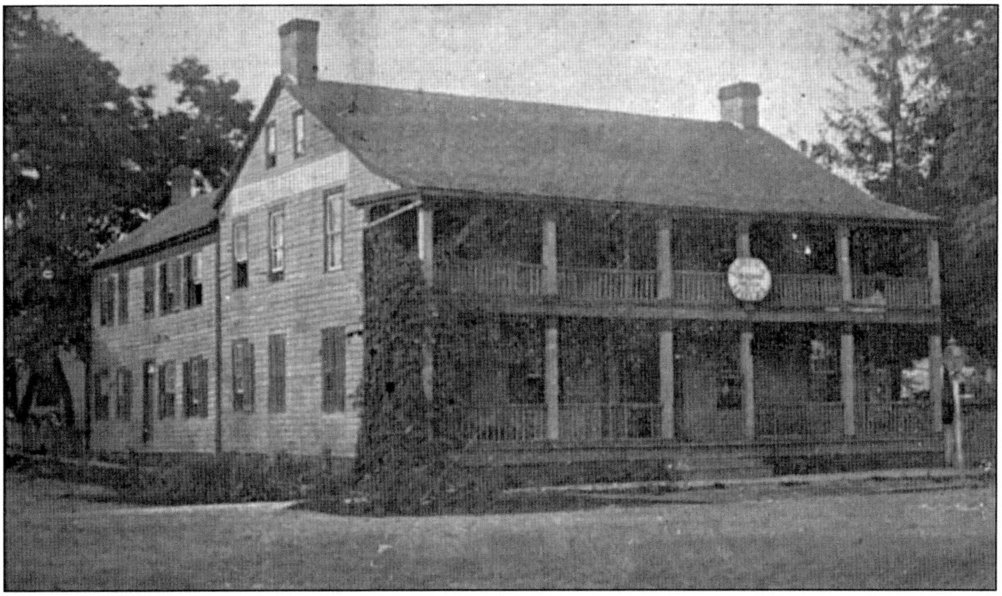

The Franklin House, later called the Hotel Eureka, stood on the northwest corner of the square. Built in the 1840s, it was owned for many years by Thomas and Lottie Smith. Their most famous guest was Abraham Lincoln, who spoke in Greenville on September 13, 1858. George Von Weise tore it down to build his new store in 1893. (Courtesy Jeff Leidel.)

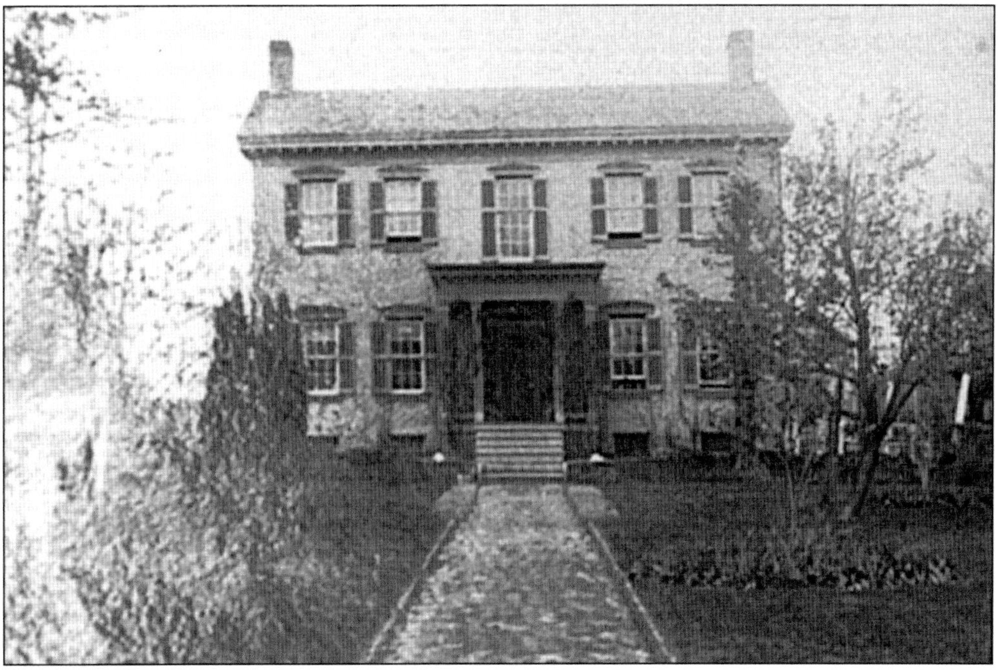

This home, located on the corner of Oak and North Third Streets, was built in 1850 by William S. Smith, a prominent banker and merchant in town. Abraham Lincoln visited with the Smiths prior to his speech in town, and it was William who introduced him to the audience. Later, the Cox and Snowden families lived here many years. Illinois Bell Telephone tore the house down in 1959 and built an office on the site. (Courtesy Kevin Kaegy.)

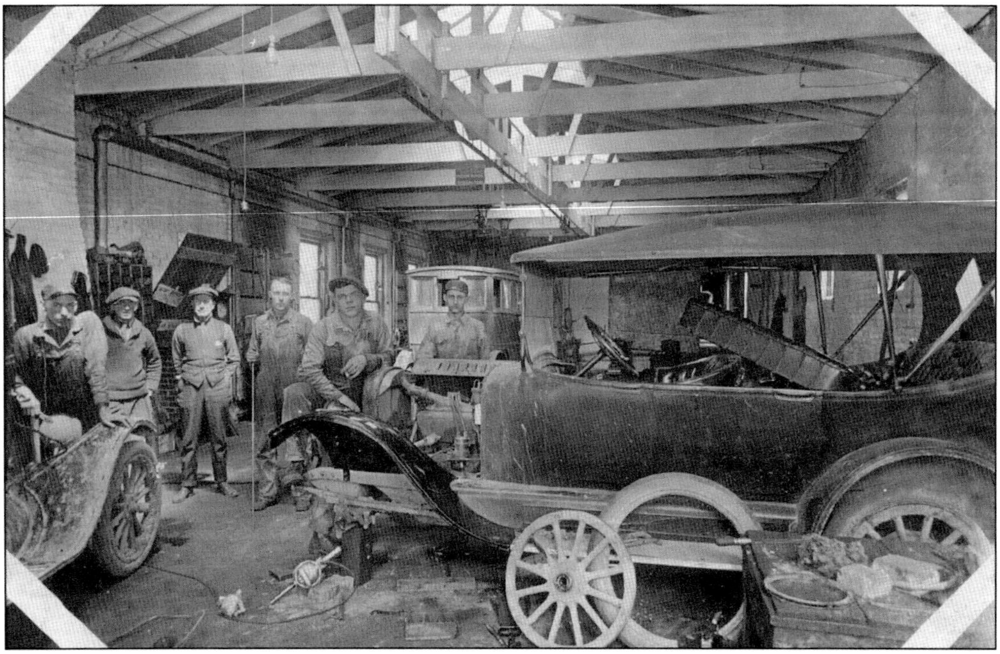

The mechanics take a break from assembling Model T autos at the Central Garage in 1920. Pictured here from left to right are Don Wannemaker, Tanner Reed, Ed Ragland, Ellis File, Frank Bauer, and Harold Gaffner. In 1932, Harold Gaffner started his own garage, which he ran until 1990. When he finally retired at age 90, he said, "There's nothing like working on a Model T. I like working on those best." (Courtesy Robert Gaffner.)

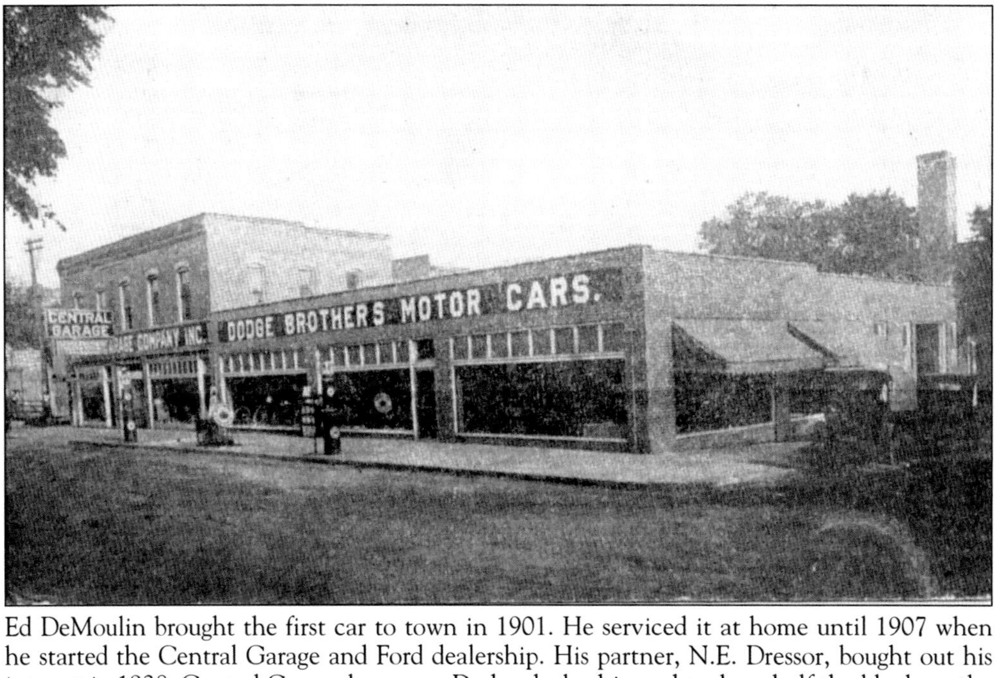

Ed DeMoulin brought the first car to town in 1901. He serviced it at home until 1907 when he started the Central Garage and Ford dealership. His partner, N.E. Dressor, bought out his interest in 1928. Central Garage became a Dodge dealership and took up half the block on the southeast corner of College Avenue and Fourth Street. (Courtesy Jeff Leidel.)

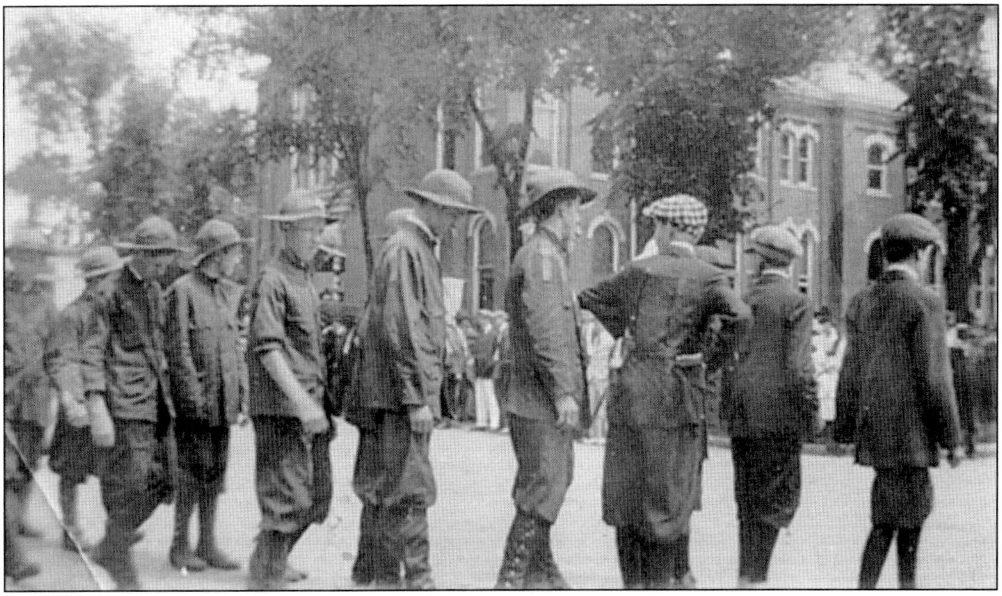

In 1915, the Greenville Boy Scout Troop No. 1 marches in what appears to be a parade at the courthouse square. The Boy Scouts of America was founded in 1910, so in just five years, Greenville had its own troop. Note their uniforms reflect the military dress of the time period, with puttees and the "Smokey the Bear" hats. Will Hoffman was leader of Troop #1. (Courtesy Velma Enloe.)

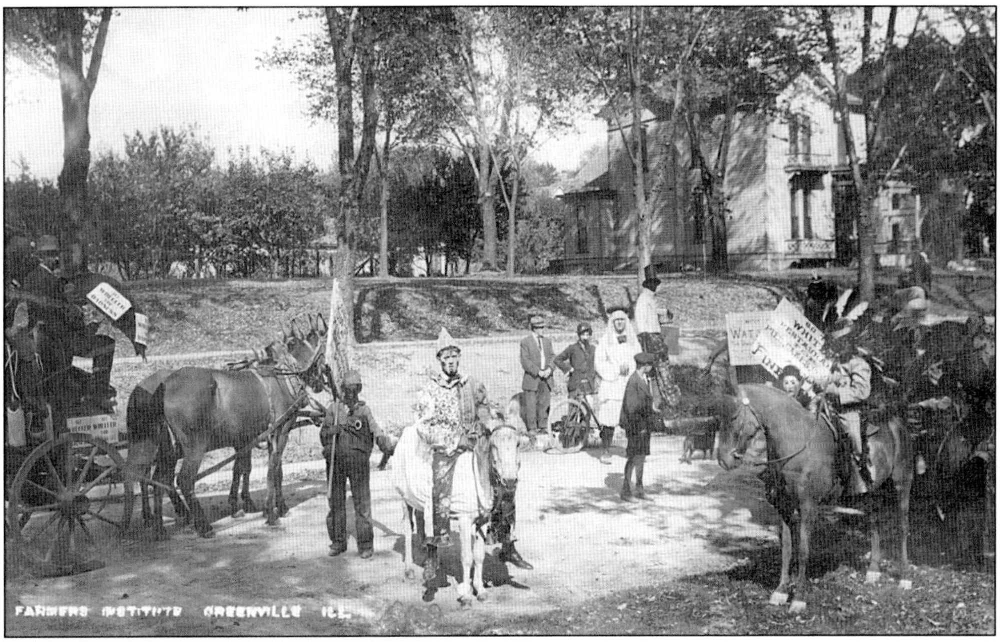

This 1908 photo shows the Farmer's Institute in Greenville before the parade, which featured riders dressed in various costumes, a horse-drawn wagon, and several advertising signs borne by participants. The Farmers Institute was founded by John Hartley in 1901. It was held around the courthouse square, showcasing county farm products, until the Bond County Fair was begun in 1948. (Courtesy Nelda Anthony.)

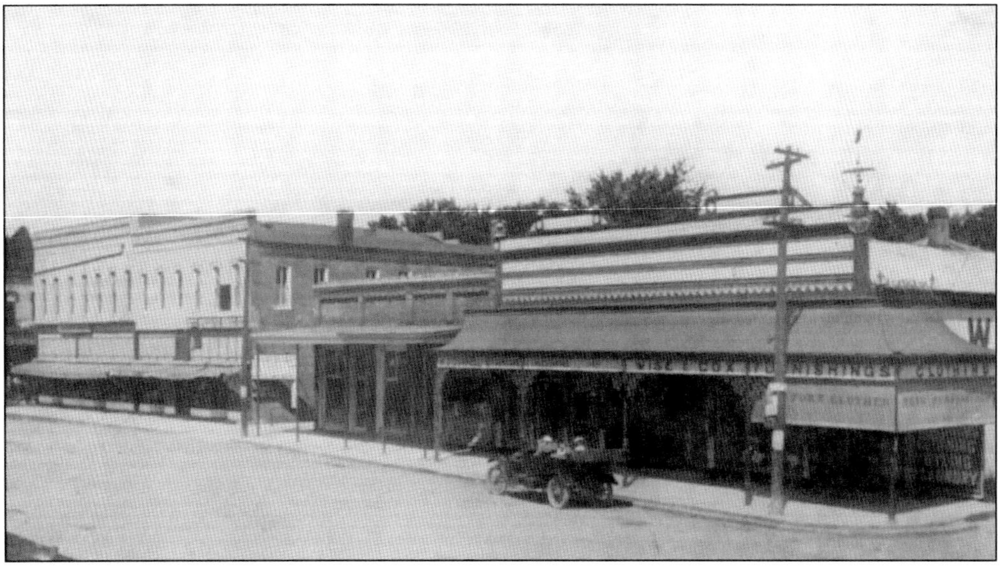

This is the north side of the square as it appeared in 1915. The Von Weise building at far left was built in 1893 and James Moss built next to it soon after. What later became Posch's store was built for Wheeler's Harness Shop. Next was W.D. Donnell Furniture and Undertaker, and at right, the clothing store owned by E.B. Wise. Wise & Cox later became Genre's men's clothing store. (Courtesy Bill Donnell.)

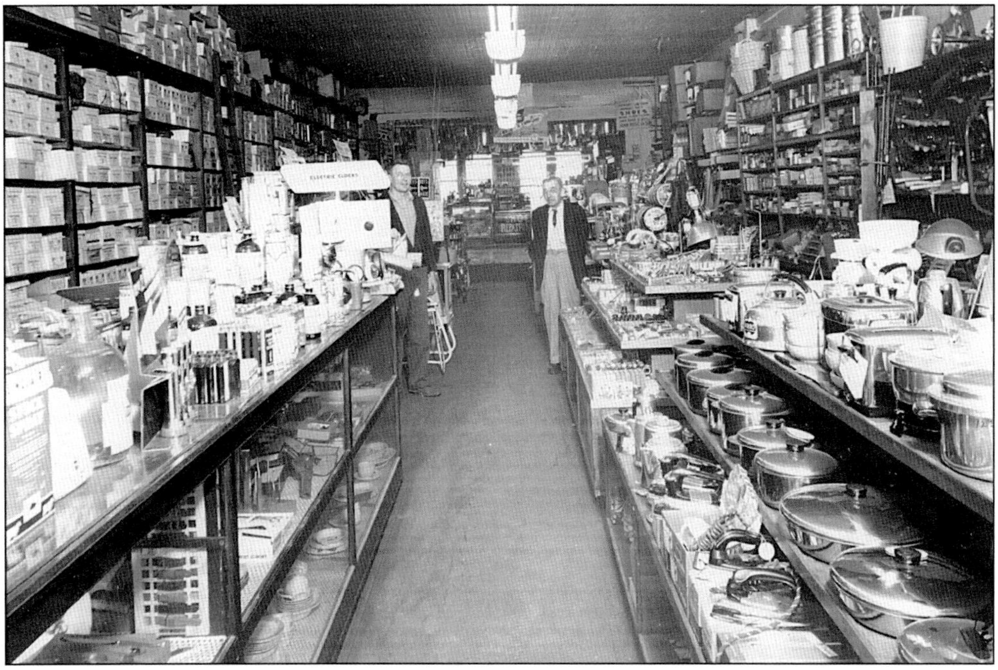

John Posch was born in Austria and came to America in 1907. He moved to Greenville in 1910 and worked as a cobbler, eventually buying out the business. John later bought the Fox Hardware Store on the north side of the square, which he operated with his son Carl, shown in this c. 1950 photo. Carl and his brother Louis continued a shoe sales and repair business out of the store, which remained virtually unchanged until it was sold in 2002. (Courtesy Marie Posch.)

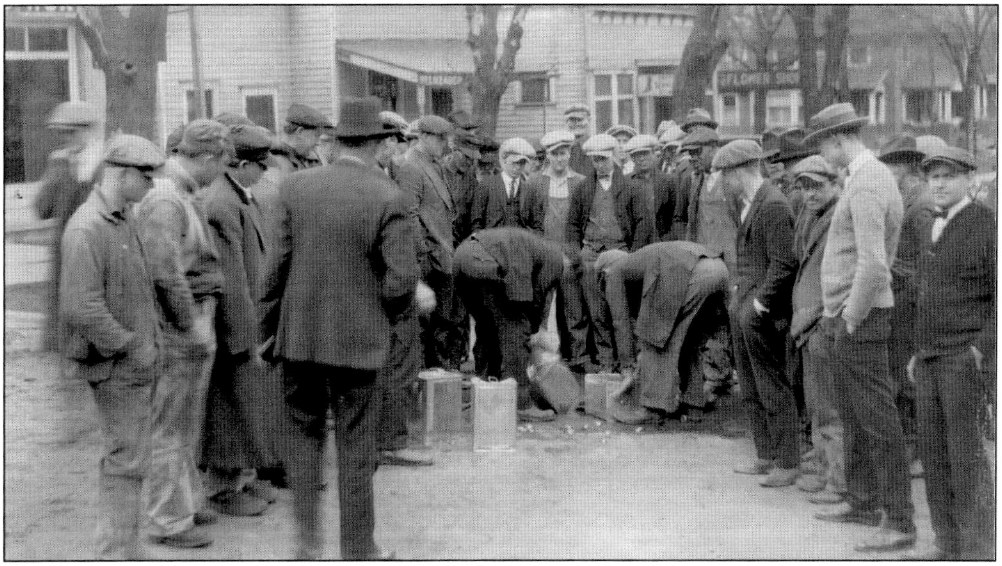

Sorrowful faces look on as county officials pour bootleg liquor down the storm sewer on College Avenue in this classic 1923 photo. These cans were held as State's evidence in the courthouse basement until two local characters snuck in for an all night spree. The pair slept it off in the local jail, and after their release, reliable witnesses found the two with tin cups at the other end of the storm sewer, catching what drops of the whiskey that they could. Producing homebrew was a thriving, albeit illegal, industry during Prohibition. (Courtesy Nelda Anthony.)

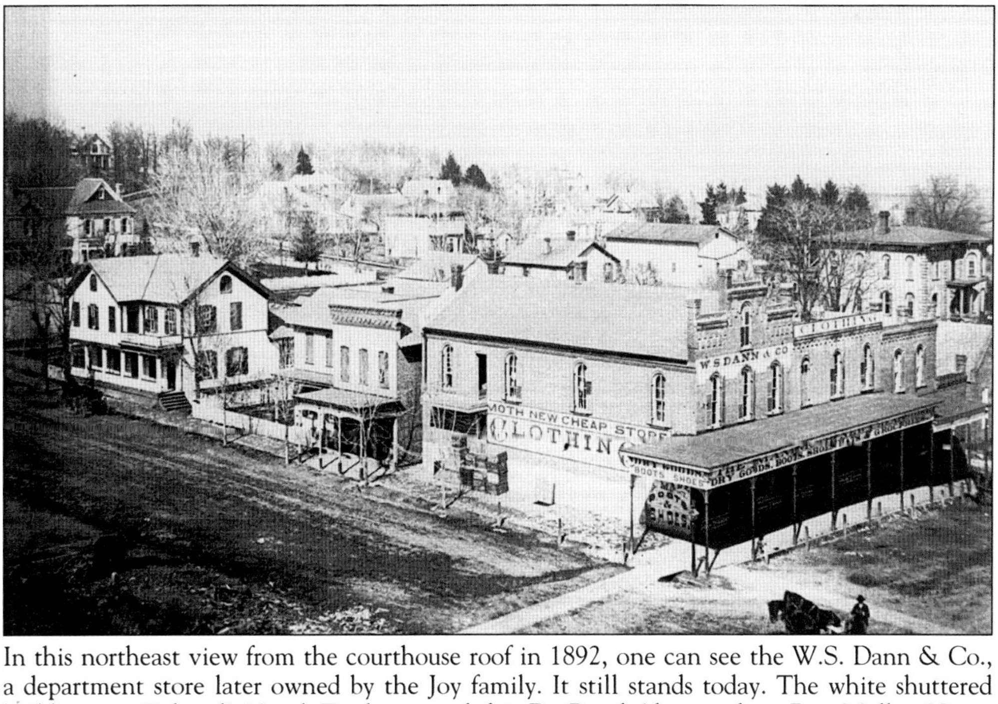

In this northeast view from the courthouse roof in 1892, one can see the W.S. Dann & Co., a department store later owned by the Joy family. It still stands today. The white shuttered building was Colcord's Hotel. To the upper left is Dr. Brooks' home where Bass-Mollett House is now. The Brooks' House was moved east and remodeled into what is now the Doug Hoiles house. This photo was taken by Edmund DeMoulin in 1892. (Courtesy of Kevin Kaegy.)

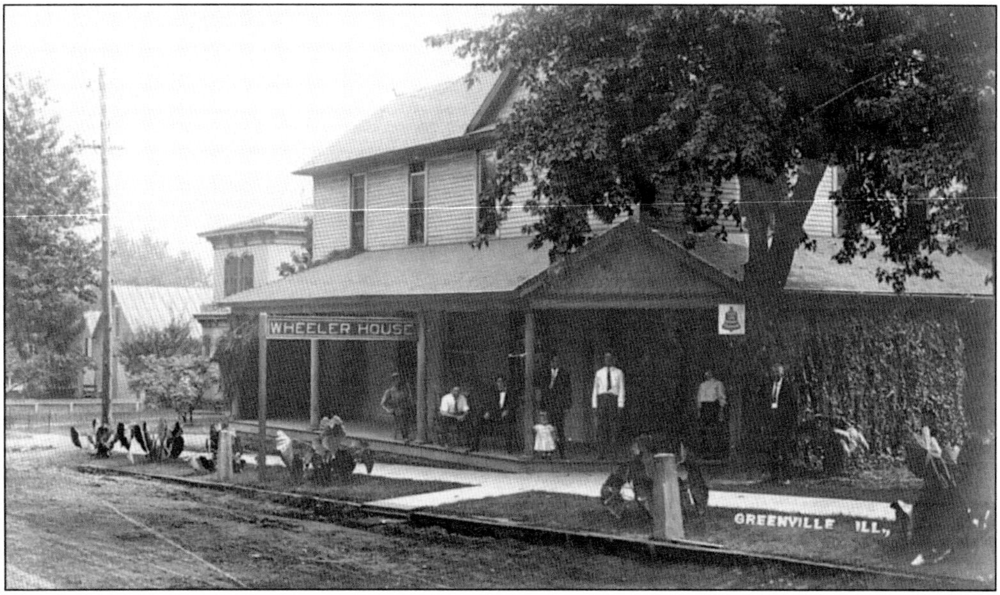

Civil War veteran J.S. Wheeler and his wife were the proprietors of the Wheeler House at the southwest corner of First Street and College Avenue. They bought the hotel around 1890. In 1926, the Wheelers sold the business to Clayton Stubblefield, who changed the name to the Hotel Clayton. Years later, the building became the Bourgeois Nursing Home. The site is now a parking lot for Bradford National Bank. (Courtesy Frank Watson.)

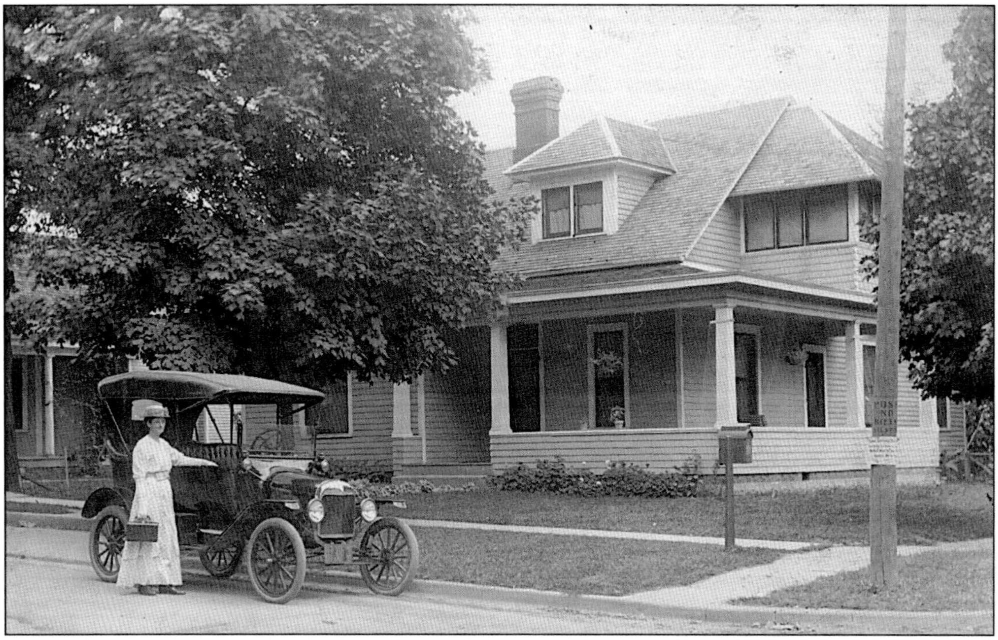

Dr. Katherine B. Luzader, the county's first woman physician, poses with her medical bag and Model T in front of her house on Elm Street at Durley in this *c.* 1915 photo. Her office was on College Avenue, just east of the square, and the small frame building still bears her name. She came to Greenville College in 1898 and graduated from medical school in 1906. Her successful practice in Greenville spanned over 50 years. (Courtesy Bill Donnell.)

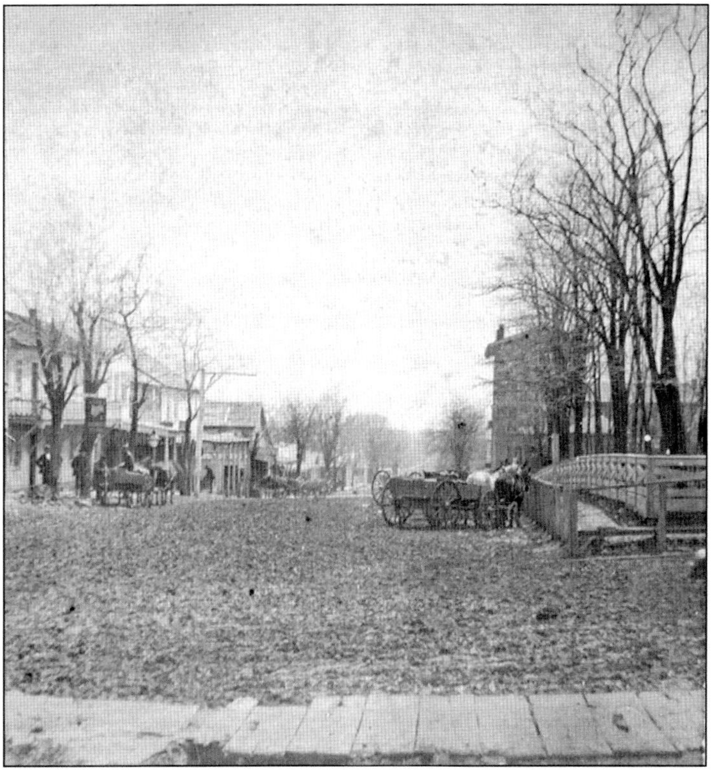

This view is looking south down the east side of the square around 1875. Stephen A. Douglas made a brief evening address from the balcony of the McCord Hotel at the far left. He was campaigning in Greenville in 1858 during the Illinois senate race. About 5,000 people had heard him speak earlier in the afternoon in Colcord's Grove. Note the fence and hitching rail at right that surrounded the courthouse. (Courtesy Bill Donnell.)

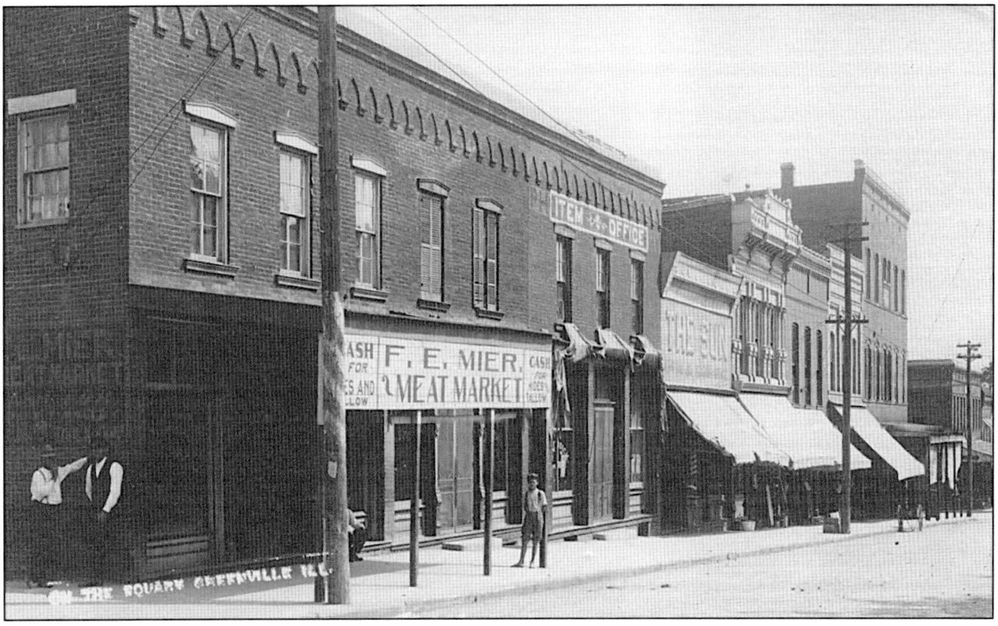

Pictured here, from left to right, are the businesses on the east side of the Greenville Square in 1910: Mier Meat Market in the north building, Bradford Bank with the *Item* newspaper offices upstairs; another newspaper, the *Sun*, was next door. In 1911, the Bradford Bank put a new stone facade with columns over their building. Except for a few alterations, all of the buildings on this side of the square have remained virtually unchanged. (Courtesy Nelda Anthony.)

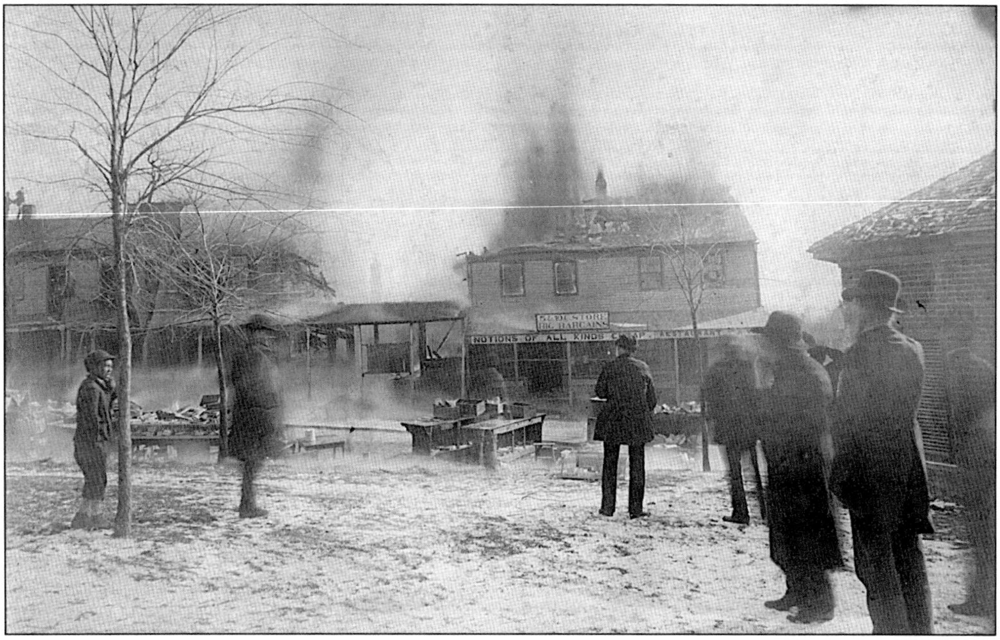

This fire on the southeast corner of the square was photographed by Ed DeMoulin on February 4, 1891. Among the businesses lost were the McCord Hotel, C.H. Shield's photo studio, and Charles Woolridge's grocery store. Four buildings replaced those structures, including the four-story Livingston Building with the Masonic Hall upstairs. (Courtesy Bill Donnell.)

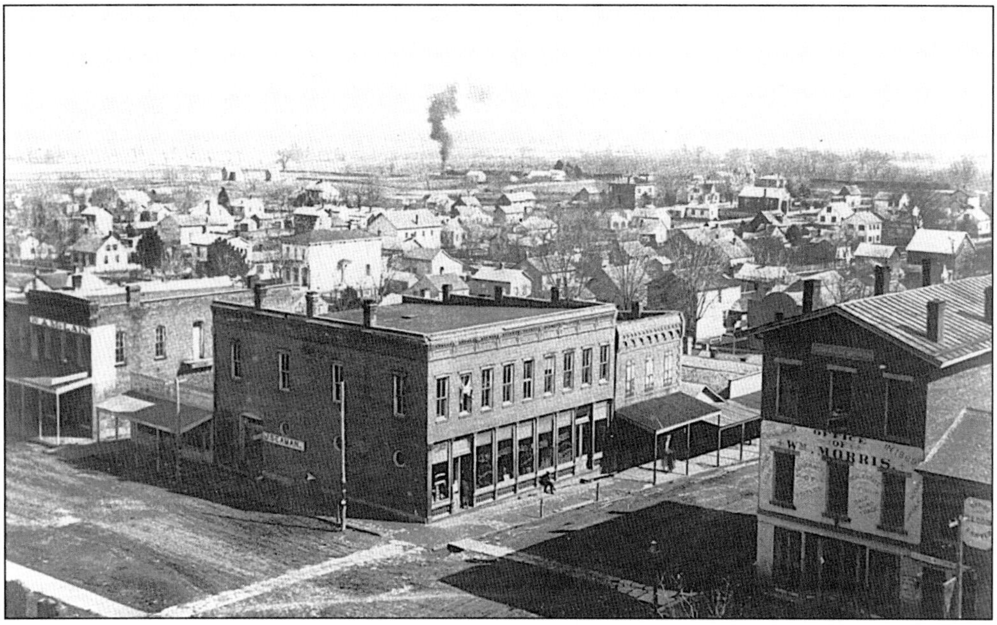

Looking southeast from the roof of the courthouse in 1892, Seaman's Hardware (now Metzger's) is in the foreground. Many of the residences still exist. Louis Wall's House at Winter and Spruce is at the southeast corner of town. Note the train smoke in the background. The three-story building at the right foreground was called the Sprague Block; built in 1859, it housed the Hoiles & Son Bank. (Courtesy of Kevin Kaegy.)

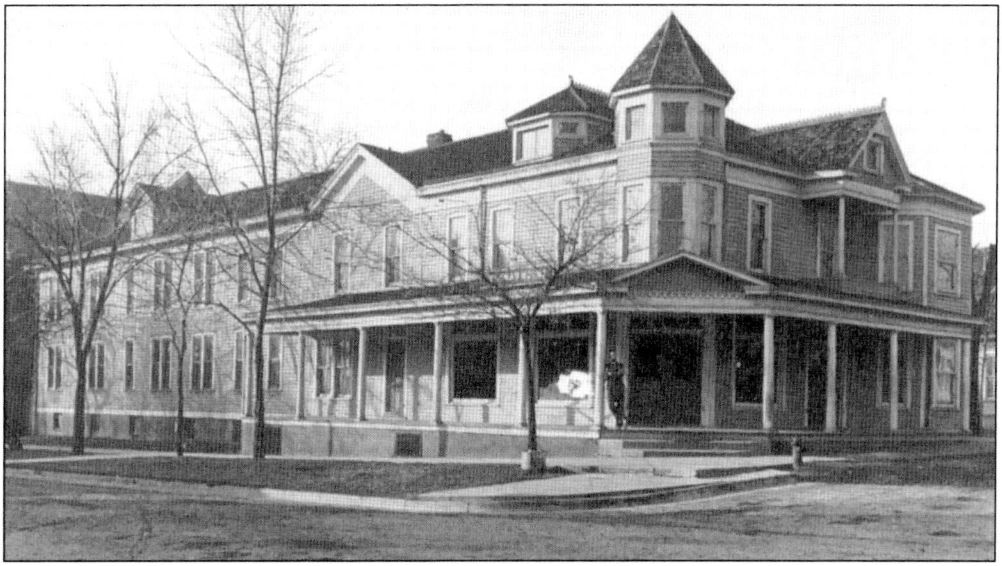

The Thomas House, pictured here *c.* 1910, was a popular hotel for area residents and railway travelers. Mary A. Thomas went into the hotel business in 1874 when she leased the old Sargent House. In 1880, she purchased the Thomas House and operated it until 1893, when her son Samuel took over. It was located on the corner of South Avenue and Second Street. The William Horsfall family were the hotel's last owners. It was demolished in 1984. (Courtesy Jeff Leidel.)

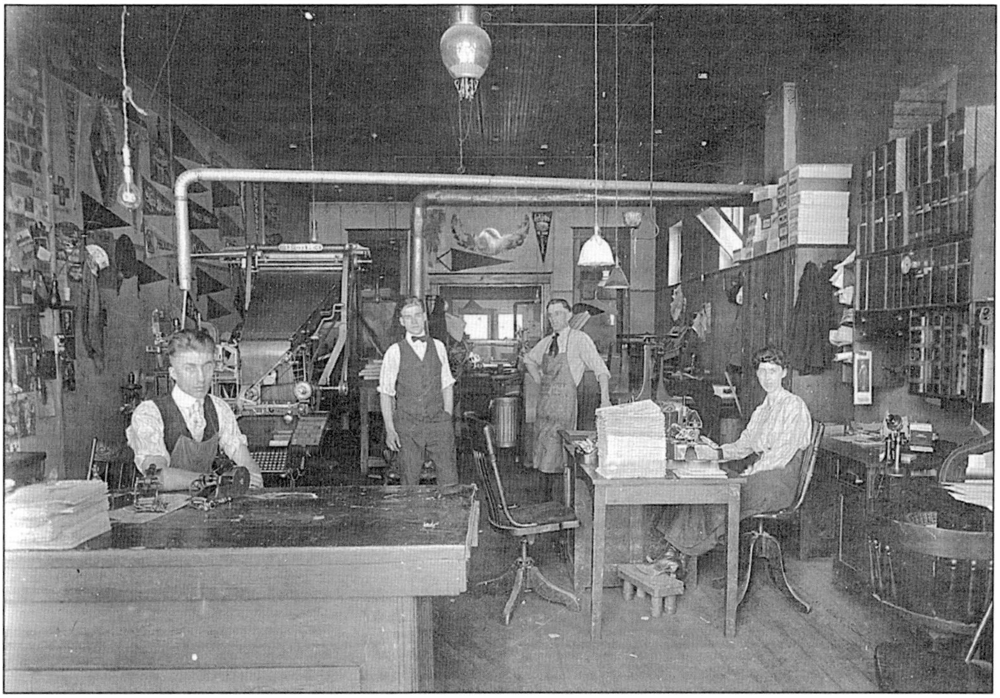

Employees at the *Greenville Advocate* take a break to have their photo taken. The newspaper was started in 1858 to support the candidacy of Abraham Lincoln for senate. The founder, Jediah F. Alexander, was a personal friend of Lincoln's. The *Greenville Advocate* is the oldest continuous business in Bond County, publishing newspapers twice a week. (Courtesy Bill Donnell.)

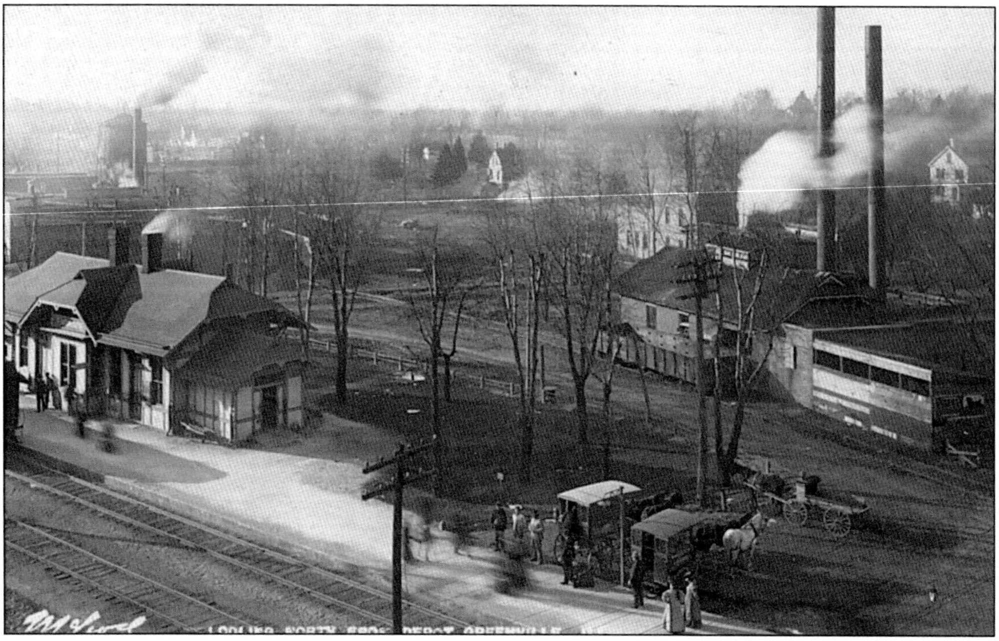

This photo was taken around 1910 looking northwest from the old water tower by the railroad tracks. The Pennsylvania depot is on the left and the Greenville water pumping station is on the right. Two horse drawn carriages wait to take passengers up Second Street to the Thomas House and Wheeler House hotels. (Courtesy Nelda Anthony.)

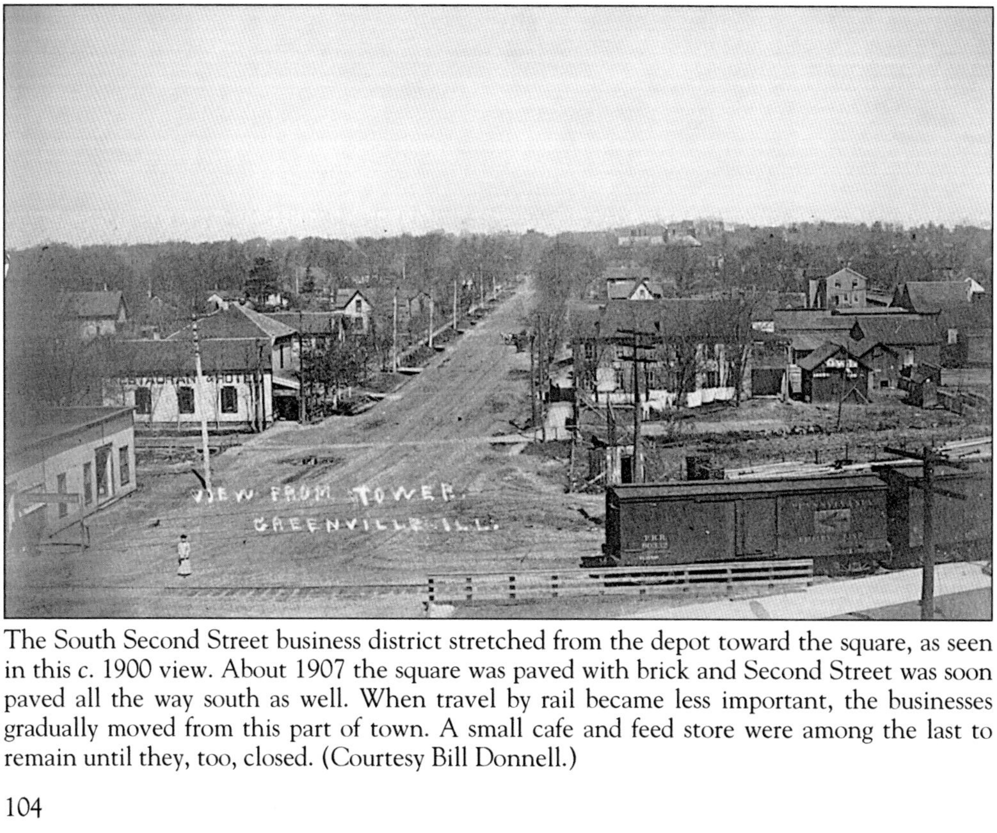

The South Second Street business district stretched from the depot toward the square, as seen in this *c.* 1900 view. About 1907 the square was paved with brick and Second Street was soon paved all the way south as well. When travel by rail became less important, the businesses gradually moved from this part of town. A small cafe and feed store were among the last to remain until they, too, closed. (Courtesy Bill Donnell.)

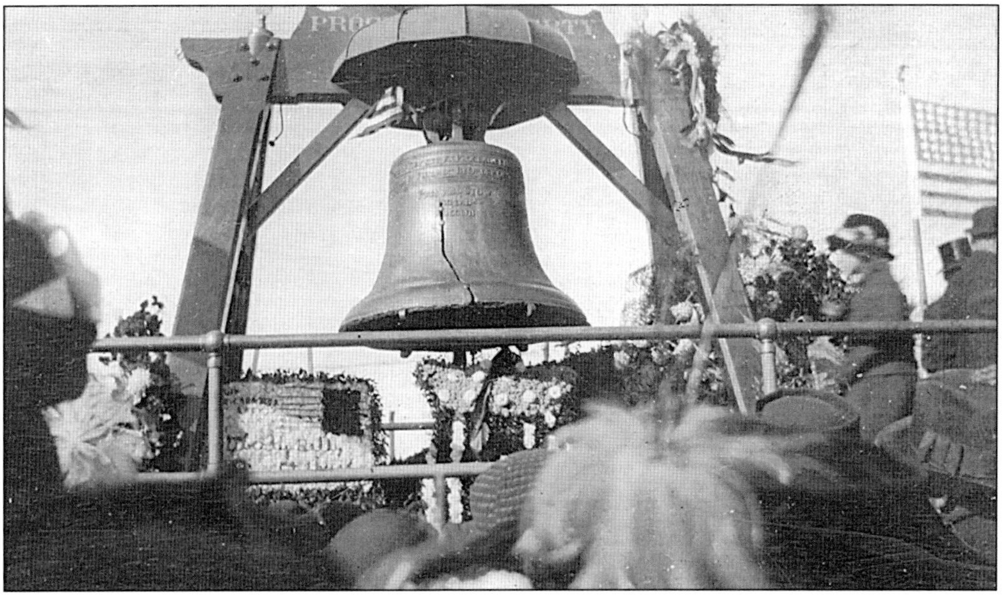

Throngs turned out to see the Liberty Bell when it passed through Greenville in 1915. The famous bell from Philadelphia was making a cross-country tour by rail and stopped at the Pennsylvania station on Sunday, November 21. Churches let out early, the Greenville band played, and the Civil War Veterans and the Boy Scouts marched to the station. The bell remained in Greenville for just five minutes. (Courtesy Frank Watson.)

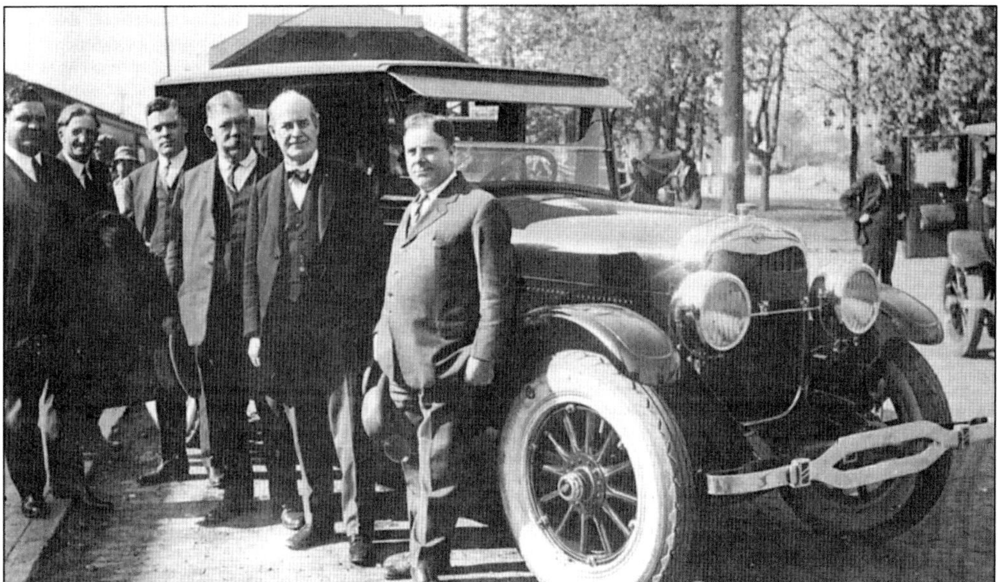

The famed orator, statesman, and presidential candidate, William Jennings Bryan visited Greenville on October 27, 1924, to campaign for his brother Charles, who was the vice presidential nominee. Pictured here at the depot, from left to right, are Judge John Biggs, C.E. Davidson, Robert Wright, Senator Hull of Salem, Mr. Bryan, and Mr. McMackin of Salem. This was Bryan's third visit to Greenville, having previously spoken during his own 1896 and 1900 presidential campaigns. (Courtesy *Greenville Advocate*.)

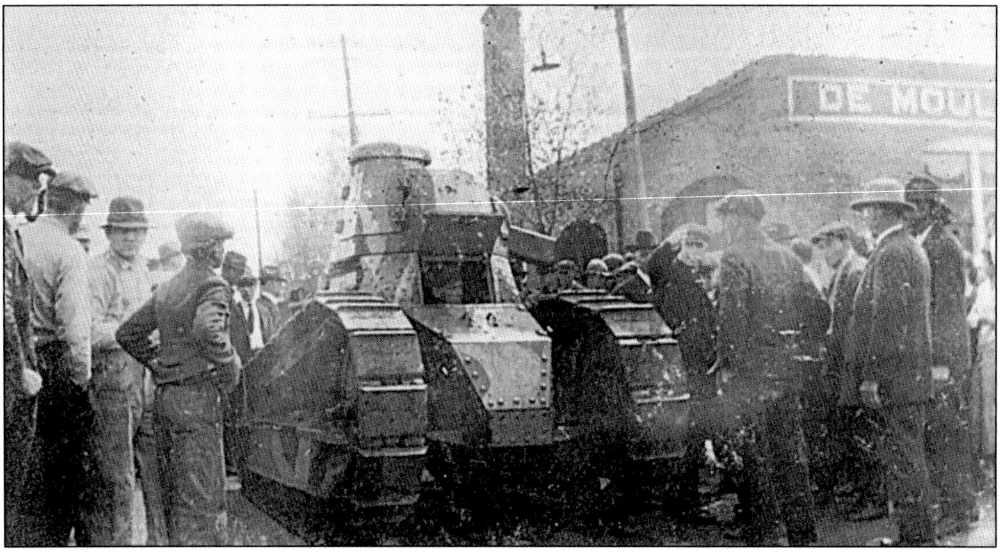

As all Americans did, Bond County residents rallied around the United States troops during World War I. In 1919, a tank visited Greenville and was parked along Fourth Street in front of DeMoulin Bros., drawing a large crowd of onlookers. On July 4, 1919, a huge "Welcome Home" three-day celebration was held in Greenville to honor Bond County's war heroes. (Courtesy Frank Watson.)

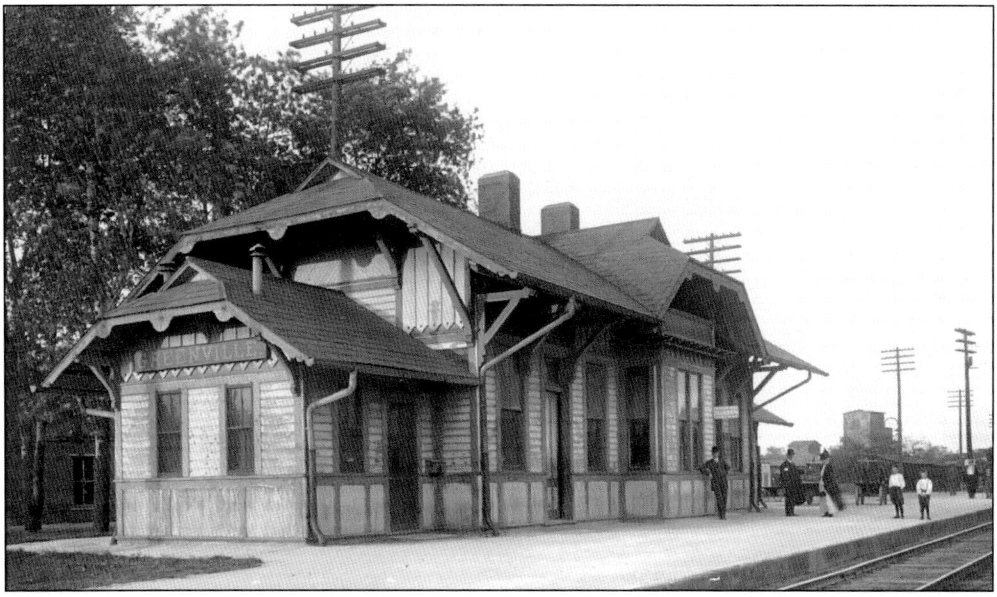

The original train depot in Greenville burned on July 22, 1884. It was replaced by this structure, the Pennsylvania Railroad Station. Both were located north of the railroad tracks between Second and Third Streets. Most of this building burned in 1975, but the small room on the left remains as Shank's Real Estate office. (Courtesy Frank Watson.)

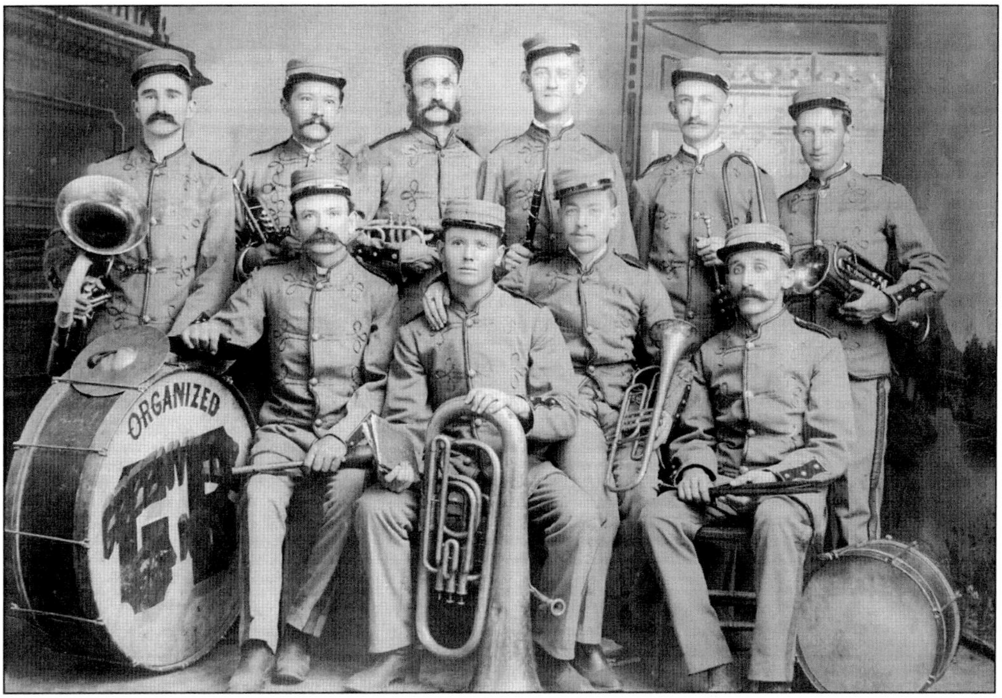

Pictured here is one of the earliest known shots of the Greenville Municipal Band, which was formed in 1896. This picture is likely pre-1900. The members are pictured here from left to right: (front row) Shelby Robinson, Alfred Shaul, Charles Riedemann, and Louis Derleth; (back row) Charlie Hueter, Ed DeMoulin, Ward Reid, Robert Morris, Frank Reid, and Joe Strueber. (Courtesy Nelda Anthony.)

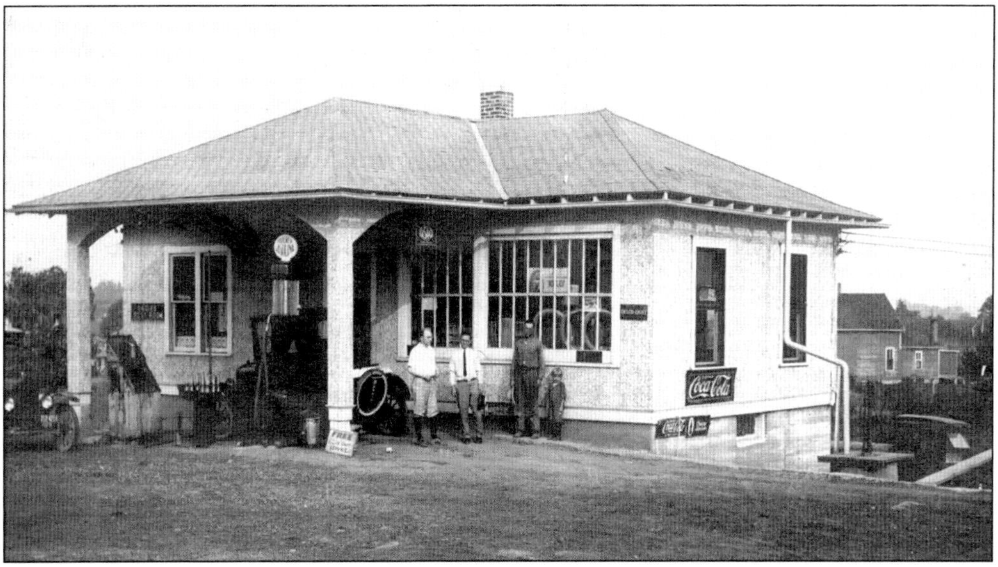

The West End filling station was opened around 1920 by Robert Marti. The garage was located in the basement. Note the vintage Coca-Cola advertising signs. In 1925, Marti traded the gas station for a farm in Mills Township. The station is now part of the Maurice Gorline residence on Franklin Ave. (Courtesy Vesper Marti.)

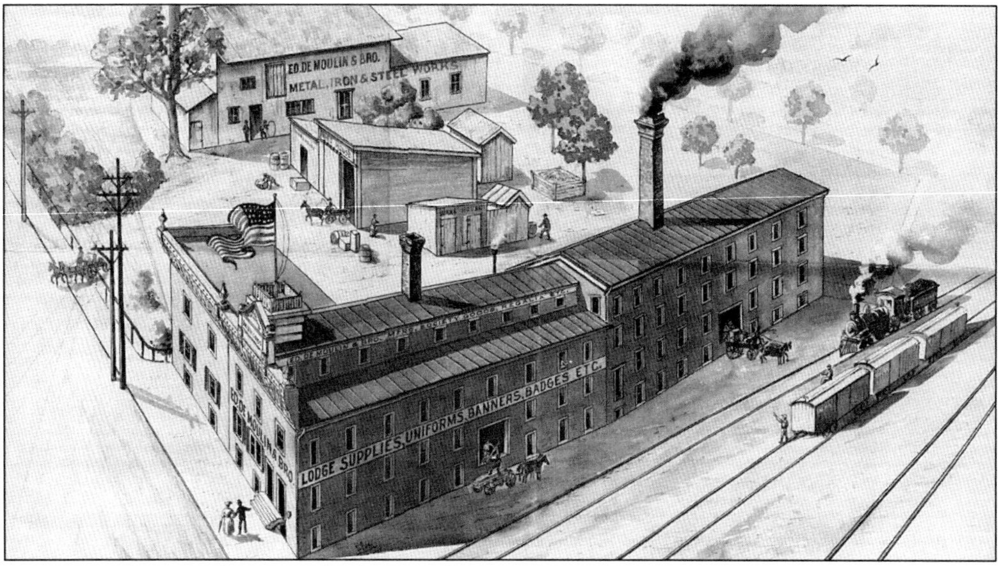

In 1892, Ed DeMoulin was asked to use his inventiveness to create some initiation devices for the Woodmen Of The World Lodge. He began to manufacture all types of lodge regalia, including uniforms, banners, and badges. DeMoulin's business prospered, and in 1896, he and his brother Ulysses built Greenville's first factory. The building (shown above) burned in 1907 and within six months the new (current) building was completed. (Courtesy DeMoulin Bros.)

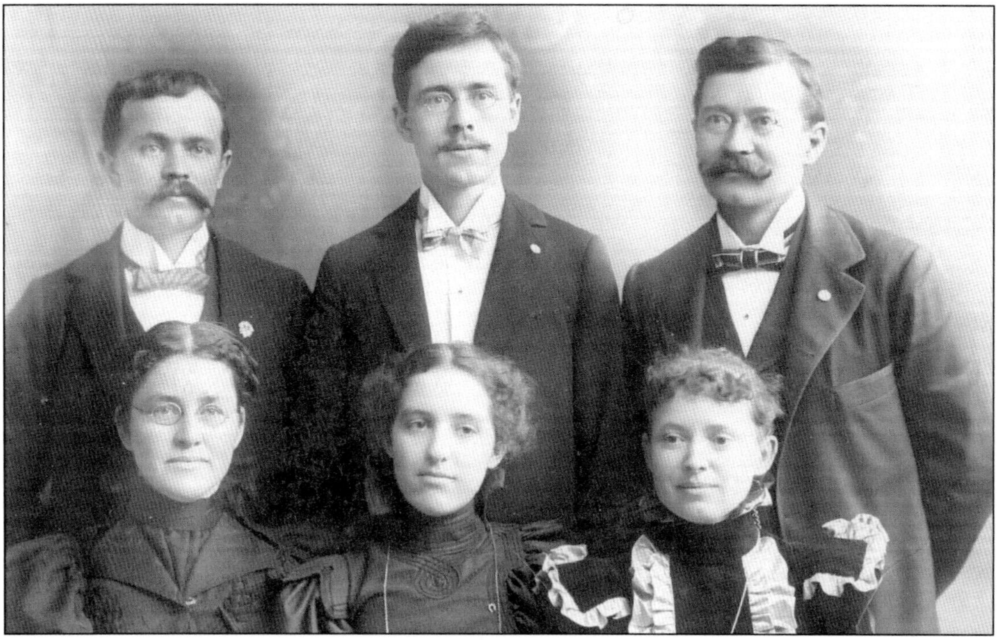

By 1900, three DeMoulin brothers ran the company. They are pictured here, from left to right, with their wives: Erastus (Ras) and Leona; Ulysses (U.S.) and Emma; and Edmund (Ed) and Constance. Ras was plant manager and, as a blacksmith, could build whatever Ed dreamed up. U.S. was the businessman who ran the company until 1955. Ed served as president, but traveled extensively and joined virtually every lodge in the country. He held 37 different patents before his death in 1936. (Courtesy DeMoulin Bros.)

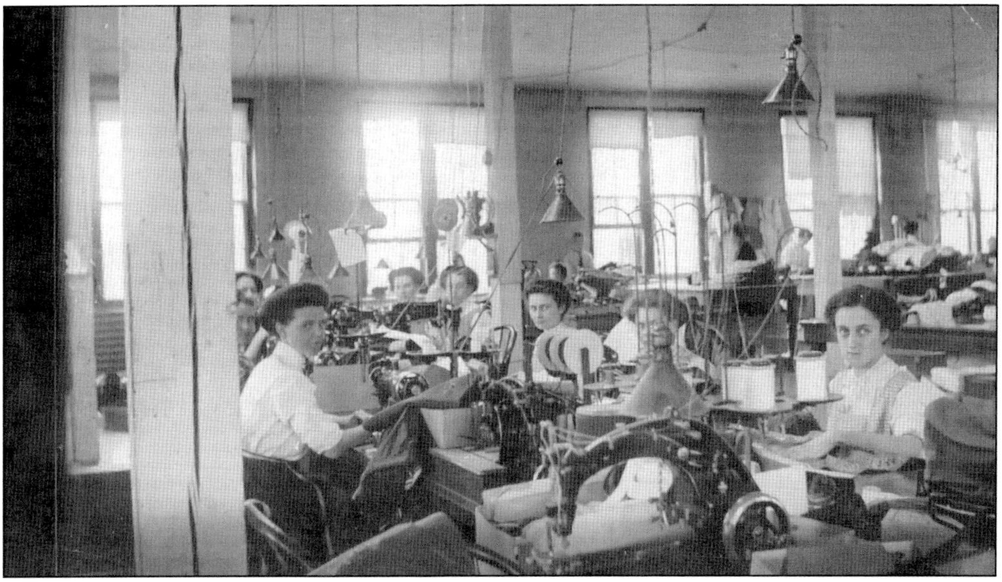

This *c.* 1908 photo shows some of the many ladies employed in the sewing room at DeMoulin Bros. The brothers, all musically inclined, added band uniforms to their costume and lodge regalia line. Later, they added a very successful graduation cap and gown line to their products. After 100 years, DeMoulin Bros. is still one of the leading producers of band uniforms in the country. (Courtesy DeMoulin Bros.)

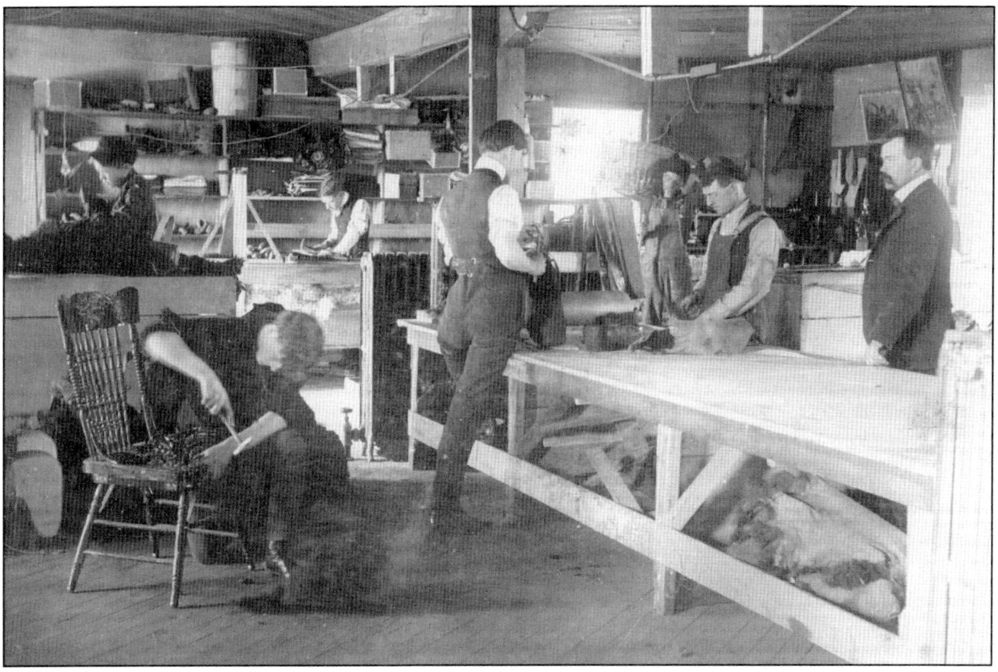

Ras DeMoulin looks on from the right, *c.* 1908, as one man (left) adjusts a collapsible trick lodge chair and others assemble a wind machine on the work bench (center). The furniture department also built the bucking goats for lodge initiations. This area of the plant was destroyed by fire in 1955 and the lodge paraphernalia line was phased out at that time. (Courtesy DeMoulin Bros.)

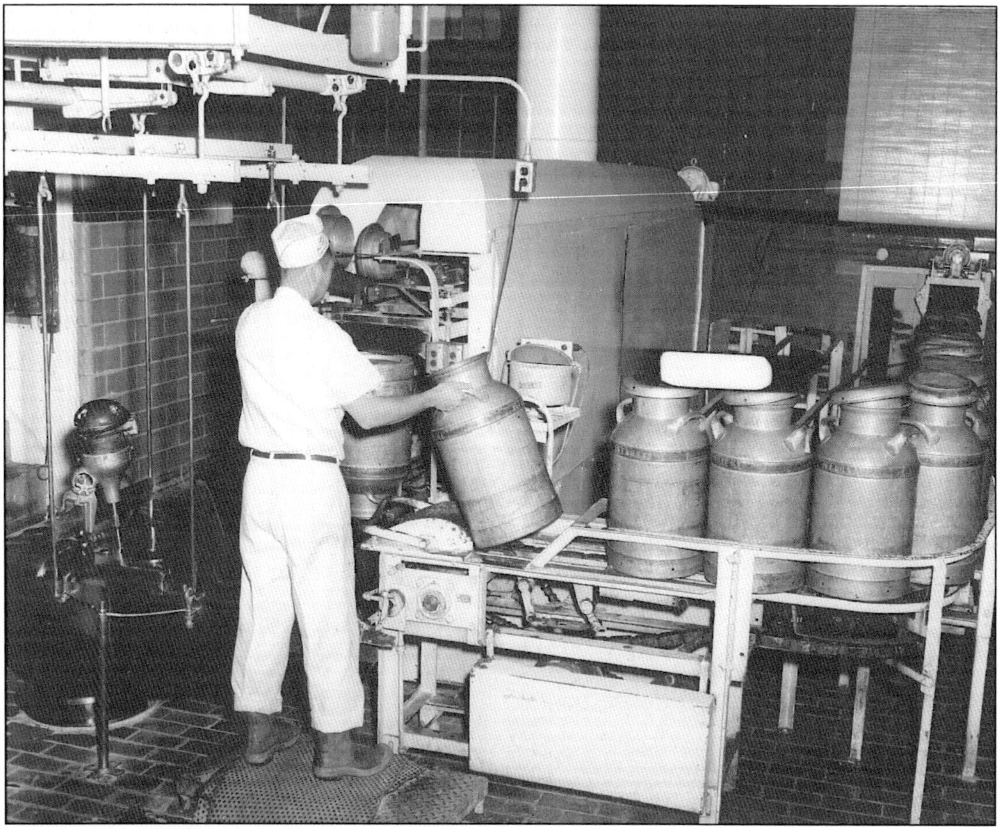

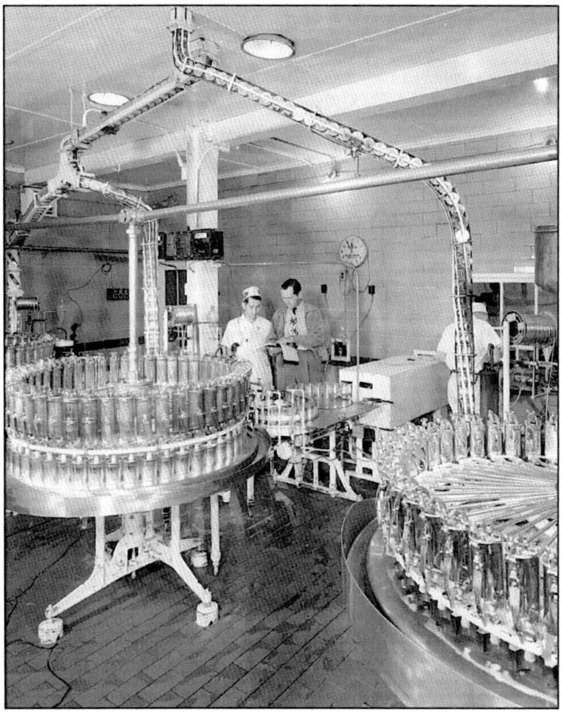

Pet Milk Incorporated was founded in Highland in 1885, as the Helvetia Condensing Company. The Greenville plant was opened in May of 1899. Local milk haulers delivered the milk to the receiving room where cans were dumped and sterilized. The milk was transferred from this room to the forewarmers. This photo, *c.* 1960, shows Richard Compton at work. (Courtesy Lloyd Redenbo.)

For many years, Pet Milk had its own can manufacturing shop. In this photo of the filling room, where cans were fed from an upstairs bin, Leroy Barnhart confers with an unidentified official. The can shop closed in April 1963. At its peak in 1959, the Greenville plant employed 221. The Greenville plant closed for good and the chemistry lab was sold to Mallinckrodt in 1992. (Courtesy Lloyd Redenbo.)

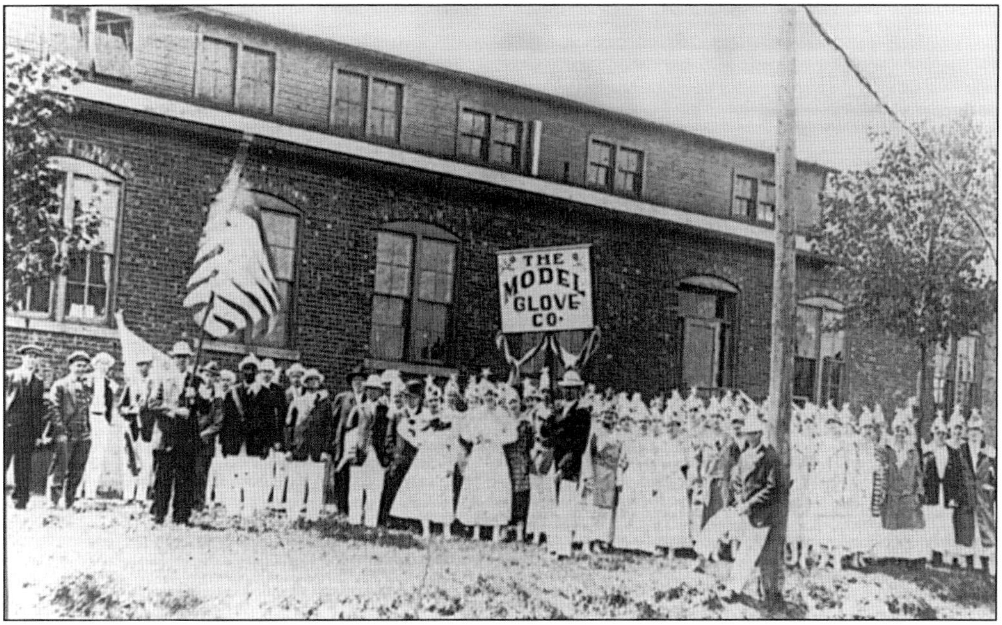

In this photo, c. 1919, the workers of the Model Glove Factory prepare for an anniversary celebration. Sam Andrews brought the company to Greenville in 1909, operating several businesses out of the same factory building on the southeast end of town and later added a larger second story. Son-in-law John Kelsey kept his law office in the west end of the building after the glove manufacturing ceased in 1958. It now belongs to Greenville College. (Courtesy Kathryn Andrews Kelsey.)

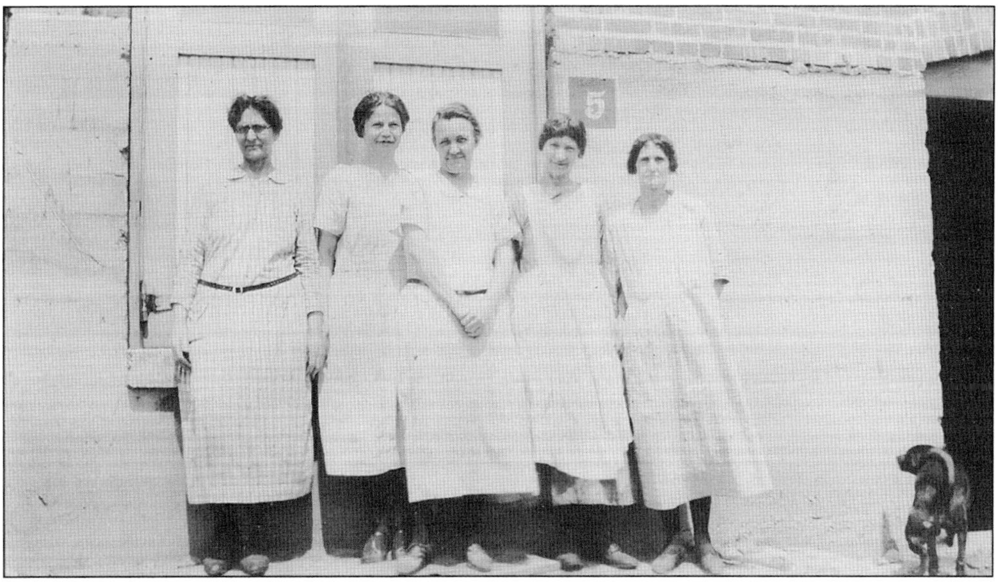

The Greenville Steam Laundry was located in the basement of the Model Glove Factory in the early part of the 20th century. This photo of the workers was taken on April 23, 1925. Pictured here from left to right are Annie Heston, Blanch Evans, Mamie Brown, Della Bryant (manager), and Nora Rule. The laundry had a one-horse closed wagon driven by Mr. DeMoulin to pick up and deliver laundry. (Courtesy Ed Heston.)

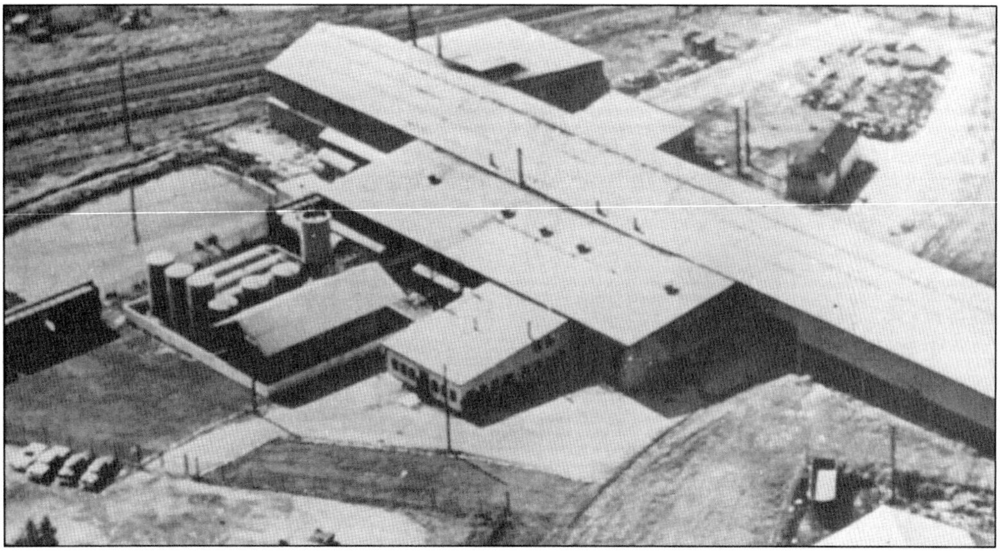

In 1924, a group of businessmen invited Coates Steel Products Co. to move a small forge shop from St. Louis to Greenville. It became "The World's Largest Exclusive Producer of Grinding Balls and Other Grinding Media." Three brothers, Robert C. Lowe, James N. Lowe, and William W. Lowe, served as executive officers for the industry over the years. The company was founded by their grandfather, C.T. Coates, in 1917. At one time the plant employed 75 persons. It closed in 1996. (Courtesy Greenville College Vista Yearbook.)

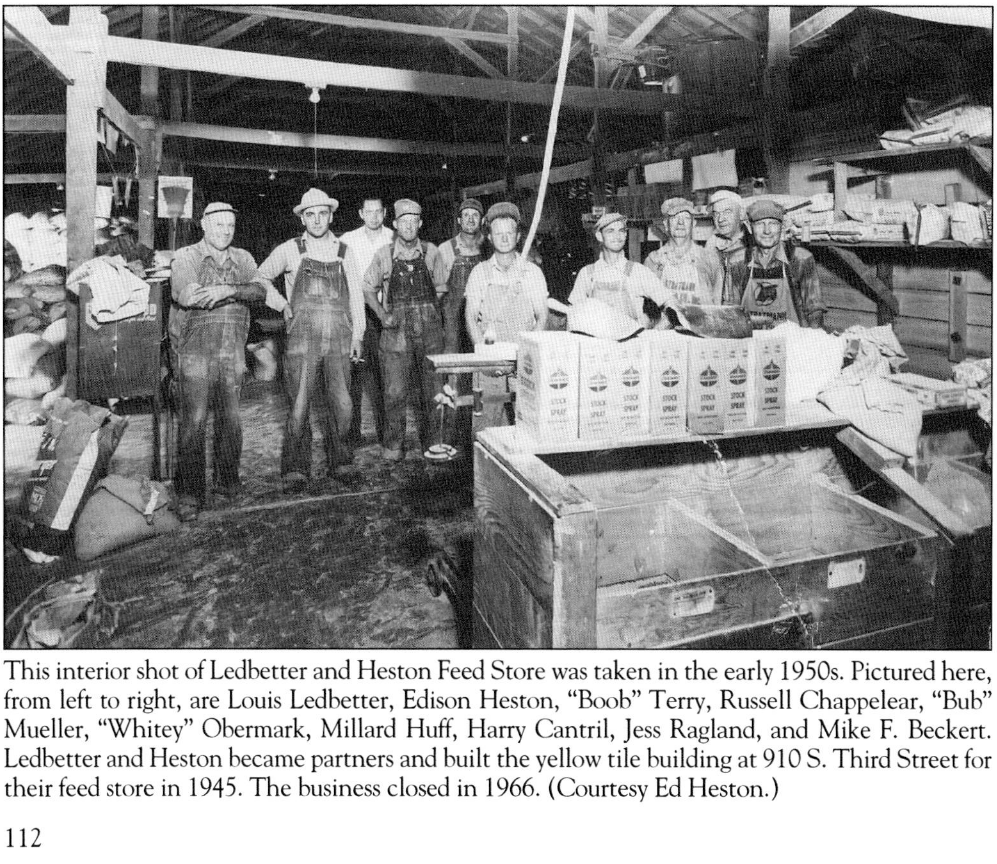

This interior shot of Ledbetter and Heston Feed Store was taken in the early 1950s. Pictured here, from left to right, are Louis Ledbetter, Edison Heston, "Boob" Terry, Russell Chappelear, "Bub" Mueller, "Whitey" Obermark, Millard Huff, Harry Cantril, Jess Ragland, and Mike F. Beckert. Ledbetter and Heston became partners and built the yellow tile building at 910 S. Third Street for their feed store in 1945. The business closed in 1966. (Courtesy Ed Heston.)

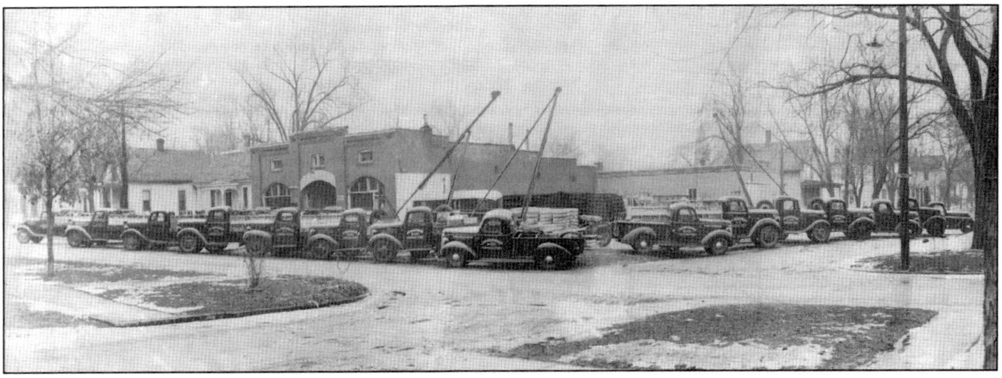

This *c.* 1938 photo show the fleet of 15 trucks owned by J.M. Hunzinger and Company Contractors. They surround the company building at the intersection of South Second Street and East Washington Avenue in Greenville. Materials for construction work are stockpiled next to the building. Chappy's Antiques and Collectibles now occupies the building. (Courtesy Jeff Leidel.)

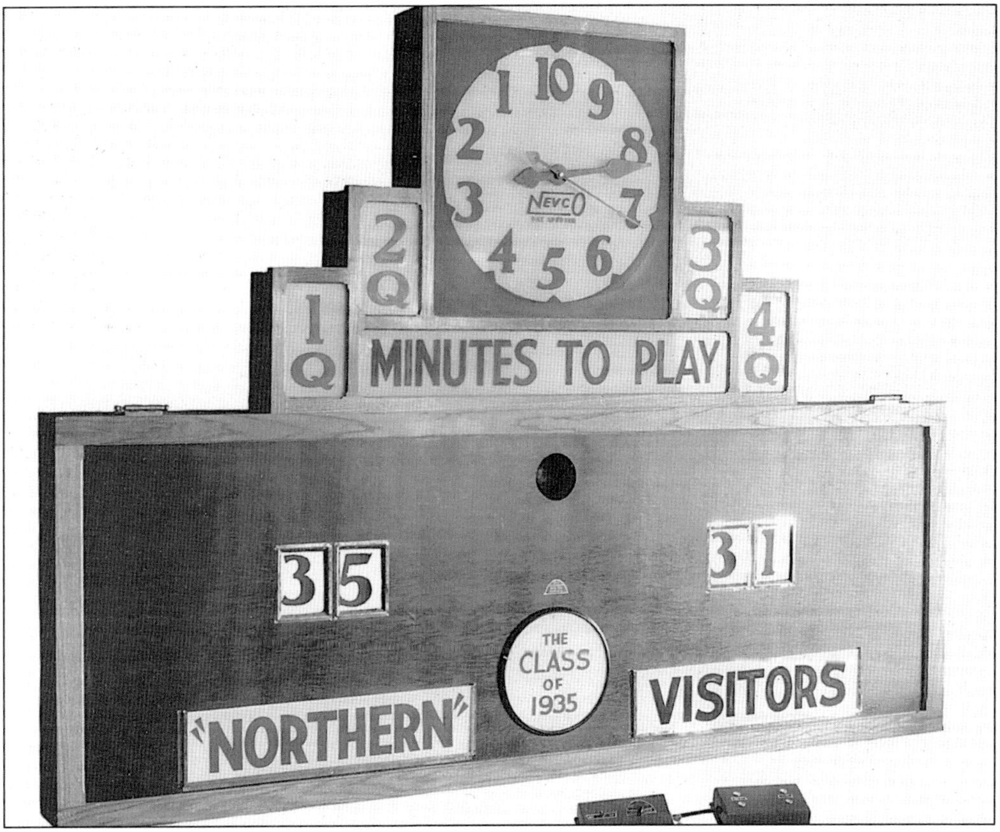

Nevco Scoreboard Company was founded in 1934 by Ralph "Bus" Nevinger. His son Jan R. Nevinger took over as president from 1973 to 1992. He brought the company into the international marketplace where it stands today as a leader in quality standard scoreboard products. Mary Gale Nevinger is the current president. This Basketball Model 35-CS scoreboard from 1935 is constructed of white oak and glass. The scoring numerals are on rotating glass dials. (Courtesy Nevco Scoreboard.)

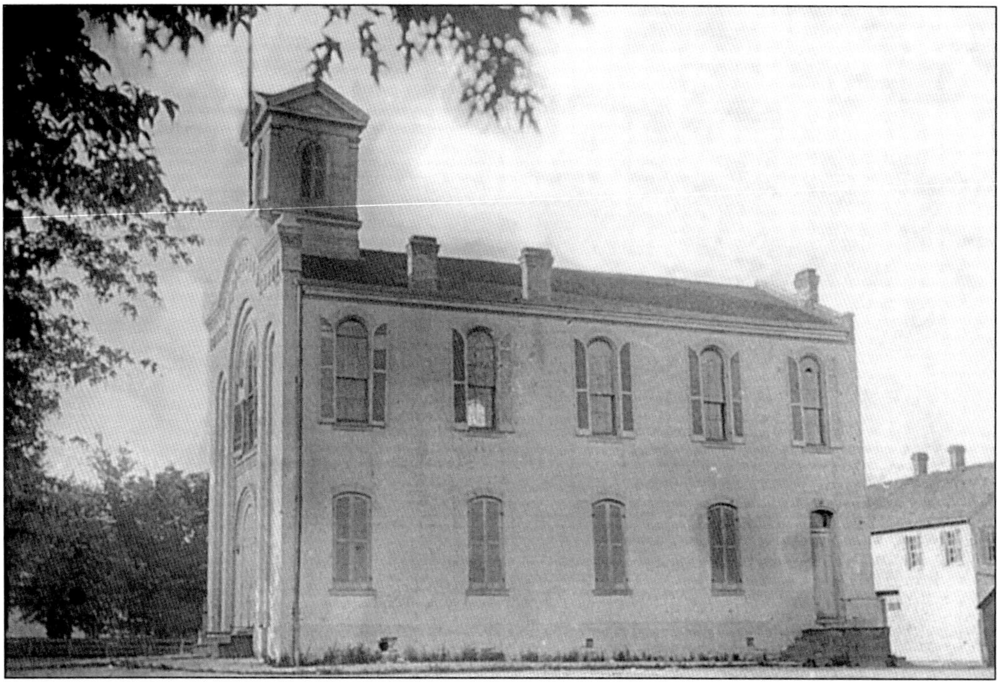

The original Central School was built in 1859. Many opposed the erection of such a large building as a wasteful expenditure of funds at the time. It served all twelve grades and also utilized the basement of the old Congregational Church. Two smaller buildings also stood on the same block and all three were demolished in 1894 for the new Central School. (Courtesy Bond County Historical Society.)

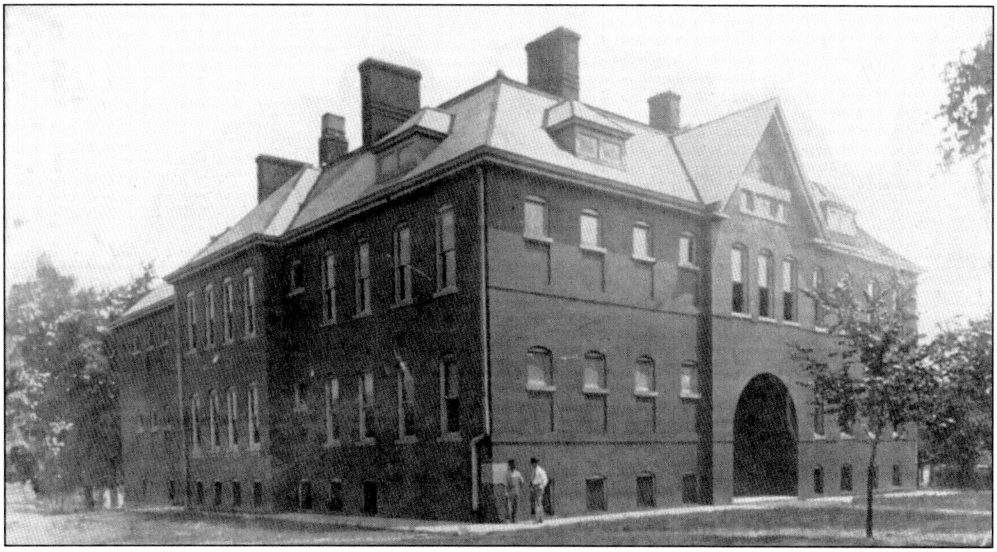

The new Central School was completed in 1895 after a special election to issue the necessary bonds to build it was carried by only 30 votes. It stood in the center of the city block bounded by First, Second, Winter, and Spring Streets. It was first used as the high school and then a grade school after a new high school was built. It closed in 1969 and was later taken down. (Courtesy Jeff Leidel.)

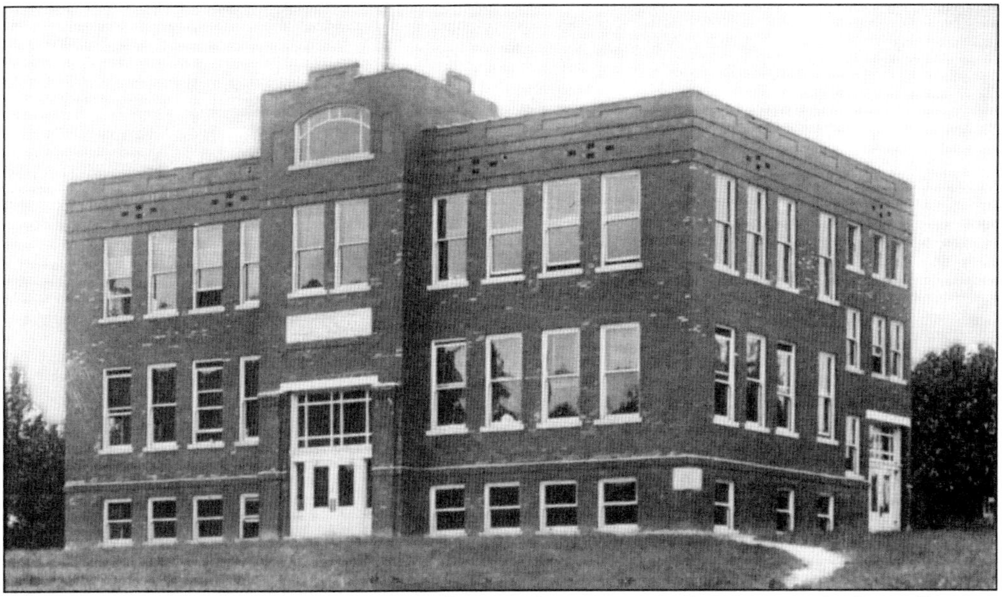

Inglis School opened on January 6, 1910 for 122 elementary students. It was built to alleviate crowded classes at Central School. Inglis School was located along Eastern Avenue between Oak and Durley Streets. It was named for Samuel Inglis, a former city school superintendent who also served as state superintendent of public instruction. It was taken down January 17, 1972. (Courtesy Jeff Leidel.)

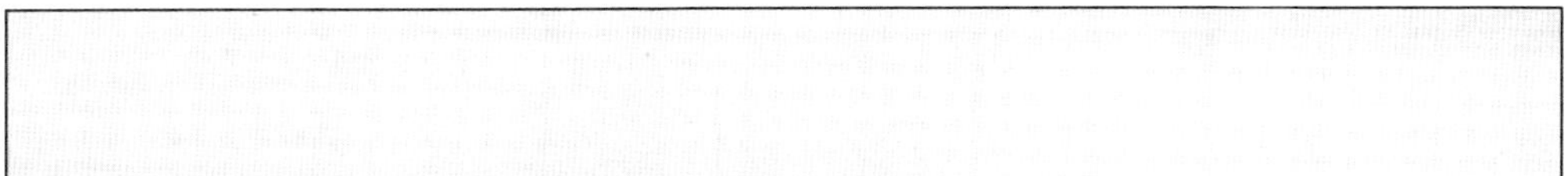

The new Greenville High School was built in 1915 on Beaumont Avenue. The gymnasium was completed in 1935. After a new high school was completed farther to the northeast in 1956, it became the junior high. Around 1968, a small earthquake caused cracks to form, necessitating the demolition of the 1915 portion of the school. The old gym along with a new addition was used as a junior high until 2002. (Courtesy Pauline Watson.)

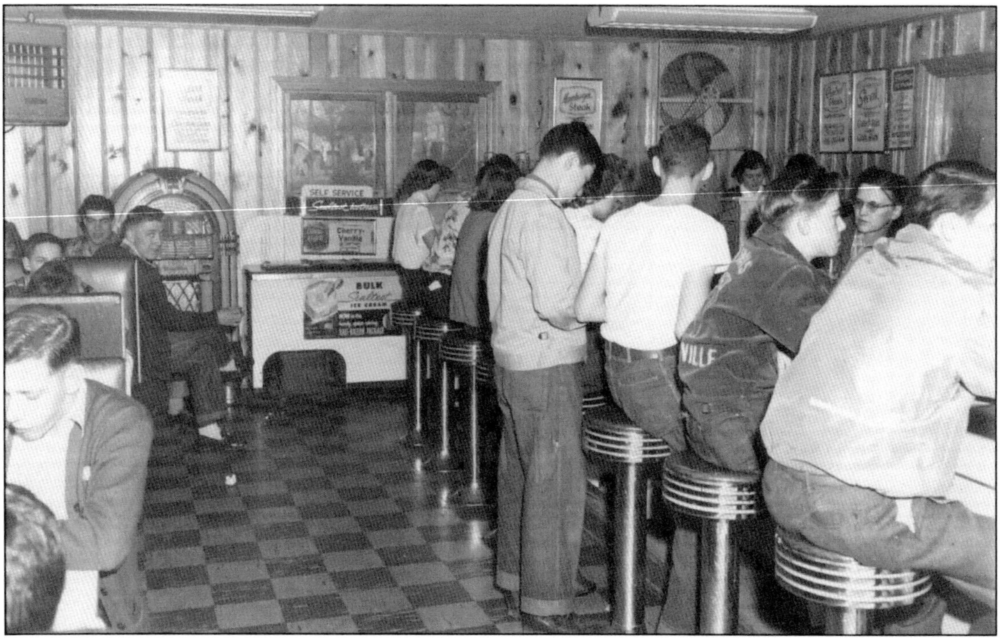

A popular eatery with Greenville High School students, the Snack Shack was originally owned by William Hentze and leased by Wayne Stone and later Jim Greek. Located at Beaumont and Asbury, the restaurant featured hamburgers, french fries, and potato salad. This photo was taken around 1951. (Courtesy Wayne Stone.)

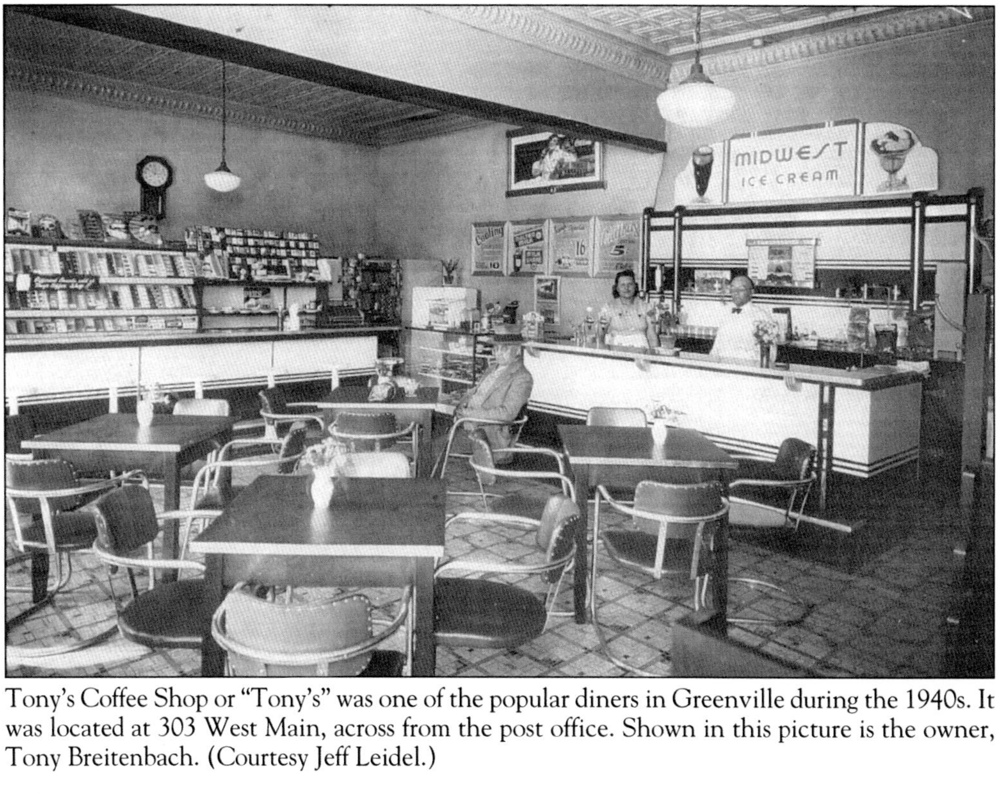

Tony's Coffee Shop or "Tony's" was one of the popular diners in Greenville during the 1940s. It was located at 303 West Main, across from the post office. Shown in this picture is the owner, Tony Breitenbach. (Courtesy Jeff Leidel.)

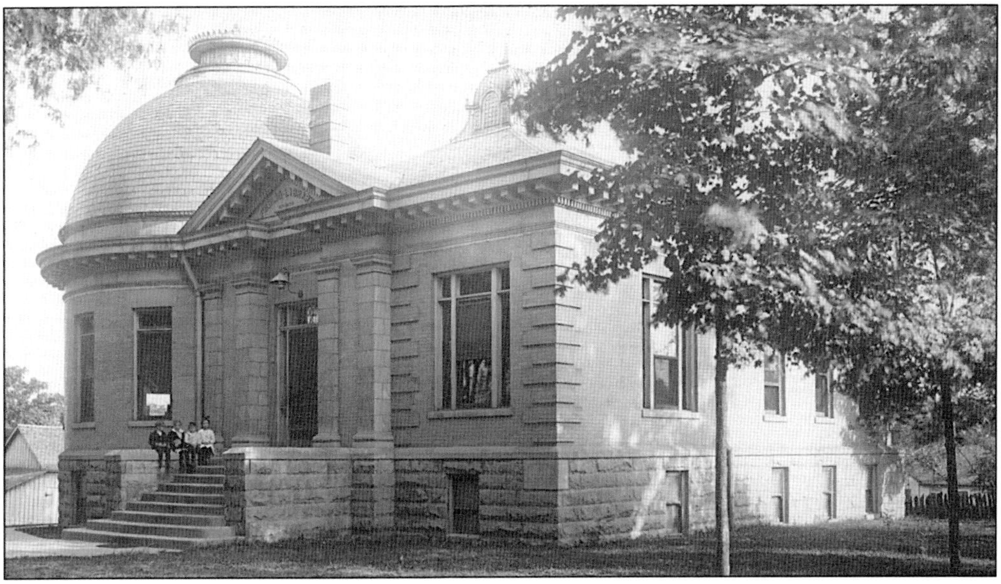

In 1902, the Ladies Library Association contacted Andrew Carnegie requesting funds for the construction of a public library. The association offered $1,000 and their collection of 4,000 books. Carnegie agreed to give $10,000, provided the city would furnish a site and levy a tax to support a library. The site selected was the southwest corner of Fourth and Main Streets in Greenville. Construction work was completed and the library was dedicated on August 4, 1905. Note the cupola and dome cap, both of which were removed long ago. (Courtesy Jeff Leidel.)

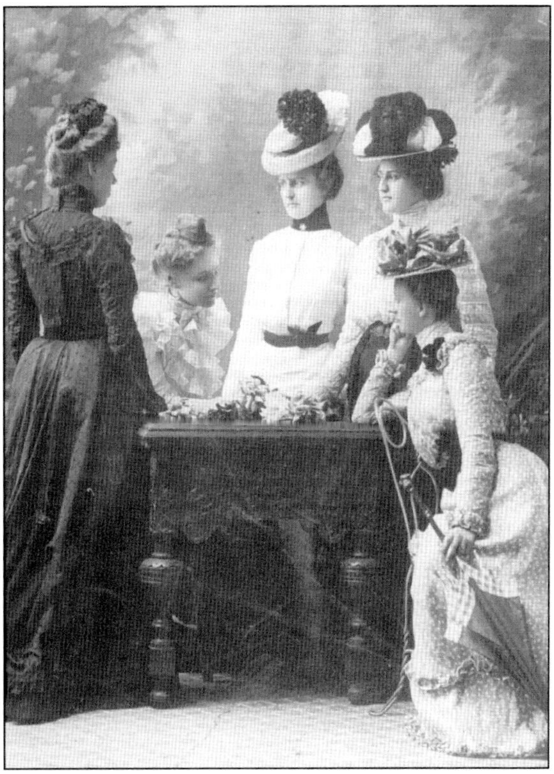

The daughters of John Baumberger pose in this *c.* 1890s photo. Pictured here, from left to right, are Louise Inglis, Katherine Donnell, Emma Hord, Alice Hoiles, and Ida Wise. Their husbands were among the most prominent men in town: Samuel Inglis, superintendent of schools; W.D. Donnell, undertaker; A.L. Hord, postmaster; Guy Hoiles, bank president and E.B. Wise, clothier. The sisters belonged to all the proper social clubs of the day and were instrumental in the building of the library and city park. (Courtesy Ruth Huffman.)

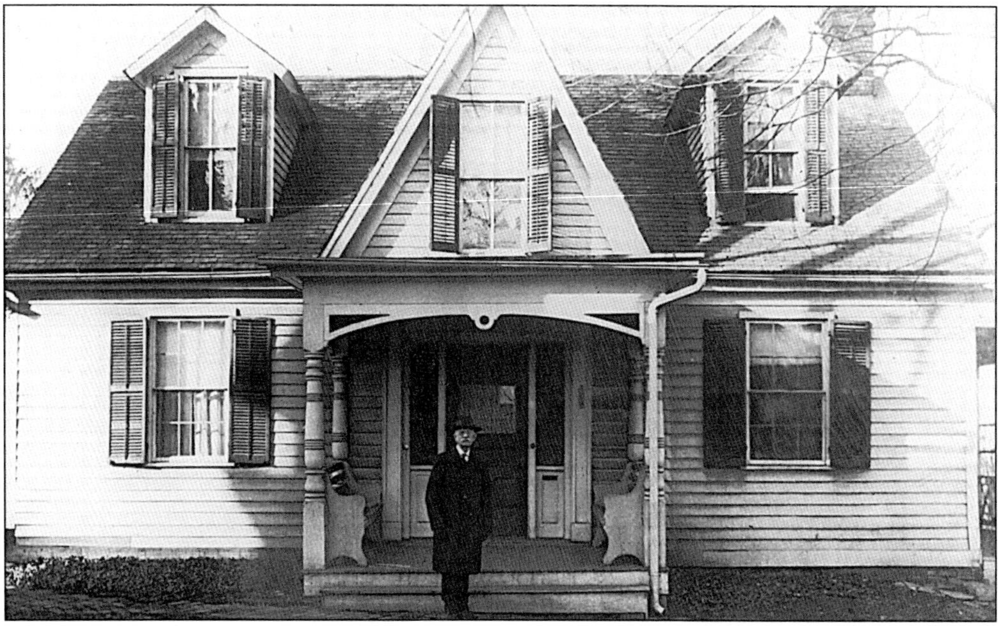

The Old Denny House at 337 N. Third Street was built around 1840 by Rev. Robert Stewart. He was a Congregational minister and an active agent for the Underground Railroad. Prior to the Civil War, Bond County had at least 17 different families who helped runaway slaves escape to the north. C.K. Denny bought this home in 1875 and it remained in his family for over 100 years. He appears in this *c.* 1900 photo. (Courtesy Mary Jane Sandifer.)

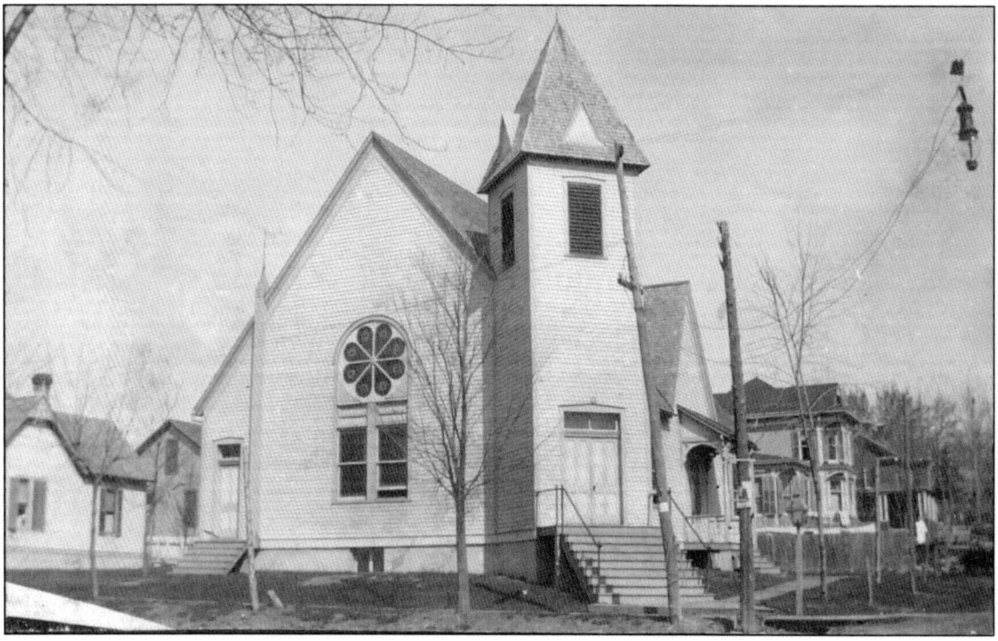

The Christian Church in Greenville was organized in 1878. The congregation grew rapidly and in 1891, built this church at the northwest corner of Main and Prairie Streets. They made several additions to the building over the years until it was outgrown. It was taken down in 1962, after a new church was completed on Killarney Drive. (Courtesy Bill Donnell.)

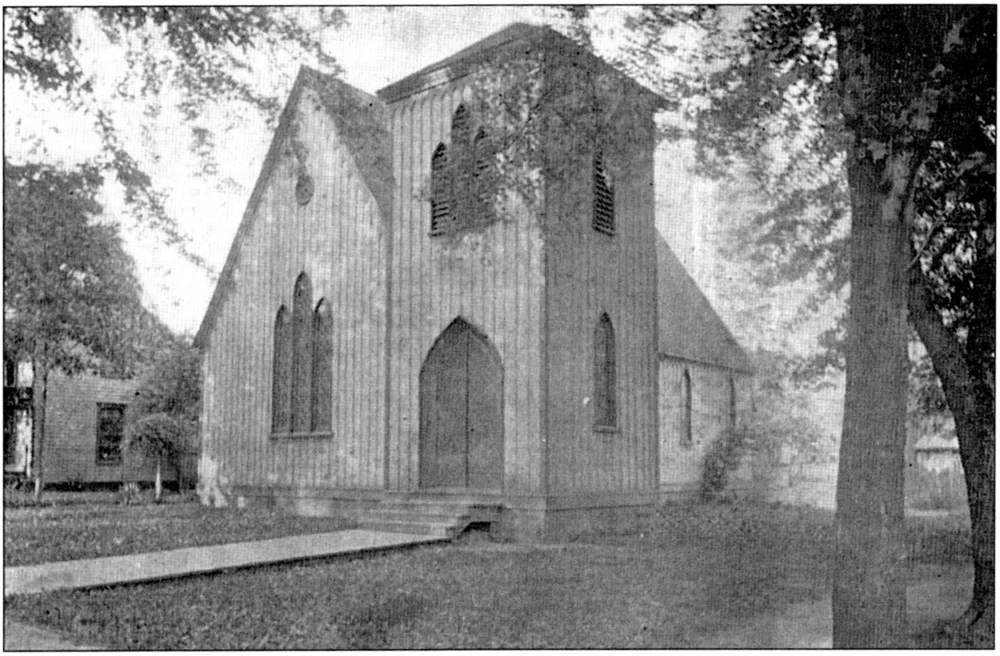

The Grace Episcopal Church was built in 1882 on the northeast corner of Third and Spring Streets. Slated for demolition, it was purchased by the Central Christian Church in 1963. They moved it to Prairie Street. Several additions have been made, but they have faithfully preserved this church's original Gothic detail. (Courtesy Jeff Leidel.)

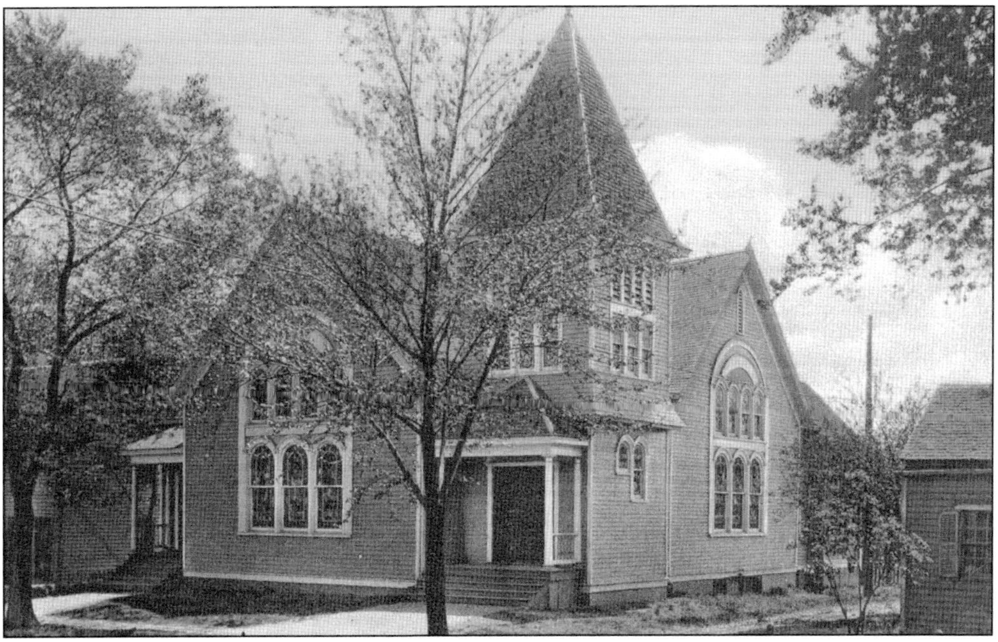

Three buildings served the First Baptist Church in Greenville. Their first church home was located on Main Street and built in 1847. Pictured above, their second church was located on South Street and constructed in 1902. It burned down in 1951 and was replaced by the current church on the same site. (Courtesy Jeff Leidel.)

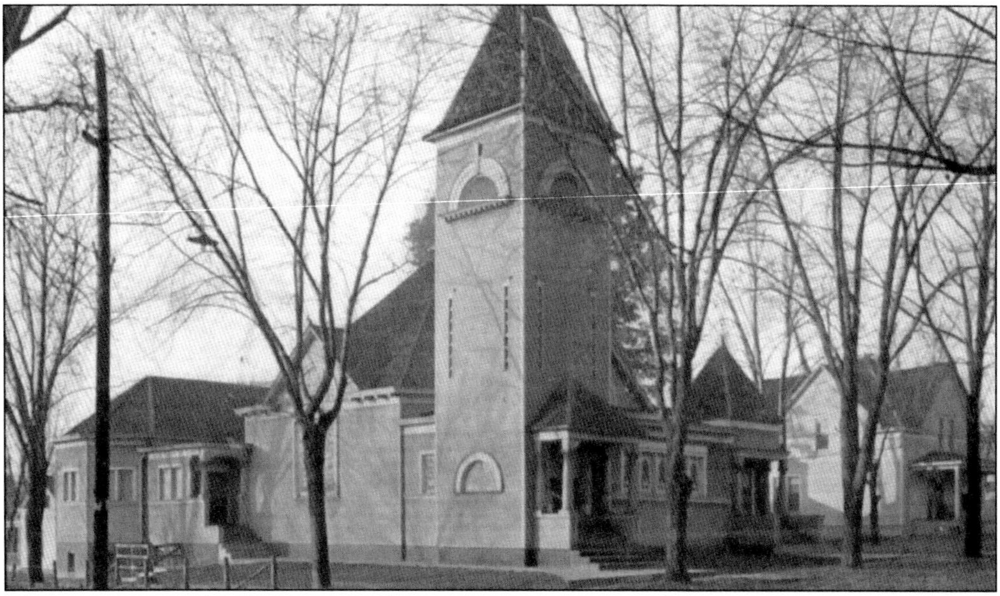

The Presbyterian Church in Greenville was organized from the original Shoal Creek congregation that was divided into three churches around 1825. This c. 1910 photo shows their 1904 church building on Main Street at Prairie. In 1969, the Presbyterians built a new church and this one was sold to the Church of Christ. They worshipped here for about 20 years before the church was taken down in 1990. (Courtesy Jeff Leidel.)

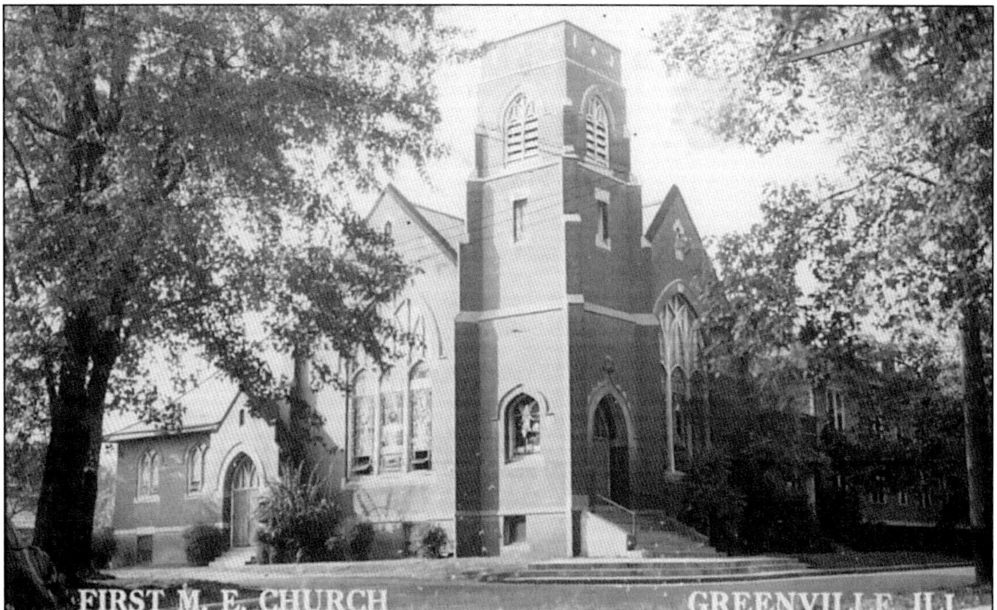

The First United Methodist Church in Greenville was located on the corner of Second Street and Summer Avenue. This was the third church, built and dedicated in 1907. It was used for 65 years until it burned on New Year's Eve, 1973. (Courtesy Jeff Leidel.)

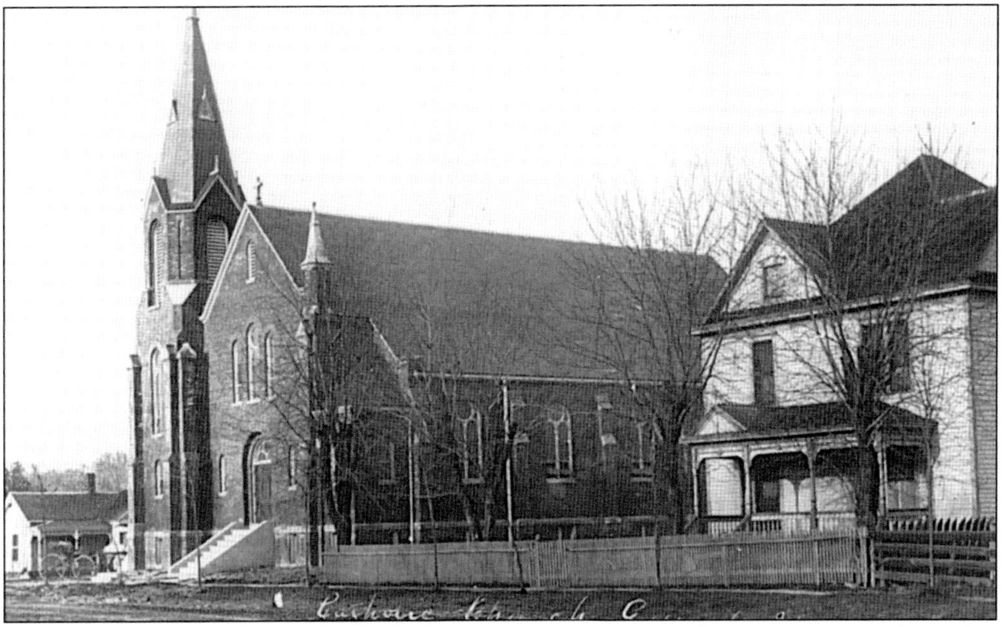

The first St. Lawrence Catholic Church was built in 1878 on South Prairie Street. It burned in October of 1910 and the new church, pictured above, was erected on the same site. This building remained their place of worship until the current church was dedicated in 1993. The old rectory, at right in this *c.* 1920 photo, was replaced in the 1960s. (Courtesy Keith Buchholz.)

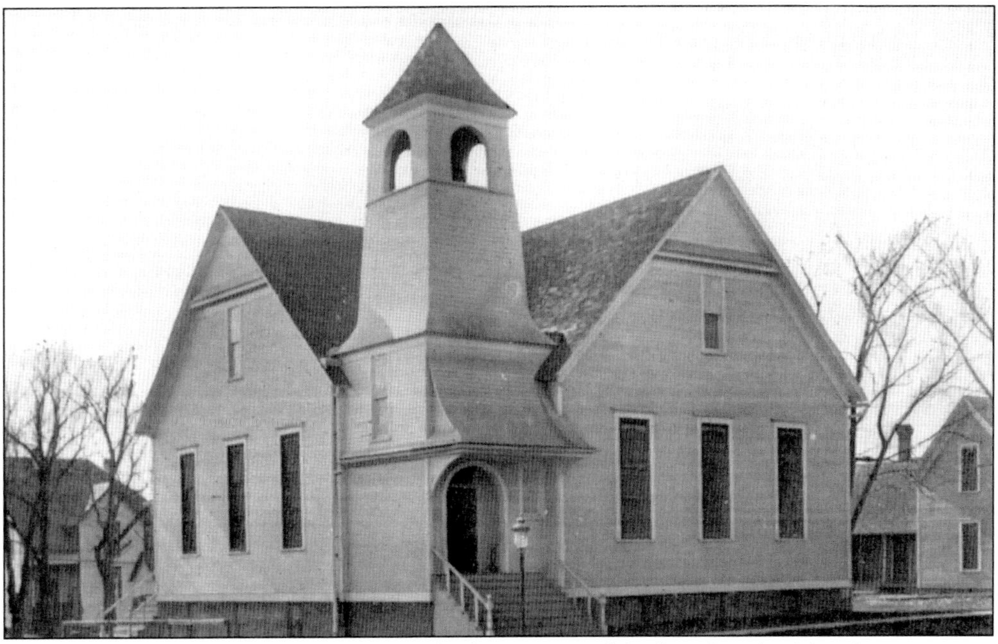

In the summer of 1881, a group of Free Methodists organized the first church of that denomination in Greenville. The original church was at the corner of Prairie and Vine Streets. The building pictured was built at the corner of College Avenue and Elm Streets in 1899. It stood until 1959 when a new church was constructed there. Greenville College has used that new church for chapel and other services over the years. (Courtesy Jeff Leidel.)

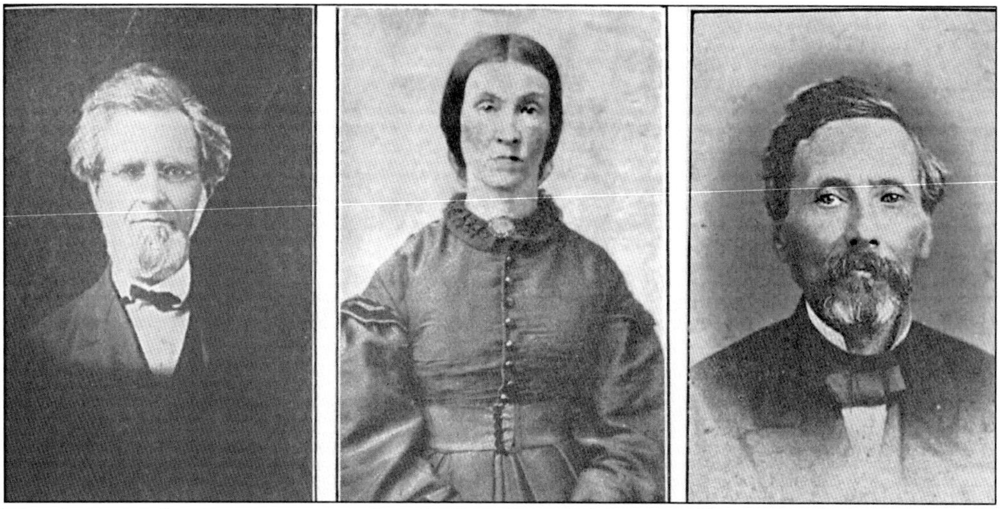

The three people most instrumental in the founding of Almira College were, from left to right, John Brown White, Almira Blanchard Morse, and Stephen Morse. White moved to Greenville in the 1830s. Morse, a close friend of White's from college days at Brown University, was a teacher in Greenville and married to Almira Blanchard, daughter of a prominent Greenville citizen. The college was named in her honor. (Courtesy Historical Souvenir of Greenville, Illinois, 1905.)

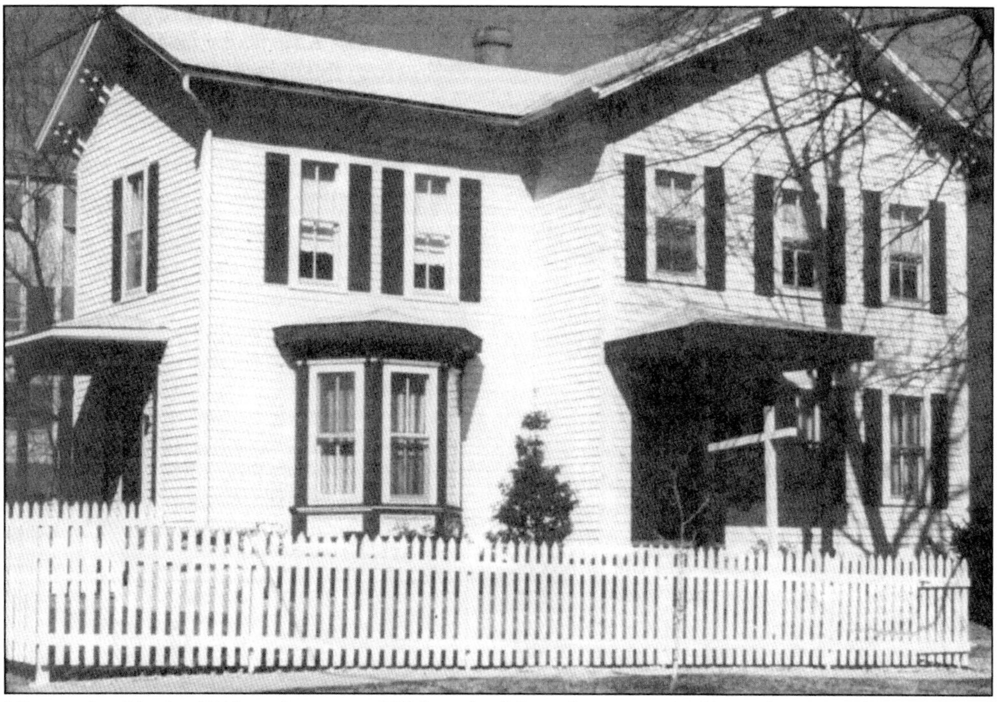

Classes for Almira College began in 1855 in the Morse home on College Avenue. White served as the first president while Morse became business manager. Almira B. Morse's endowment of $6,000 allowed property to be purchased on the east edge of Greenville for a permanent college building. As Almira College House on the Greenville College campus, the Morse home is now a museum for the Richard W. Bock Sculpture Collection. (Courtesy Kevin Kaegy.)

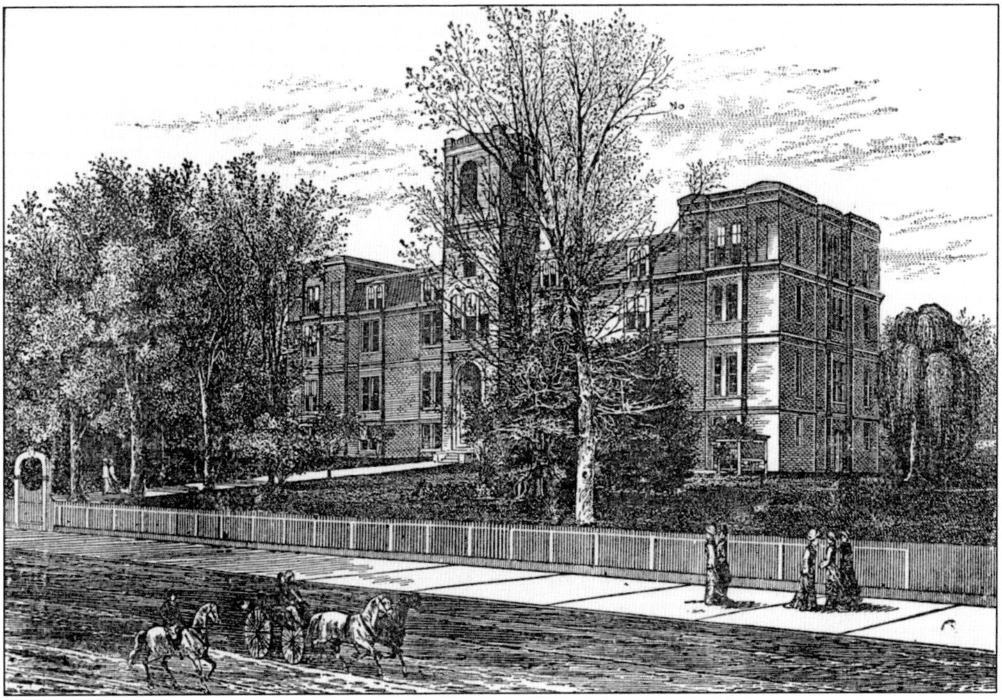

Built in 1858, "Old Main" was so-named because it served as dorms, classrooms, administration, and dining commons. In spite of a growing enrollment, continuing financial struggles forced Almira College to close its doors in 1891. It was purchased by the Free Methodists in 1892, and was renamed Greenville College. "Old Main" is now known as Hogue Hall, the administration building. (Courtesy Greenville College Archives.)

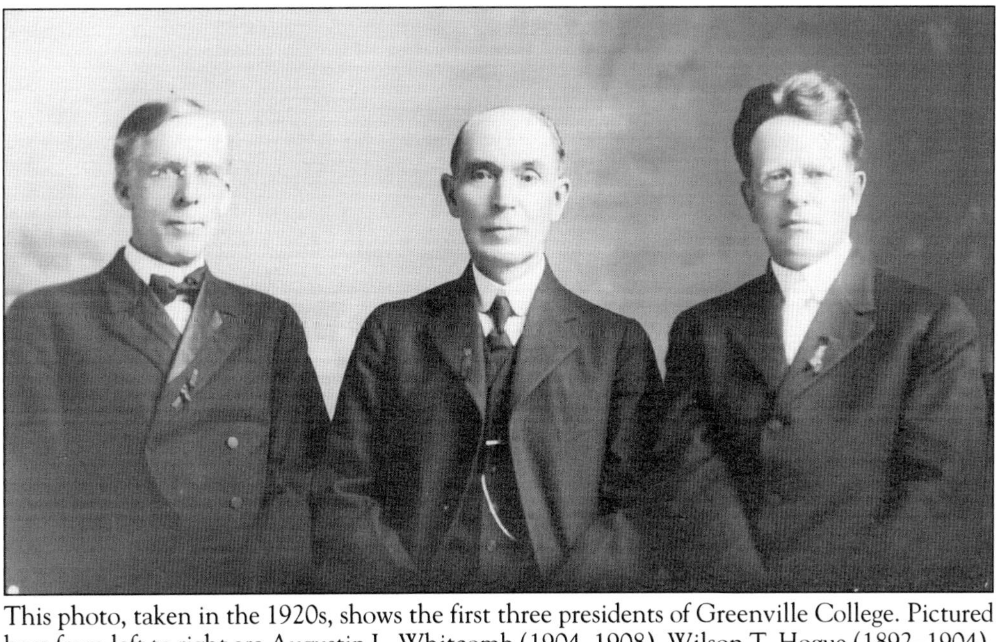

This photo, taken in the 1920s, shows the first three presidents of Greenville College. Pictured here from left to right are Augustin L. Whitcomb (1904–1908), Wilson T. Hogue (1892–1904), and Eldon G. Burritt (1908–1927). (Courtesy Greenville College Archives.)

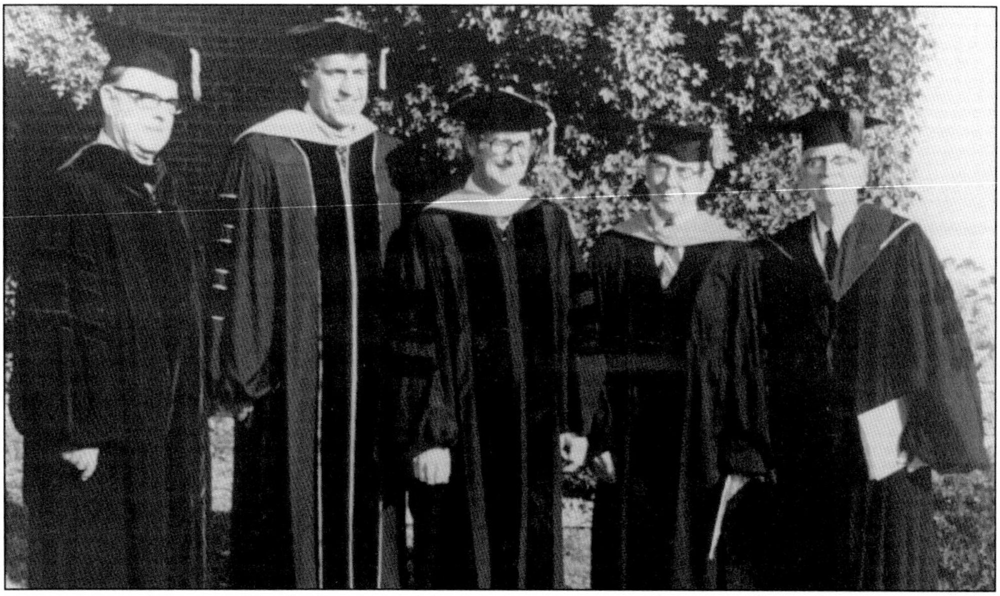

Representing 66 years of leadership, six of the recent presidents of Greenville College pose together on the occasion of Dr. Richard Stephen's inauguration. From left to right, they are Glenn A. Richardson (1962–1970), Orley R. Herron (1970–1977), W. Richard Stephens (1977–1993), H.J. Long (1936–1962), and Leslie R. Marston (1927–1936). (Courtesy Greenville College Archives.)

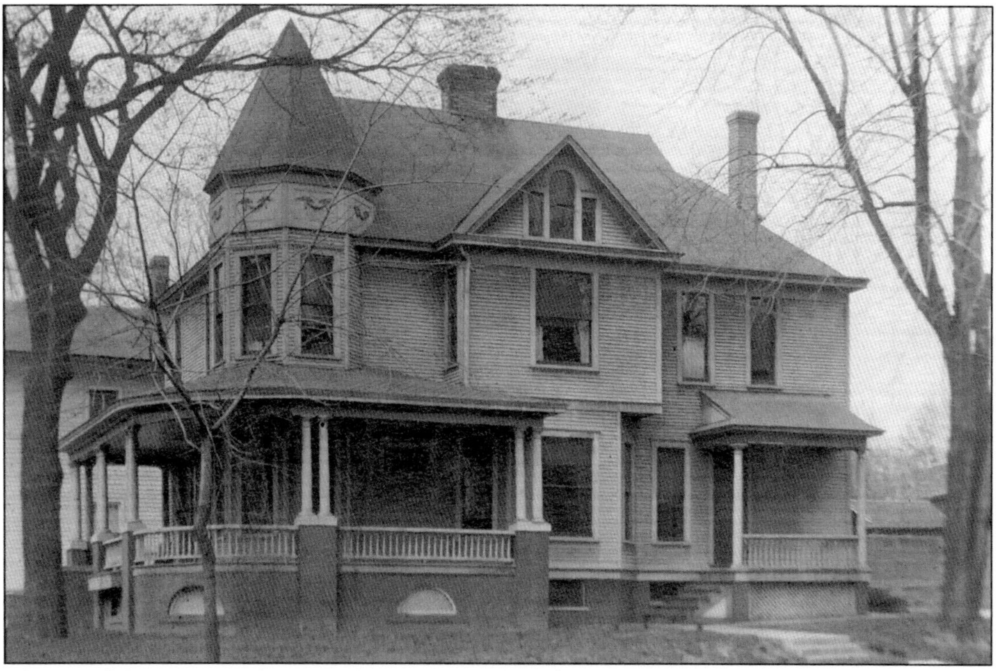

This grand Queen Anne house with a turret was built by Ward Reid about 1905 and stood at the northeast corner of College and Spruce Streets. It served as the college president's residence for many years. Dr. H.J. Long lived here for 26 years, the last president to do so. It was taken down in 1961 to make way for the Delbert E. Sims Student Union. (Courtesy Greenville College Archives.)

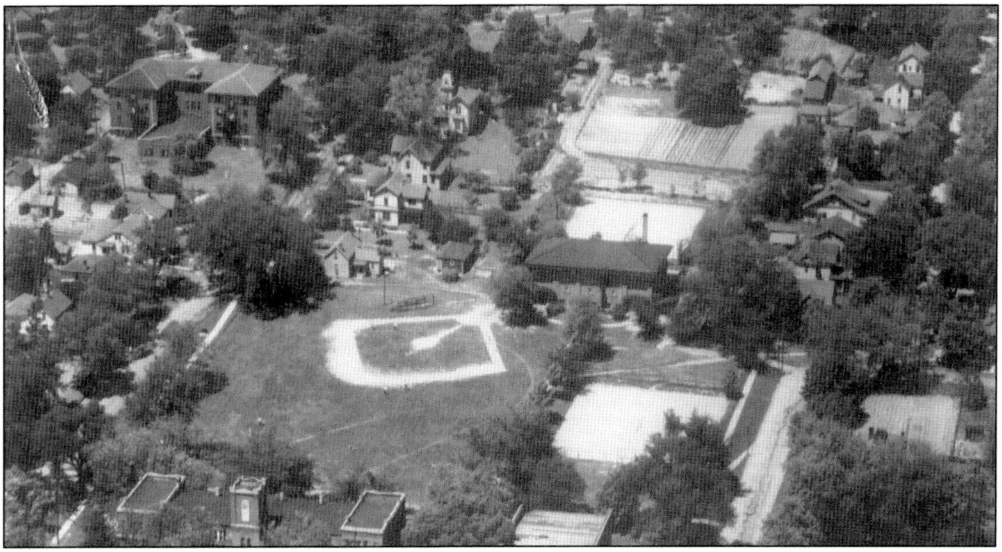

Here is an aerial view of the Greenville College campus taken sometime after 1915, looking north. Note the ball diamond behind Hogue Hall on what is now Scott Field, the original old Burritt Gymnasium, the many private houses on campus along Spruce Street and Burritt Hall on Beaumont Avenue, the women's dormitory named for Carrie T. Burritt, wife of President Eldon G. Burritt. (Courtesy Greenville College Archives.)

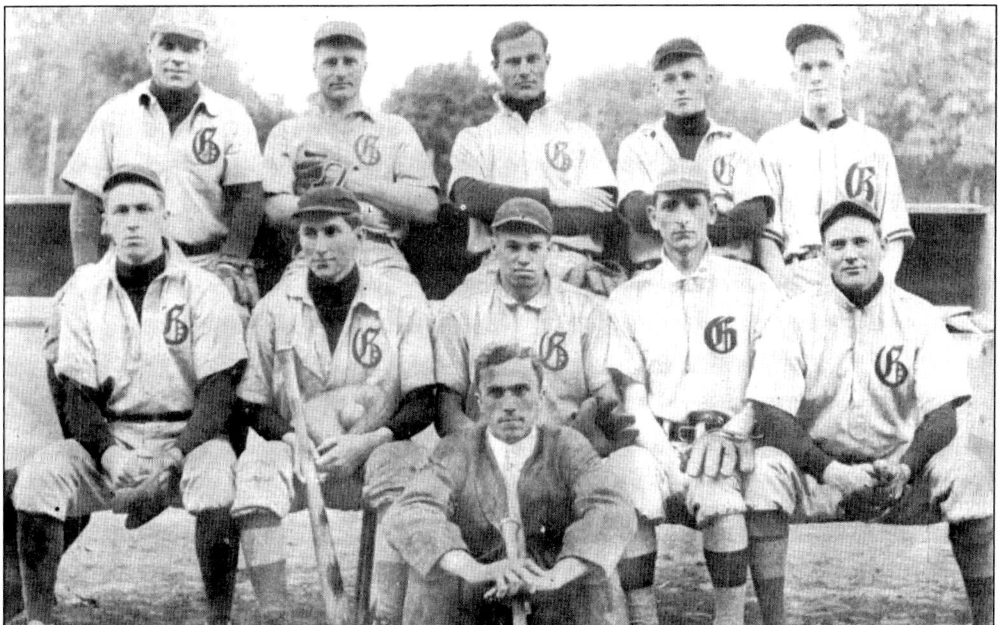

The Greenville College Sophomores Tournament Champion Baseball Team in 1914 included the following team members, pictured here from left to right: Henry Taylor (front center), (front row) Wilson R. King, James Earl Secord, Merlin G. Smith, Arthur W. Secord, and Albert Grigg; (back row) Francis M. Harden, William S. Hoffman, Richard E. McDougall, Alva E. Harford, and Leslie R. Marston. Several future ministers and college professors are in this group, as is one future Greenville College president. (Courtesy 1914 Greenville College Vista.)

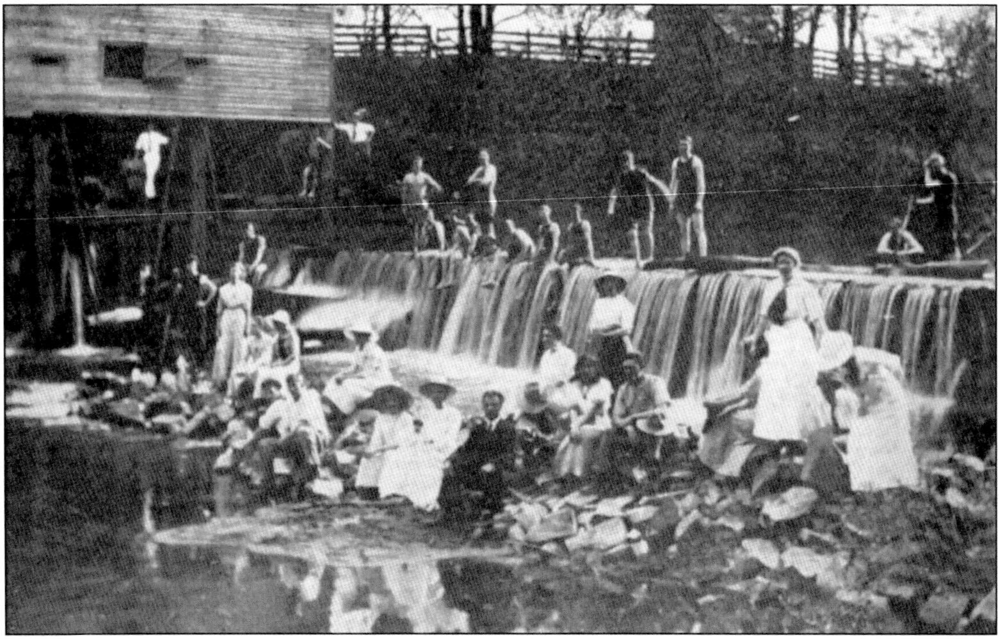

A group of Greenville College students pose on the dam of Brown's Mill in 1913. In the early days of the college, students frequently took hikes to remote areas of the county. This tradition continues with the "All College Hike" to Durley Camp. The distance from the campus to Brown's Mill was ten miles. (Courtesy 1913 Greenville College Vista.)

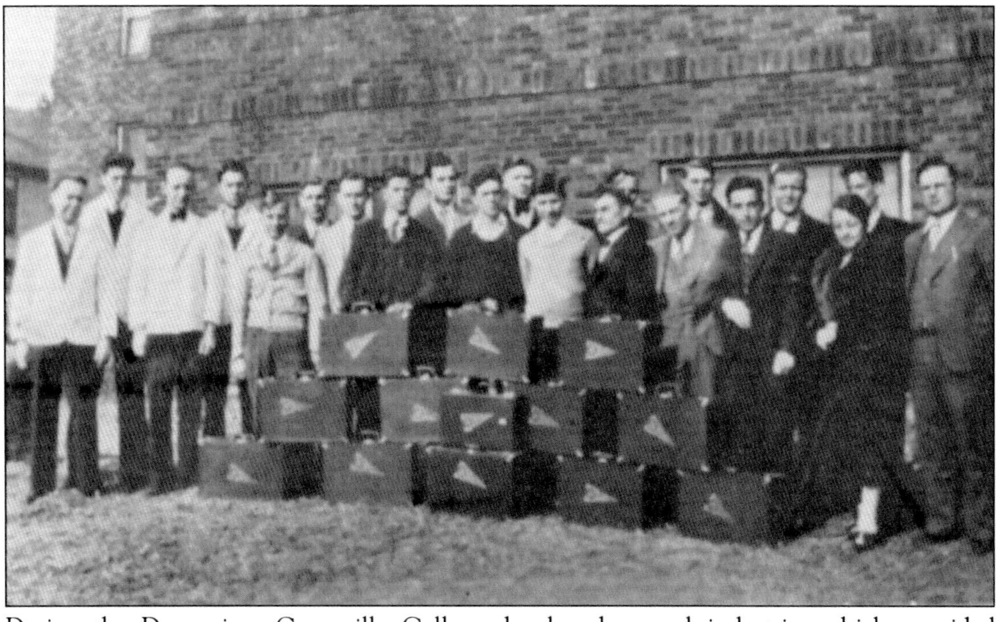

During the Depression, Greenville College developed several industries which provided employment for students. Tower Products offered a variety of home necessities, including extracts, cleansers, home remedies, and toiletries. At far right, Dr. H.J. Long, Chemistry Professor, stands with students who created these products in the laboratory and then dispersed throughout the county to sell them door-to-door. (Courtesy *Greenville College Quarterly*, 1933.)

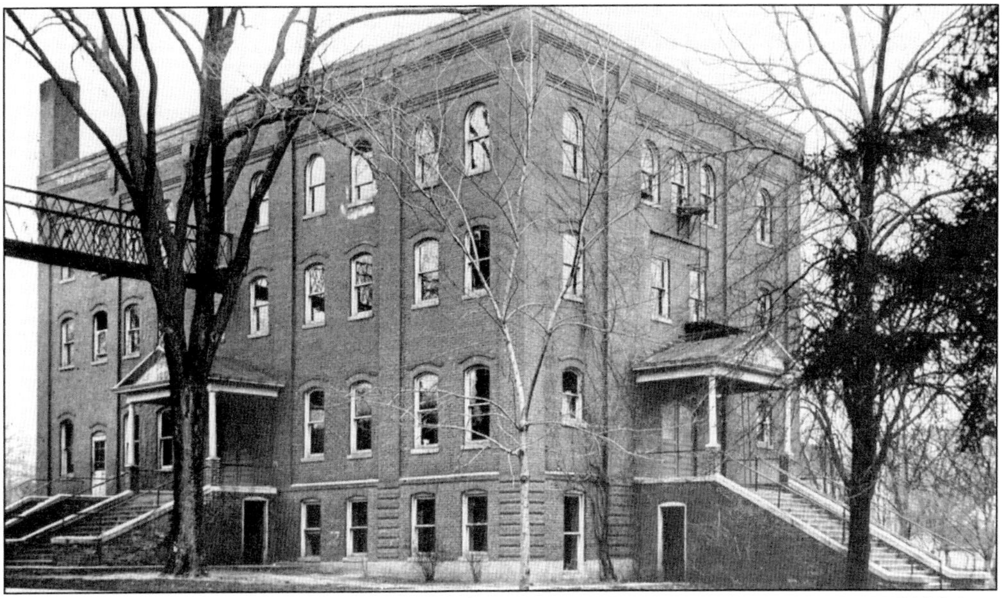

Built in 1905, LaDue Auditorium was the first campus construction project since Old Main was built in the 1850s. It was named in honor of Professor John LaDue, a long-time professor of religion. His son, Dr. Wilson Ladue, taught language for 30 years. Wilson's wife, known as Aunt Mary, taught piano for 30 years. Marston Hall was added in 1962, with its six classrooms. The cat walk, at left, still exists, connecting to the third floor of Hogue Hall. (Courtesy 1922 Greenville College Vista.)

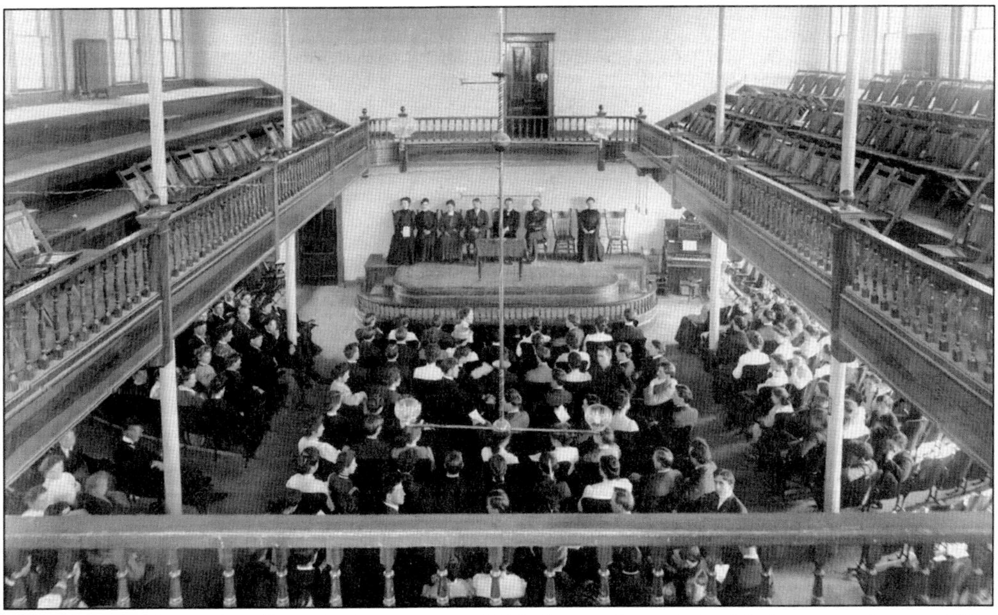

This interior shot of LaDue Auditorium c. 1905 shows the original balcony and stage. The building was extensively renovated in the 1980s and is still in use. According to Dr. Enoch Holtwick, a student prankster once dropped a live chicken from the door above the stage onto the bald head of a speaker during chapel service. The door was subsequently removed. (Courtesy Greenville College Archives.)

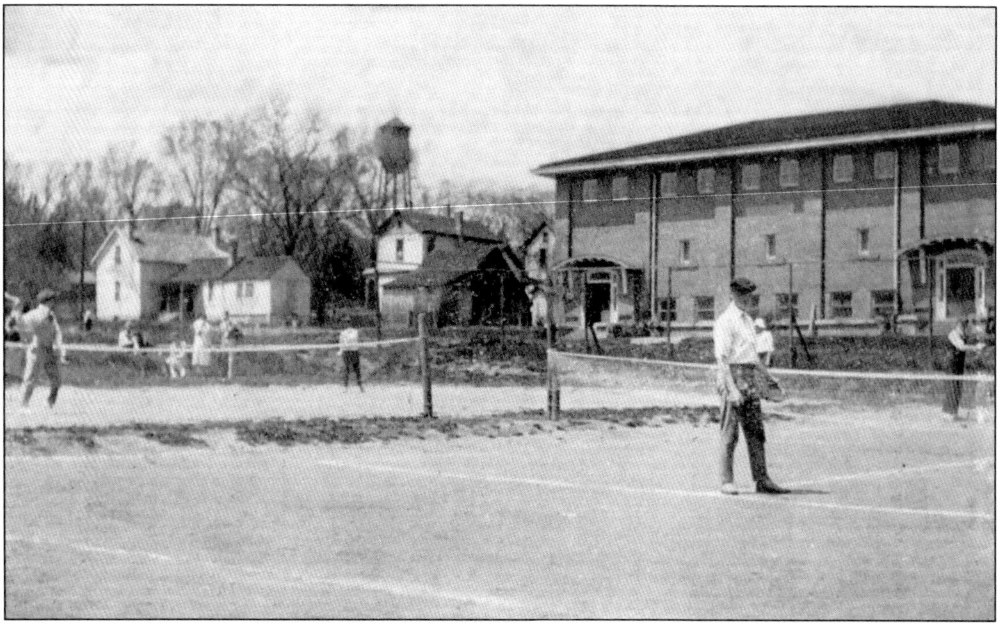

The Greenville College tennis courts in 1918 were located south of the Burritt Gymnasium. The students raised money and contributed manual labor to complete the gym, which opened in January 1915. The houses along Spruce Street to the west were privately owned at that time. Spruce Street is now a campus mall. (Courtesy 1918 Greenville College Vista.)

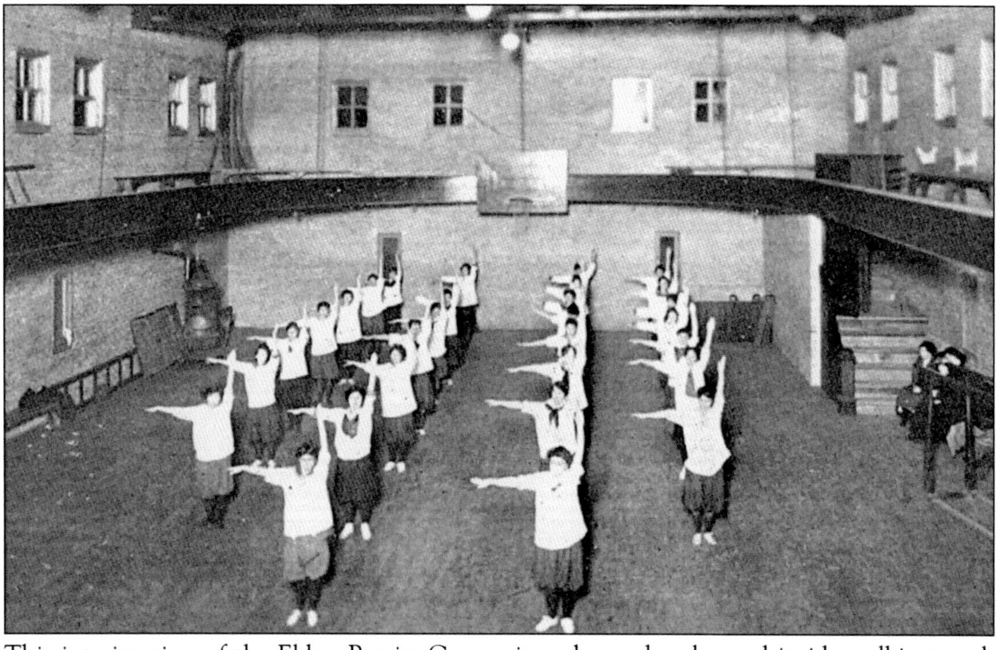

This interior view of the Eldon Burritt Gymnasium shows the elevated inside walking track that is suspended from the walls. Below, female students perform calisthenics in their regulation bloomers. Part of the track has been removed, but the old gym is still intact within the current Crum Recreational Center and H.J. Long Gymnasium. Restoration of the existing old gym interior is underway. (Courtesy 1915 Greenville College Vista.)